Shack Notes

Moments While At a Writing Retreat

Shack Notes

Moments While At a Writing Retreat

by Satsvarupa dasa Goswami

GN Press, Inc.

Persons interested in the subject matter of this book are invited to correspond with our secretary:

GN Press, Inc.
R.D. 1, Box 837-K
Port Royal, PA 17082

Printed in Port Royal, PA
United States of America
ISBN: 0-911233-91-1

Library of Congress Cataloging-in-Publication Data

Gosvāmi, Satsvarūpa Dāsa, 1939-
Shack notes: Moments While At a Writing Retreat/by Satsvarūpa dāsa Goswami.
p. cm.
ISBN 0-911233-91-1: $13.00
1. Gosvāmi, Satsvarūpa Dāsa, 1939-. 2. International Society for Krishna Consciousness—Biography. 3. Spiritual life (Hinduism) 4. Krishna (Hindu deity) I. Title.
BL1285.892.G67A3 1992
294.5'512—dc20 91-38509
CIP

Cover design: Madana-mohana dāsa
Photographs: Kṛṣṇa-arcanā-devī dāsī

Special thanks to The 1991 Lunar Calendar, Nancy F.W. Passmore, Ed., Luna Press, publisher, and R.D.K. Perrens, for use of the moon drawings that appear in this publication.

Keep on with this business of writing articles: In the midst of your heavy duties, go on writing something glorifying the Lord, and put our philosophy into words. Writing means to express oneself, how he is understanding this philosophy. So this writing is necessary for everyone.

—Śrīla Prabhupāda

Contents

Preface	i
Week One	1
Week Two	83
Week Three	197
Acknowledgements	314

Preface

Shack Notes is almost undefinable, at least in the sense of examining a particular book's genre. It is autobiographical, yet is it not an autobiography; it is diary, and yet it is not a collection of diary entries; it is self-exploration, yet it is done in the context of seeing the external world. *Shack Notes* is special. To write *Shack Notes,* I have deliberately slowed down my outer experiences in order to think out Kṛṣṇa consciousness on the page. It is an attempt to explore the writing as Kṛṣṇa conscious experience in itself. I have attempted to push it to the limits in hopes that writing would bring me deeper into my personal Kṛṣṇa consciousness. It is also an inside look at a writer's thinking.

The discovery of *Shack Notes* came from the actual process of writing it, and thus it would be fitting to cull from the book some of the definitions of the work as they came to me.

"This is a book about writing in devotional service. I like to think of it as a book *for* writers, helping them through the process of writing and recognizing the challenges writers face. Those who are not writers can apply these principles to their own attempts in devotional service."

"This book describes three weeks of my life. There is something very wonderful in trying to let go, in trying to quiet myself so Kṛṣṇa can come forward. I am not saying it so clearly, but I think you know what I mean. I have allowed myself to become congested in spirit, insipid, and afraid over the years. To acknowledge that and let those parts of myself go is a blessing."

"*Shack Notes* means spending three weeks in a wholehearted attempt to live entirely occupied by writing. The writing is centered on repeated attempts to evoke Kṛṣṇa consciousness. Each attempt must start from scratch. I accumulate markings, some direct hits, sometimes a feeling of going nowhere . . . but gradually, I am gathering a growing conviction that writing itself is *bhajana.*"

"I love to write. That is why I keep doing it. It is awkward, tainted, flawed, I know: but it is love, and a love that helps others. I can learn to sing better, to compose more expertly."

"This has been my aspiration in writing *Shack Notes,* that I can honestly translate physical and mental experience into Kṛṣṇa conscious action, and that I can delve into my own inner meanings. I can only pray to Kṛṣṇa to help me, and pray also that the experience of writing *Shack Notes* will become a meaningful spiritual journey."

Shack Notes was born out of my having time between the writing of other books. It started out as writing practice, something personal just for myself, an experiment. As I gradually freed myself up and allowed myself to flow with the writing, I managed to accumulate a lengthy manuscript. Then material was selected from it and edited into its present form (what is presented here is only sixty percent of the total writing). I hope my readers will flow with me through this adventure in writing, and that they will find something useful in these pages.

Week One

July 1, 1991, 6:30 A.M.

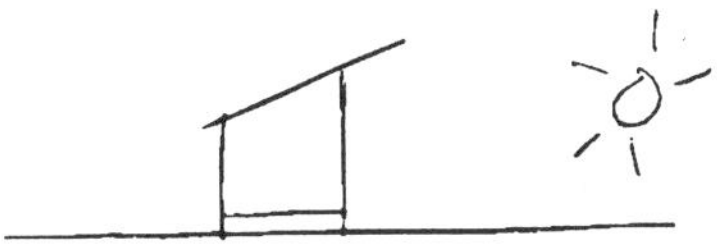

The routine of the writing retreat is quiet and protected. I can't complain. If anything, there is so much comfort that I may lack a certain struggle, a sense of hunger. My disciples pamper me. Despite the comforts, I don't indulge in sense gratification. I follow a simple routine: I don't overeat, I get up very early, I don't mix with women. O Kṛṣṇa, I desire to serve You by writing.

❦

This Moment

A plane overhead. Hunger in this guy's belly. At last he harkens again to the voice within, looks at his watch—can't you even go for thirty minutes?

In between writing projects. I don't know what form to submit to.

Robins and a wood thrush. I saw a fox yesterday, watched him unobserved. Big pink flowers blossoming on a tree, just brushing the screen of this outdoor shack in my host's backyard.

Trucks are moaning on the highway. Tires are rushing by outside the boundary of the forest. Route 80, Stroudsburg, Pennsylvania.

On the walk this morning, I thought of a few disciples who don't write to me anymore. One tried hard to live in ISKCON temples, and he sent his child to *gurukula.* Somehow it didn't work out for him, and now I hear he has moved back to his native country, has a full-time job in the city, and not much Kṛṣṇa conscious practice. It's not his fault, but it is unfortunate.

I thought of him, and I wondered how to help. By keeping in touch I can remind him of the importance of spiritual life. Now I hear from another disciple that she *is* hanging in there with her *sādhana*. She has an extremely heavy workload—a medical internship. She chants "carjapa," and she plays Kṛṣṇa conscious tapes when she's home relaxing as background sound. ("Better than spooky sound," she says.) I encouraged her. What else could I do? Should I tell her not to be a doctor, that she should live in a temple? It's not easy to advise people like that. There is no single solution for everybody's problems.

I just try to encourage them.

Anyway, let me stay present with whatever comes up. Hear the robins and the traffic, and keep reading the mail.

❦

Yesterday I completed a major work (sorry if that sounds puffed-up), *Prabhupāda Meditations,* Volume 3. Now I am jobless, seeking employment.

The present moment is an arc of time. It is not just 6:58 A.M., July 1, 1991, but an arc (like a rainbow) stretching from birth to death. I am in the homestretch—harvest time—last years with full facility for health and concentrated work. It's now or never. That's the present.

❦

Shack Notes, like former Gītā-nāgarī "creekside notes," are tangible. They are what I have now. The past is gone; it can never be recaptured. Don't falsify it or try to relive it just to create writing.

The present: Lord Nṛsiṁha's photo on the cover of my diary. I am trying not to be anxious about not being employed in a writing project. I *am* employed in writing *practice.*

12:00 P.M., Writing Practice

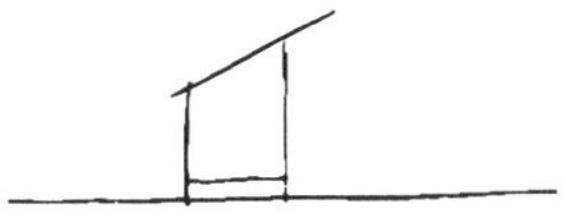

Who, me? Writing boring, silly stuff? Me, having nothing valuable to say? Me, needing a list of topics for writing practice? Naw, I'm an old hand at this. Or is it that I'm afraid to face the truth about myself? Anyway, I propose to write through it. Give me the moment; stay present with whatever comes up.

❦

A description of the shack: Its dimensions are about ten feet by ten feet. It's elevated about three feet off the ground on stilts. The sun is falling through in patches now, but it never gets bright and sunny in here. The trees are too dense. It's just a backyard in the suburbs, with a constant highway drone that becomes part of life.

Just now I heard a locust, the first I've heard this year. It vibrates and then stops. Forgive me for being happy.

No doubt about it, the locusts have arrived, vibrating against the patchy sunshine as it softens the green of the trees. The wood thrushes are as common as daisies now; all sure signs of a summer that has taken hold.

❦

The shack is screened in. There is a desk here, and gradually I am starting to pile it with books. There is also a sitting bench. Baladeva comes out at 10:00 A.M. and reads aloud to me from *Kṛṣṇa* book. This morning's reading was, "Kṛṣṇa Opens His Mouth and Shows Mother Yaśodā the Universal Form." I hear the pastime and then speak a "visualization" of it. I will tell you more about that as it develops.

❦ ❦ ❦

July 2, 1991, 1:30 A.M.

My legs are crossed as I sit on a chair at a desk in the bedroom. It's so early in the morning, but the highway roar never slows. It sounds almost like the ocean surf at Jagannātha Purī. I try to think about it like that, but it's hard to forget the big trucks.

We have been reading Kṛṣṇa's pastimes. I am preparing for a seminar of twenty lectures on "Kṛṣṇa's Vṛndāvana Pastimes" for the Vṛndāvana Institute for Higher Education in India this October. The lectures are prepared, but I still feel inadequate. Everyone has already heard these "stories" many times. How can I bring them to life just by presenting the same old thing? I don't really want to research esoteric texts to find additional stories of *kṛṣṇa-līlā;* I have faith that whatever Śrīla Prabhupāda has given of *kṛṣṇa-līlā* in the *Kṛṣṇa* book and Tenth Canto is sufficient. There is a challenge before me: how to speak about Kṛṣṇa with sincere *bhāva?* The blissful relationship of Kṛṣṇa with His devotees is the real nectar. How to capture it?

The reading we are doing now, with visualization of the scene, is providing me the added dimension. I am learning how to participate more in the pastimes of Kṛṣṇa. Śrīla Prabhupāda encourages this. After reading a verse with many visual details, such as describing Mother Yaśodā churning butter, Prabhupāda writes that we "should contemplate the bodily features of Mother Yaśodā . . . Therefore, this description is provided here. Advanced devotees must cherish this description, always thinking of Mother Yaśodā's features—how she was dressed, how she was working and perspiring, how beautiful the flowers were arranged in her hair, and so on. One should take advantage of the full description provided here by thinking of Mother Yaśodā in maternal affection for Kṛṣṇa" *(Bhāg.* 10.9.3).

The Franciscans have a tradition dating back to fourteenth century England of preparing texts, both to guide the common people through the scriptures and to encourage them to participate in the scriptural teachings. In a book called *Meditation on the Life of Jesus Christ,* the author describes a familiar gospel passage and then elaborates on some of the daily life details to provide the reader with a visual and familiar setting for the passage. Although the "additions" may not be found in the scripture itself, the details faithfully follow the mood of the scripture. Then the author invites the reader to respond to the descriptions, to admit their own failings or doubts, and to pray to lead a better life in obedience to the Lord.

We can do this when we hear Kṛṣṇa's pastimes—we can employ the imagination without falsifying or concocting anything. Śrīla Prabhupāda says that we should always think of Mother Yaśodā's features, how she was dressed, how she was working, how the flowers were arranged in her hair . . . We may have to imagine what kind of flowers they were. Was it a small garland, or flowers arranged here and there? Were they *mallika?* Fragrant jasmine? And when I feel resistance to thinking of Mother Yaśodā, why is that? Do I think she is "just a mother?" Then I can disallow my negative mood or my turning away from this image of Mother

Yaśodā—and I can pray, "Lord Kṛṣṇa and Śrīla Prabhupāda, please allow me to stay in the shelter of these pastimes. Teach me how to think of them."

> A very poor man living in Vṛndāvana forest presents the following appeal at the lotus feet of Vṛndāvana's King and Queen . . .
>
> Although I am the lowest and You the highest, although I am a fool and You the greatest philosopher, although I am wicked and You the most saintly, and although I commit offenses when I think of You, still, O King and Queen, the shadow of whose holy name delivers one from a host of sins, please be kind to this person who sometimes chants Your holy name.
>
> —From Rūpa Gosvāmī's *Stavā-mālā*, "A List of Requests" texts 1, 16

❦ ❦ ❦

2:10 A.M.

This early morning is precious time. A writing retreat is also precious. I unlock my door to see if any typing or notes have been left by Baladeva. I am trying to develop processes and projects that I can continue wherever I go. *Prabhupāda Meditations* is like that, an open-ended format I hope I can always pursue. I hope I never think, "That's finished."

I remember the joy of those weeks in Europe when the historical fiction came to me. Now it has left me and I am seeking something more. One project comes and goes, but I am always up early, writing. Writing is valid *bhajana* . . . just be ready to leave it all when Kṛṣṇa desires you to . . . and when the providential force pulls you away. Until then, "A poor person living in Vṛndāvana," a speck of dust in the wind, desires to worship and desires to share worship.

6:35 A.M. 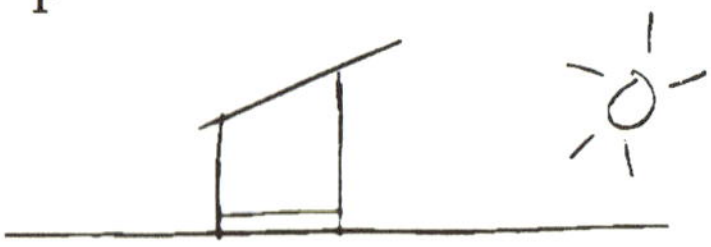

It's light enough around 6:15 to write in the shack. The birds are up at 4:45. I am a clock-watcher.

❦

The highway really revs up at this hour. The birds too. Everyone is hungry. The day's coming is announced by crows.

I can stop writing and look at my mail, but this is a writing retreat. It's better I don't do that. I will be defeated if I have to go answer mail now and can't write. Keep at it.

When I answer a letter, I force myself to speak straight. No nonsense. I tell them what they should do: "Don't give up your chanting of sixteen rounds." I am together when I speak in the letter, although sometimes I admit I am not perfect. How did Rilke put it in one of his letters to the young poet? Something like: "Do not think that the writer of these lines has reached the ideal he suggests that you should follow. No, his way is very difficult and he is struggling like anything, etc. . . . "

❦

No one can completely understand what another person is going through. Communication helps, but I sometimes rush my reading of a letter, or force my answer to it. Does that mean that everything will come out the same whether or not I write the letter? No, I cannot believe that. I just have to try my best.

❦

I don't want to make these "shack notes" into clever literary reflections, like some spiritual version of André Gidé musing and moodling in his home library. Gidé used to go out to cafés in the day and record what he read or what he overheard people saying in their conversations; he also wrote of his previous "reflections" on life.

But what is my alternative? Give you "the moment"?

Give us something edifying. You mean you've got nothing in there, nothing at all?

Well, I can choose a *Bhāgavatam* verse and speak on that . . .

❦

I just peeked into the mail bag. There is a letter from a father of a devotee in England. He became interested in Kṛṣṇa consciousness through his daughter. She used to write to me, but no longer does. However, her father and I exchange letters mostly because we share an interest in the writing craft. By occupation, he is an illustrator ("Work comes in short sprits . . . tomorrow, who knows? I manage to survive"). He writes poems, and in his last letter he said, "I think my own poetry is going through a sort of change at present. I feel the need to make direct statements. Whether I am bold enough is another matter." He sent this poem dedicated to his daughter, who recently got married:

For Laksmi-priya

Your spiritual master's garland
hangs withered on my rowan tree
blessing young branches—bright new leaves.
As I pass, I remember your wedding—
the *mahā-mantra* murmur
filling the temple room.

This perhaps describes my present creative
limbo;

I have crossed the line.
I have left it behind.
Yet it still holds me.

I need to detach.
Creativity lessens.
It seems unimportant.

It seems to say nothing.
I've left it behind.
I have crossed a line.

No pose of creation.
No poem but truth.
No drawing but skill.
—James Hall Tompson

I like the poem and told him so, but I couldn't understand the last line. "No drawing but skill"?

Isn't there more to art than skill? Skill and Kṛṣṇa consciousness, and inspiration and honesty—dedication—improved skill, human feeling . . . Rūpa Gosvāmī, for example, is a highly skilled Sanskrit poet, but there are others who are highly skilled in Sanskrit. Rūpa Gosvāmī is a pure devotee of Kṛṣṇa. Become a devotee (even if not yet pure), and then you can write and draw something worthwhile. That is our contention. Artists of the world, especially skilled ones, please become devotees and save yourselves. Then give the world pleasing, edifying work that will live long after you are gone, work that will please the Supreme Lord.

Noon

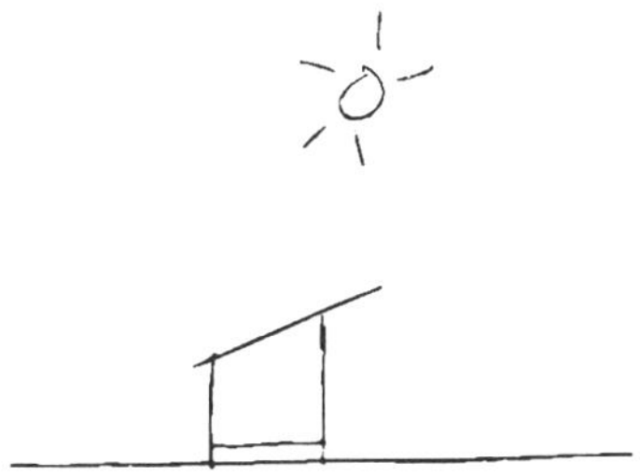

These "shack notes" must be temporary. We are scheduled to leave here by July 21, so I have until then to do something. I will continue beyond this time, of course. Yet each writing piece is my last chance. Put as much quality into these notes as possible.

But the fact is that although I am faced with the countdown, and although I have at least a small audience, I spend my time performing a soft shoe dance routine, juggle my top hat, make a few jokes . . . someone shouts from the audience, "Where is the perfection?" I reply, "It's the struggle, Prabhu, observe the struggle." The attempt to perfect devotional service.

❦

I have been recording my dreams, trying to remember them. I have heard that dreams can teach us something and that we can learn to dream in more favorable ways. My dreams are mostly weird or distressing. One book offers an explanation as to why we often dream of people and events from the past (like my travels to Staten Island and the U.S. Navy). "After all, the emotional 'you' that exists today is a product of those earlier people and events; so your mental computer is doing its work, even if it appears to you as a roundabout method."

The dreams are like a "computer" within myself which is trying to work things out, express things . . . It is the powerful unconscious self. I know just from the viewpoint of a writer that my dreams are more expert tales and more tangibly powerful "poems" than I can come up with when I try to create consciously. The only problem with the dreams is that they make no sense and their Kṛṣṇa conscious content is usually peripheral. (That is a very humbling fact. It makes me see that my Kṛṣṇa consciousness is merely a thin top layer of my conditioned self.)

If the dream life can be reached and even directed favorably, it can be another material thing to be used in the service of Kṛṣṇa. We are dreaming in any case, so why should we dream only on behalf of *māyā?* Why not have more Kṛṣṇa conscious dreams, dreams helpful for improving devotional service? And if the dreams can help me release my *anarthas,* that's certainly a gain.

Right now I am not much interested in "interpreting" my dreams or asking anyone to do that for me. Let me just start remembering them and see if just by giving them some attention, some of the signals from the "computer" will become obvious. Then it will be up to me to use the information in the right way.

The book I am reading talks of how dreams can solve problems and how scientists and writers have gained from their dreams: "It is not always the dreams themselves that are important. It is as though dreaming enables you to enter some sort of subconscious sorting-house so that the ideas arrived at when you awake are of greater significance and clarity."

The best thing happening these days is the reading of *Kṛṣṇa* book and Tenth Canto. First I relax and try to enter a submissive, receptive mood. Devotees might think it strange to see me counting down to relax: 10, 9, 8, 7, and then saying aloud, "Now I am going to enter the company of the pure devotees who are discussing the pastimes of Kṛṣṇa. They have invited me, and Śrīla Prabhupāda wants me to go there. Kṛṣṇa is in His pastimes. I can be with Him by hearing." It only takes me five minutes to prepare myself like this, but it gives the whole reading and discussion an aura of meditation (it turns into prayer too) and delightful participation.

4:30 P.M.

Now I am a bit stuck. Maybe because all day it's been gray and rainy. A siren (not uncommon) starts up on the highway. The rain patters all over the forest leaves and floor. Why should I be "stuck"? I have just spent a half-hour reading in the *Kṛṣṇa* book, gleaning the main points from Nārada's cursing of the two sons of Kuvera. No, I am not stuck, just a little quiet, uninspired, and dumb.

Heart beat, heart beat steady. Plane overhead, grumbling and scratching through the big clouds . . . I am in my home country doing something today which I hope will not be useless or eventually forgotten. How little we are aware that each passing day is subtracted from our calendar total. Only Vedic knowledge gives us the complete picture—it will happen to everyone, and not just once, but again and again *(mṛtyu-saṁsāra)*. The world mostly ignores Vedic truth, but a few of us have been drawn to it. Prabhupāda, let us live true to your order. Although we are unaware of the future, we have the assurance that at least we are making progress.

What is it like to cross from one life to another? Who remembers? Why can't I become more serious? When will I begin to perceive the reality of the material and spiritual worlds? When will I open up to my true nature and help others? That is what's important.

❦ ❦ ❦

July 3, 2:00 A.M.

This book has little going for it in terms of form. You are honest in telling the things you are doing—exploring a better way to read scripture, trying to recall your dreams—but is this the way to become a better devotee? What about travel and preaching? Yes, I will do that too. Try to tell your own truth, and if possible, the greater truth.

This shack is the place to write about Lord Kṛṣṇa in the spiritual world. You feel empty as you write—the inside of your cheek is chewed on, you are older by another day, you have some early morning indigestion—this is only the body.

You are not the body; nor are you the mind. You are spirit soul and "soul" means person, servant of God. That nature is revealed to you by serving the spiritual master. You hope to be stimulated by something from outside (like an interesting book arriving in the mail), but, finally, you have to become fully satisfied in the simple process of chanting and hearing.

Don't worry about failing on this page. *Serve here.* What if you had to render your entire service to Kṛṣṇa by writing on this page? How would you serve? Hare Kṛṣṇa, Hare Kṛṣṇa, Kṛṣṇa Kṛṣṇa, Hare Hare/Hare Rāma, Hare Rāma, Rāma Rāma, Hare Hare.

I am reduced to chanting and hearing. The best thing I am doing is reading *Kṛṣṇa* book for two hours a day with my friends. We are trying to participate in it by describing our feelings as we enter the scene of the *līlā,* and we discuss the impact the *līlā* has on us. Then we offer a prayer asking to improve our devotional life and to be allowed to continue hearing Kṛṣṇa's pastimes *(puṇya-śravaṇa-kīrtanaḥ).*

There is nothing to lose in this kind of writing.

❦

As for dreams, I am sometimes doubtful about their value. That is my mood this morning. I overslept a half hour and dreamt that I had lost the proper identification I needed for travel. I didn't realize it until we were already at the airport and the immigration official asked me for it. Although I had some ID with me, it wasn't acceptable and he didn't let me through. We had to stay in some place that resembled Florida. In the dream, I just accepted the fact that I was stuck.

What should I *do* with this dream? What does it mean? The subconscious may be revealing something, but how does it help me now that I am awake? The dream has reverted back to the shadows. It's intangible now. Is it enough to say, "I am a groping preacher who lives in shadows and whose body is affected by *tamo-guṇa*"?

❦

Writing is important to me. It's my service. I have written in the prescribed forms of biography and *BTG* essay. Now this plain and simple talking in the morning. Please accept it.

May I tell you about my Deity worship? We are reading Kṛṣṇa's Vṛndāvana pastimes, and I am especially attracted to the Lord in His Vṛndāvana form. It is the form He loves most, where His best devotees don't care to know that He is God. They love Him as a child, as a friend. His father Nanda Mahārāja says, "Kṛṣṇa, please bring my slippers."

I began to think I should worship a Kṛṣṇa *mūrti* in this Vṛndāvana mood. Then I realized that the pictures I worship are pure Vṛndāvana, and my worship of them is simple, like Vṛndāvana. If I had Rādhā-Kṛṣṇa Deities, I would have to worship Them in opulence according to regulation, serving the Lakṣmī-Nārāyaṇa forms within Them.

I have one picture of Rādhā-Dāmodara at Gītā-nāgarī, another of Rādhā and Kṛṣṇa as young children standing by the Yamunā, and another photo of the Six Gosvāmīs standing on the earth of Vraja with beautiful Vṛndāvana trees in the background—all pure Vṛndāvana persons. I also have a photo of the mystical Pañca-tattva. It is a copy of the Bengali painting Śrīla Prabhupāda brought with him to the U.S.A. as his only deity. The effulgences behind Lord Caitanya and the other members of the Pañca-tattva remind me of auras rather than the usual artistic rendering of halos. I am worshiping in the Vṛndāvana mood with these pictures, and I have my solid, three dimensional *mūrtis* of Lord Jagannātha, Subhadrā, Baladeva and Lakṣmī-Nṛsiṁha.

Vraja's importance is being awakened in me in a natural and safe way by Śrīla Prabhupāda's books. Too soon, however, we will have read through the few hundred pages describing Kṛṣṇa's Vṛndāvana-*mūrti*. I hope to continue the participatory method of reading in the other cantos, but will it be the same without Vṛndāvana? Śrīla Prabhupāda told us to read all his books. We can find Vṛndāvana pastimes described in many of Prabhupāda's books —*Nectar of Devotion, Caitanya-caritāmṛta*—and I can read and participate in them by Prabhupāda's mercy. And when I read *Caitanya-caritāmṛta,* I can participate in the life and teachings of the best devotee of Kṛṣṇa's Vṛndāvana pastimes, Lord Caitanya.

Thank you, Lord Kṛṣṇa and Śrīla Prabhupāda, for awakening me. It is not sufficient to be awakened from bed—that is still sleepwalking. I mean, thank you for awakening me in Kṛṣṇa consciousness.

I seek to enter the best life of hearing and chanting. When I engage in my other more external duties of traveling and meeting people, I want to remember to read and participate in Kṛṣṇa consciousness by hearing. Learn how to do it. And write about it to my friends.

❦

O Lord, O Energy of the Lord, how I neglect You in this most accessible form of Your holy name. Last night, after hearing and speaking *Kṛṣṇa* book, I thought, "Now let me chant the names in which the Lord is *most readily* available." What we preach about to the nondevotees is right here—*harināma* and books about Kṛṣṇa. They will want to know, "What do you people get from this? Does it change your lives? What do you experience? How does it solve problems in the world and in yourselves?"

We can respond to this by saying, "Although it is not easy for the members of the Hare Kṛṣṇa movement to surmount the entire material world, Kṛṣṇa consciousness makes some immense and deeply personal changes. Māyā is Kṛṣṇa's energy and is very powerful, and the devotees are in many ways still nondevotees; but to the degree we practice devotional service, our experiences are sublime. We worship great devotees who are entirely devoted to Kṛṣṇa, such as Śrīla Prabhupāda and the previous *ācāryas*, and we try to serve their Kṛṣṇa conscious mission. In this way, we increase our devotional service until surmounting the material energy becomes easy."

Highways roar past all over the earth. Soon I will be joining that mechanical river and will be rolling along. Madhu is fixing up a new van for us so we can travel to the European temples. I am looking forward to the Czechoslovakian farm because the devotees are simple and not much experienced. They are an easy and attentive audience when topics of Kṛṣṇa are discussed. I will tell them, "You didn't know God like this before. Kṛṣṇa is God's most intimate feature. Accept Him wholeheartedly." I want to tell this to others also—the Carmelite monk in Belgium, and the devotee who is disillusioned with how he has been treated by ISKCON—and in private asides, "I am reading *Kṛṣṇa* book. *He is the best.* Don't give up on Kṛṣṇa. No other manifestation of God is as relishable." I am trying to fully understand this myself.

6:40 A.M.

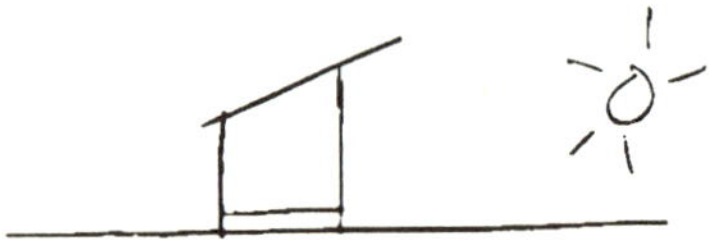

What is the quality of life as I know it?

I look out from the darkness of the forest shack, the dark morning, cloudy sky low overhead. Through the green I see part of the house and a glimpse of Baladeva pacing back and forth chanting *japa.*

I feel ambivalent toward the scene, and a little detached from it, but I am also aware that my experiences are what comprise my life. And sometimes when I attempt to verbalize my experiences, something wonderful occurs. Kṛṣṇa is the art of writing; He is all the alphabets from A to Z; He is the willingness of readers to decipher the printed symbols in a book. He is the love that is shared.

Writing is a way of life. We have already been told that we should not live a vicarious life in a world of books. We must meet life on our own; only then can we write. But what of spiritual books? Should we live in their world? And how can we gain the experiences told about in spiritual books so that we can meet spiritual life head on? Is there anything in our present experience to help us understand the depths of the spiritual exchanges we read about in spiritual books?

For example, I hear of Kṛṣṇa responding to the cries of the fruit vendor. He quickly grabs some grains in His small hands and runs down to barter with her. By the time He finds her, He has dropped most of the grains, His hands are so small. The fruit vendor is charmed by Kṛṣṇa's childish manner . . . What in my life corresponds to this pastime? I know fruit vendors, but none who love Kṛṣṇa like this. I know boys with small hands, but none even come close to being like Kṛṣṇa. We have no direct experience of *kṛṣṇa-līlā,* and, therefore, we can live entirely in a book like *Kṛṣṇa, Śrīmad-Bhāgavatam,* or *Bhagavad-gītā.* These books are where we gain our direct experience of spiritual life, and the sages who compiled these books also tell us about the world *we* live in, helping to usher us out of the material world and into the transcendental realm. They give us the correct vision.

❦

A wood thrush is singing and another is replying. Pan pipe tunes and whistles. I know it is not Vaikuṇṭha.

❦

About a month ago I went back to Katan Avenue (Staten Island) and walked, but I felt foreign there. I don't belong to my Guarino family. Devotees were waiting for me in the car, and I felt too odd sitting in the Great Kills train station. How long can I go on like this? I am hitting against walls. I cannot find Kṛṣṇa by this process.

There is not much depth to me; right now I cannot communicate much Kṛṣṇa consciousness. I am spiritually poor and yet I pick up a dictaphone and confidently dictate letters to aspiring devotees who ask, "If I become your disciple, how would you instruct me? I hear that you let devotees go in their own directions and you don't reprimand them much. How shall I know who my guru is?"

This is it, the essence of my reality. Truth flows. I have nothing else right now. It is a wonderful moment of life—my body working, my will striving, my intelligence dictating, "Let go."

Let's go to that deeper, quiet, peaceful place before we go inside the house for breakfast. Let me say something about Kṛṣṇa. He has butter-smeared footprints. He sits on the wooden mortar and gives out stolen butter to the monkeys. He is God, but His friends in Vṛndāvana aren't concerned with that.

Before I go into the house, a quiet word with You, Kṛṣṇa.

Look within for a vignette. Maybe a memory of Śrīla Prabhupāda about the upcoming twenty-fifth anniversary of ISKCON at 26 Second Avenue. I will tell you what I think—I don't know where they will be able to park all their cars. It will be a hectic, crowded event in the little storefront, with people making speeches on July 11, 1991, about what it was like twenty-five years ago, and about what it is like now and in the future, and everyone expecting something to happen . . . No one has invited me, but it is a general open house, so I will go too. But that is not the vignette.

The thrush is singing his head off.

I know the truth is in both voluntary and forced surrender. I am doing all I can.

I love Prabhupāda's purports to *Bhagavad-gītā* 12.2. Śrīla Prabhupāda describes a devotee's life as very simple. He says that the devotee chants or reads, or sometimes goes to the market to purchase something for Kṛṣṇa. Sometimes he cleans the temple or *washes the dishes.* And in all these activities, the devotee is in *samādhi.* I really like that description.

I also like to think of Śrīla Prabhupāda living such a simple life in his Rādhā-Dāmodara rooms. We can see in his account books how much he spent for charcoal, how much for postage to mail manuscripts and letters. I like to think of him typing *Śrīmad-Bhāgavatam* there on his small typewriter.

When we go to India, we can also visit those Rādhā-Dāmodara rooms and meditate on Prabhupāda in this way. But it will never be the same as when Prabhupāda was actually there and carrying out these activities. It's like the twenty-fifth anniversary of ISKCON at 26 Second Avenue. I am sorry if I say that everything falls short of expectations. It's not always true. Some things are much better than we expect. They're just never the same, that's all.

12:15 P.M.

Write what you can. Ananta dāsa has just come back from the Boston Ratha-yātrā. He is intent on cultivating personal, confidential relationships, and he wants to discuss how we may improve ourselves. He wants honesty—no more hiding behind religious roles. I would like to do this with him, but I have my schedule and writing work and correspondence. We spoke together today and decided to travel together for a few months. "Then," he said, "I will have to strike out on my own, be honest with others, and develop my own service."

❦

Ananta, Baladeva, and I spoke after hearing Kṛṣṇa's pastimes from the *Kṛṣṇa* book. We read how the families moved to Vṛndāvana in their ox carts, how Mother Yaśodā and Mother Rohiṇī were very happy holding Kṛṣṇa and Balarāma on their laps. The cowherd men protected the procession. We spoke of what impressed us. I liked the *Kṛṣṇa* book's mention that the boys were speaking with Their mothers. I wondered what they were talking about, but realized that I am not qualified to hear that conversation. Baladeva noted that the mothers and children were free to "bubble over" with happiness because the men took on the anxiety of protecting them. Ananta noted the noise of the carts creaking, the wheels and the bullocks' movement over the road. Then I spoke more extensively about how an outsider would doubt the reality of Kṛṣṇa's killing the calf demon. I liked what I said, thought it was eloquent, something I could repeat in the classroom in Vṛndāvana.

I joked, "What if we become so addicted to hearing Kṛṣṇa's pastimes that we become mad unless we are actually hearing them? The psychologists would use this against us in court cases. They would say, 'At first they started out just hearing two hours a day, then they increased it . . .'"

Now I am alone, scratching the page. Rain drips down around me. Birds and squirrels sometimes attract my attention as they crackle old leaves on the forest floor.

I was joking about what won't happen—becoming mad to hear of Kṛṣṇa's pastimes constantly.

❦

I want to discover a best way of writing. I love the flow of ink.

❦

I want to be part of the big group moving to Vṛndāvana with Kṛṣṇa. I want to be walking behind one of the carts and sometimes catch sight of Kṛṣṇa. I would like to compose poems to Kṛṣṇa. There is quite a bit about that in the Tenth Canto. Prabhupāda says that Mother Yaśodā used to compose poems and sing them while she was churning butter:

> It was formerly a custom that if one wanted to remember something constantly, he would transform it into poetry or have this done by a professional poet. It appears that Mother Yaśodā did not want to forget Kṛṣṇa's activities at any time. Therefore, she poeticized all of Kṛṣṇa's childhood activities, such as the killing of Pūtanā, Aghāsura, Śakaṭāsura, and Tṛṇāvarta, and while churning the butter, she sang about these activities in poetical form. This should be the practice of persons eager to remain Kṛṣṇa conscious twenty-four hours a day.
>
> —*Bhāg.* 10.9.2

I heard Śrīla Prabhupāda talking about composing Kṛṣṇa songs during a meeting with *gurukula* teachers in France, 1976. One of the teachers told Prabhupāda that they were sometimes composing simple songs for the children. Was this all right? Prabhupāda said yes. Then he said, "*Kṛṣṇa* book is already easy, but if you want to make it more easy, that is all right." He seemed to be hinting that he thought the *Kṛṣṇa* book was fine the way it was, but on other occasions he instructed devotees to put *Kṛṣṇa* book into verse form.

I somehow get the impression (although maybe it is my imagination) that Mother Yaśodā was making up her songs with little attention to rhyming lyrics or Sanskrit rules. There is also a mention of singing songs when Kṛṣṇa's family and friends moved to Vṛndāvana: "As they rode, they began to chant with great pleasure the pastimes of Kṛṣṇa." Prabhupāda explains, "They used to pass their time either by taking care of Kṛṣṇa and Balarāma, or by chanting about Their pastimes."

Śukadeva says that after some wonderful activity by Kṛṣṇa, the boys would then "declare the incident loudly." Prabhupāda states, "It was the practice of the inhabitants of Vrajabhūmi to compose poetry about the incidents that occurred in the forest when Kṛṣṇa performed His different activities of killing the *asuras*. They would compose all the stories in poetry or have this done by professional poets, and then they would sing about these incidents" (*Bhāg.* 10.11.53).

Of course, one cannot do this unless he has *bhāva*. I hope that as I go on hearing and reading, I will develop appreciation and deep respect for those pastimes. There is nothing better than attaining this taste. Then no matter where you are, you can think of Kṛṣṇa and sing of His pastimes, and be free of all material disturbances.

4:00 P.M.

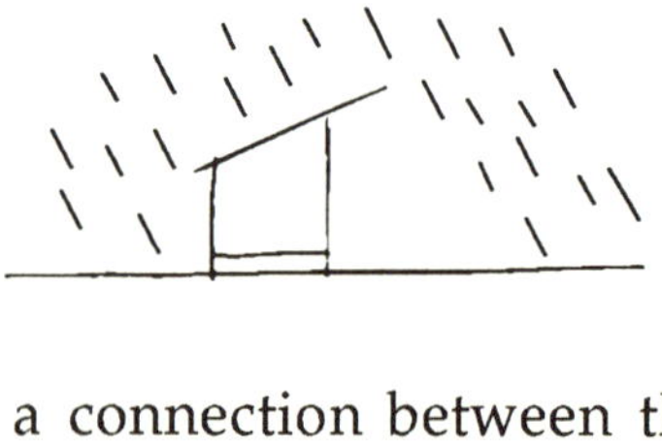

There is a connection between the *Kṛṣṇa* book reading and this writing. I don't want it to be only the obvious one.

I want to describe it, but can't yet. I have heard enough about left brain and right brain theory to desire to race ahead of left brain. If there is wholeness, it is in Kṛṣṇa.

I did one of those nonlinear exercises called, "Writing the Natural Way." I put the word "flame" in the middle. Then you are supposed to write down words as fast as they come, and circle them, radiating out from "flame." After doing that you pause, and something is supposed to click. Then you start writing in sentences. I put Kṛṣṇa in there in such a way that He is in all things.

Flame

Cluster never seems to work for me.
So burn it up.
All gets burned up
in Śiva's dance
the sun god's planet,
a match
to incense
waved before the Deities.
Flame of digestion,
my old flame—
can't pull it all together, so
I'll put it all to flame.

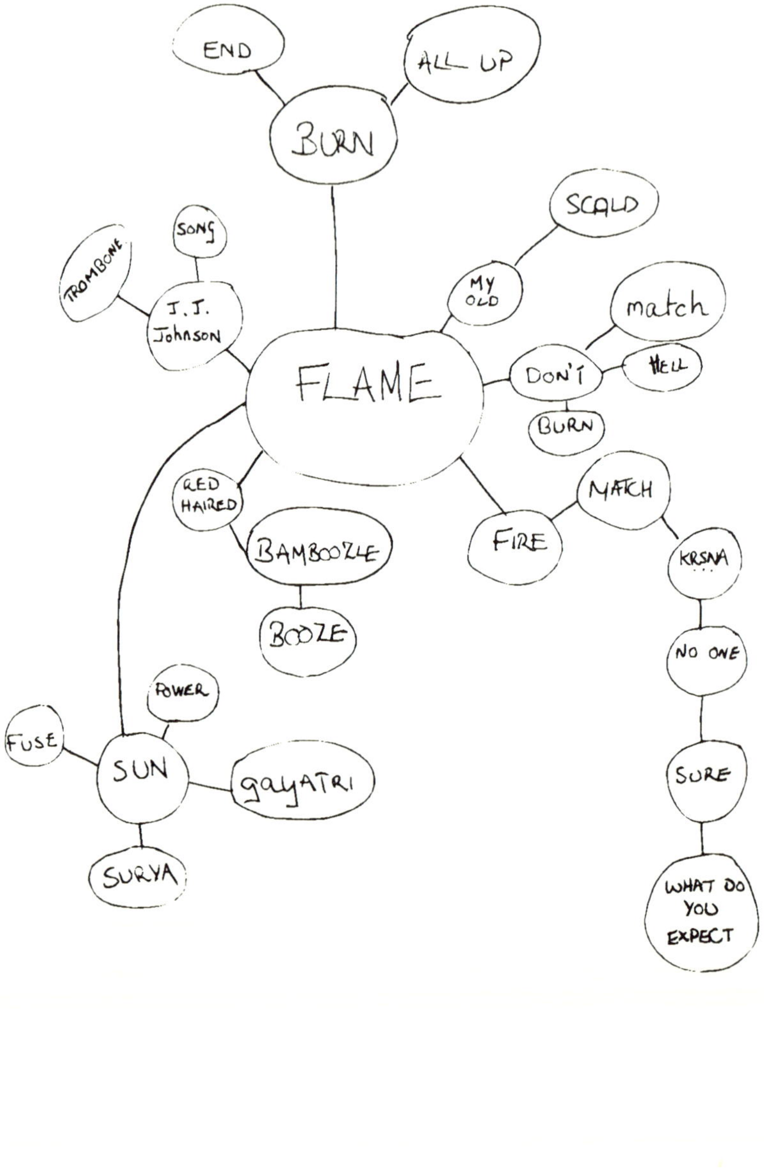
FLAME
BURN
END
ALL UP
SCALD
MY OLD
match
DON'T
HELL
BURN
MATCH
FIRE
KRSNA
NO ONE
SURE
WHAT DO YOU EXPECT
SONG
TROMBONE
J.J. Johnson
RED HAIRED
BAMBOOZLE
BOOZE
POWER
FUSE
SUN
gayatri
SURYA

The author of *Writing the Natural Way* talks about right brain. Design mind. Okay, but what is the method whereby the soul can speak? I don't think there is any way except by the blessings of Supersoul: "Please speak like this. I know you want to praise Kṛṣṇa in a way that is intelligible to others. Try this." He sits down before the Deity of Kṛṣṇa and the Lord dictates to him many volumes of prose and poetry. Baladeva Vidyābhūṣaṇa wrote *Govinda-bhāṣya* in that way, and Kṛṣṇadāsa Kavirāja says he is a puppet writing only what Madana-mohana tells him.

I cannot claim that connection, but I do work for You, dear Bhagavān. I serve You through my spiritual master.

I heard Śrīla Prabhupāda talking with *gurukula* teachers. A teacher said, "Śrīla Prabhupāda, someone here wants to educate their own child." Śrīla Prabhupāda said, "Yes, he told me that his child wasn't getting good education [in *gurukula*]." Śrīla Prabhupāda said it was all right to educate him at home. The *gurukula* teacher had to swallow it. Then Śrīla Prabhupāda said, "Yes, it is the parent's responsibility to somehow see that the child gets Kṛṣṇa conscious education. That is our whole principle, whether singly or in a group, as long as they grow up in Kṛṣṇa conscious education." This confirmed what I thought—that Śrīla Prabhupāda is less concerned with a particular method, even if he taught that method, than he is with the result. He wants strong Kṛṣṇa consciousness, good preaching, and a life-long commitment to devotional service.

I can apply that to writing—there is no one way it *has* to be. Surrender, be Kṛṣṇa conscious, be honest, cry with *laulyam,* be free in your desire to serve: that's the writing method.

❦

Now be peaceful. Take a deep breath. Hear the rain. You have eighteen days left here. Go back inside the house for a *Kṛṣṇa* book reading. It will be nice. First, do your ordinary service. You have much to learn.

We are starting to hear how each demon killed by Kṛṣṇa represents an *anartha.* Discuss these things.

As the cowherd men protected Kṛṣṇa and the other devotees while they all moved in bullock carts to Vṛndāvana, so I must post guards to fight the demons of doubt: the Western world swarm of wasps and other attackers who say Vedic knowledge and the *Purāṇas* are *kalpana,* mythology, imagination.

❦

Left brain: The "primitive" efforts are all right, but don't make a big bombast out of it. Admit you are just making some loose notes in between more serious work.

❦

Some may say, "Hey, Satsvarūpa is trying to reach Kṛṣṇa by the ascending process."

I say, "Not true. But if I write before Kṛṣṇa speaks through me, I state, 'This is only me talking from the point of view of material life. I know I cannot reach Kṛṣṇa just by an exertion of will. I am begging

Kṛṣṇa to please engage me in His service.' What you are hearing is my cry."

"But why print that? If you are just crying, do it in your closet. When Kṛṣṇa actually enlightens you, then speak."

"That doesn't sound right to me. The cry is the early stage of devotional service and has its place. Anyway, you can decide for yourself whether or not to listen."

I like to remember that purport where Śrīla Prabhupāda says we cannot make nice prayers like Brahmā or Śiva, but that Kṛṣṇa wants to hear our prayers anyway. Go ahead, He accepts your good intentions.

Acknowledge He is everything and offer obeisances to His lotus feet.

❦

Seventeen days left to go.

❦ ❦ ❦

July 4, 1:30 A.M.

When we say you should write as if it is your last piece, this means you should write soberly and with as much Kṛṣṇa consciousness as possible, to help people. It means you should go to the heart of spiritual sentiment and surrender, like Mahārāja Khaṭvāṅga.

❦

After attending an hour of our *Kṛṣṇa* book reading sessions, Ananta said, "It helps me to understand Kṛṣṇa as a person." Last night we discussed the killing of the Baka demon, a stork with a sharp beak.

❦

When there is nothing to say, it means you are not able to speak. There is *so* much to say, but the censors and inner controllers edit out the burdensome weight of the emotions. They soften or trivialize the actual situation, as if you couldn't bear it. Yet you want to write as evocatively as possible, to nourish and entertain readers. The artist's predicament. Therefore, you make little forays into the realm of inner knowledge, try to sneak past the editorial board. Ultimately, you accept whatever vocalization the intelligence *is* willing to give.

❦

A devotee repeats the message of Kṛṣṇa in his own words. Śrīla Prabhupāda was strong on the need for realization. He did not encourage us to speak like parrots. A parrot can be taught to repeat the Hare Kṛṣṇa mantra, but when it is being choked, it only squawks. Our utterance of Hare Kṛṣṇa mantra should be made with personal conviction, but should be parrot-like in the same manner that Śukadeva Gosvāmī was parrot-like—he added sweetness to the mango of Vedic knowledge he had received from his father.

"Know, O thoughtful men, that *Śrīmad-Bhāgavatam* is the mature fruit of the tree of Vedic literature. It emanated from the lips of Śukadeva Gosvāmī. Therefore, this nectarean fruit is all the more relishable for liberated souls" (*Bhāg.* 1.1.3). Śrīla Prabhupāda: "Śrīla Śukadeva Gosvāmī describes the *Bhāgavatam* from its very beginning and not whimsically to satisfy the mundaner who has very little knowledge in transcendent science."

So where is *my* "last piece sobriety"?

Wait until the right message appears on the screen before writing it down. Unfortunately, we have cluttered screens (vision) and so much junk in our pasts. We cannot say whatever comes to mind and pass it off as Kṛṣṇa conscious instruction. The materialists conclude that they have nothing to say; they speak whatever occurs to them. They refuse to repeat or to faithfully sweeten scriptural truths. I must not fall into imitating them in their worship of the hovering mental plane or *muni*-like mental agitations.

I want to give Vedic truths.

Yet there is value in trying to "cut through to first thoughts," in listening to the uncorrected flow of ideas. There is good advice available there.

My contention is that the life of a struggling devotee is worth hearing about by other devotees.

Some devotees, however, think this is whimsical. They want to read only perfect truth. I agree that we must speak the truths of *Śrīmad-Bhāgavatam,* and that we should sweeten them with our realizations. But there must be time for devotees to speak heart to heart, even to expose their misgivings. We must be compassionate toward fellow devotees, and should desire to hear from them in this way. We should find our own confidential friends who will hear from us. We will get real strength from these confidential exchanges. The Absolute Truth is perfect; we are not. *Our not being perfect is of importance to us.* Therefore, it is neither whimsical nor taboo to discuss these topics.

Another challenge: Okay, but the *writer* in Kṛṣṇa consciousness should be perfect, or if he isn't, he should not express his imperfection in writing. He should serve only as an instrument of perfect truth when he writes. If he is too obsessed with his hang-ups and attachments to the mundane, then he should not write. In Vedic society, only a liberated person can write.

But I have already gone ahead. I speak what I know, including the troubles.

❦

So what are my sober last words? One urges everyone to be good, one says it as a teacher and as a departing, flawed, but repentant soul: "Don't make the same mistakes I made." I remember reading the dying words of Aldous Huxley, "I should have been kinder." Words like that are edifying, even if one was previously a rascal. We want honest testimony.

Speaking of last words, former U.S. President Dwight Eisenhower said, "I have always loved my wife. I have always loved my country." There is some piety there, but it is not the transcendental wisdom the living need to guide them. If we follow Ike and love this world, we will have to come back to this world.

Bhaktisiddhānta Sarasvatī Ṭhākura's last words: "Please bear in mind that our sole duty and religion is to spread and propagate service to the Lord and His devotees." And shortly before that he said, "Please do not give up the service of Godhead in spite of all dangers, all criticisms, all discomforts . . . do not give up your own service, which is your everything and all, neither reject the process of chanting and hearing . . . "

Honesty, therefore, as candid expression is not enough in itself. Hold your tongue when a nonsensical or offensive thought wants to be uttered. Practice *mauna.* Kṛṣṇa conscious *mauna* is to vibrate *kṛṣṇa-kathā.*

Some reject their life's work with their last words, but a man's writings assume an independent life of their own regardless of his later rejection of them. Are the poor utterings of a faulty *bhakta,* one who begs for advancement, who is trying to love, and who tries (and fails and tries again) to rid himself of *anarthas*—are they in the category of "literature in pursuance of the Vedic version?"

Is the writer himself supposed to know for sure?

In *Bhagavad-gītā,* the Personality of Godhead says that in the *Vedas* there is nothing but the urge for searching after Him, Lord Kṛṣṇa. Thus the questions that pertain to Kṛṣṇa are the sum and substance of all the Vedic inquiries . . . Forgetting Kṛṣṇa, we have created so many objects of questions and answers, but none of them are able to give us complete satisfaction.

—*Bhāg.* 1.2.5

❦

This morning I am feeling selective. I am rejecting most of the impressions and memories that are coming to the surface of my mind. Writer's block.

❦

I like to hear someone correct himself, admit his wrongs. But don't keep making mistakes and then correcting yourself. It has to be edifying to follow a person's life (in writing or otherwise), see his error, and see him struggle to correct it by repentance and humble reform. This is the victory we all seek in our own lives.

❦

Sometimes when we admit what goes on in our minds during *maṅgala-ārati* or *japa,* it gets a laugh from a fellow devotee. They know, too. Actually, a devotee's failure to think of Kṛṣṇa is always sad. We need to laugh at our failure, but there is a certain poignancy there. There is an absence of direct Kṛṣṇa conscious thought in our lives, yet Kṛṣṇa is present even when He is *not* in our thoughts. That is the sadness of the faulty utterance.

But it is our reality, that faulty utterance. We chuckle, "He didn't think of Kṛṣṇa. He was distracted." We do get beyond it *sometimes;* we want to get beyond it *all* the time. Our desire brings an added note of poignancy: our awareness of the ideal compared to our ability to attain it, or even *really* try for it. And so we tell ourselves, "At least I was at *maṅgala-ārati*. I saw the Deities. I chanted my rounds."

❦

Ah, this is it—this is the urgency and
  soberness of last words,
declaring—I was there,
I loved my life in Kṛṣṇa consciousness,
I valued it,
(unlike Ike's loves)
I loved Prabhupāda,
I failed him. My tears,
he witnesses, "I'm sorry I failed."
And I can tell others, *don't do like this.*

Somehow you have to do better. But at any rate, don't quit.

6:30 A.M.

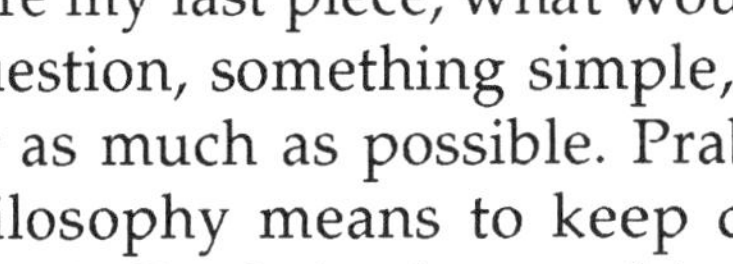

If this were my last piece, what would I say? This is a plain question, something simple, and I should face up to it as much as possible. Prabhupāda tells us that "philosophy means to keep death in your front." Mahārāja Parīkṣit phrases this question with relevance to all of us: "I am therefore begging you to show the way of perfection for all persons, and especially for one who is about to die" (*Bhāg.* 1.19.37).

It's another dreary, overcast day. I finally saw the elusive wood thrush. It was high up in a tree, singing in plain view on a dead branch. It had a whitish breast—the dawn light gave its breast a silver glow —and it had a dark, brownish head and back. I had a good view of it, but when I shuffled my feet to look from another angle, it flew away.

And that is one of the things I want to say in my last piece. Even when I am intent on a spiritual activity like reading scripture, I am liable to remark to a brother about the weather or a bird song. It's small talk, *prajalpā,* and I don't go on about it at great length but you see, there are birds and weather and trees in Kṛṣṇa's abode. He doesn't live in a vacuum. He and His friends talk about these things:

> Some of them gladly followed the peacocks and imitated the onomatopoetic sounds of the cuckoo. While the birds were flying in the sky the boys ran after the bird's shadows along the ground and tried to follow their exact courses . . . some of them imitated the dancing of the peacocks.
>
> —*Kṛṣṇa,* p. 80, 1982 edition

We see a thrush, are thrilled, can't deny it, and we soon talk about Kṛṣṇa and what He does in Kṛṣṇaloka. What's the harm in that?

❦

Śrīla Prabhupāda continued translating *Śrīmad-Bhāgavatam* right up until the end. He did not write a separate "death piece" or feel the need to reject his life's work at the last minute. He was translating the Tenth Canto, "The Stealing of the Calves and Cows by Lord Brahmā." He worked right up to the point where Lord Brahmā was humiliated, when he saw the glory of Śrī Kṛṣṇa. Just as Lord Brahmā was about to make his wonderful prayers (14th Chapter), Śrīla Prabhupāda stopped. He left us with the impression that he continued until his last breath, preaching and glorifying Kṛṣṇa.

Śrīla Prabhupāda was always speaking and writing with death in his front. He was solidly giving the "medicine" to save others at the time of death. His work is full of substance.

❦

O wood thrush on the broken branch,
your silver-white breast attests
to creation,
song,
—or never mind that—
you are who you are.
I frightened you and you vanished.
I had my beads in my hands,
looked up to you. I paused in
japa to see you—you ought
to thank me, or be impressed
at least, that I took time out
to see you. But no, you don't care.
Better you go anyway,
after a brief look,
so I can get back to chanting
and I did.
I strode down the dirt hill,
happy to chant and move outdoors,
singing *mahā-mantra*
to myself in the woods
grateful to walk and chant.

Devotees need to heal themselves; they need to heal as communities and in their friendships. It is essential work and falls within the purificatory process known as Kṛṣṇa conscious self-realization. Not all devotees agree. Some devotees shy away from open friendships. They want to keep their relationships strictly in terms of devotional duties and speak only of perfect Vedic teachings.

But speaking personally to each other can include discussion of our inadequacies. It is not just "dwelling on the problems." Our problems can only be solved by the application of chanting and hearing, but even our own chanting and hearing can be helped along by being able to reveal in confidence the truth about our inabilities to chant and hear properly. This is part of inner life.

Recently, someone was encouraging me to speak out about this point. He wants me to decry the widespread rejection of healing and intimate friendship. But are open relationships something one can advocate? Is it not a private matter which each individual has to decide for him or herself? Better to allow for that freedom. For those who want openness, let it be; let the others be also.

❦ ❦ ❦

Noon

Everything material becomes ruined, goes through changes. One minute the shack is a summer paradise, surrounded by cool breezes, patchy sunlight, and the calls of birds, and the next, the neighbor starts up his power saw. His dogs begin to bark, and he shouts commands to his son . . .

Kṛṣṇa runs through the field with His friends, but there too disturbances come. The demigods were afraid of Agha, but the friends of Kṛṣṇa were unafraid. They knew Kṛṣṇa would save them.

Ananta, Baladeva, and I visualized the scene: Kṛṣṇa walks ahead of the others a short distance to enjoy a scenic spot. The boys race to see who can touch Kṛṣṇa first. I started to run and felt my false ego-self in competition with the other boys, as happens in ISKCON. I thought, "I have no friends. And I am not a friend to other boys—not like it is in Goloka." Then I left that conception behind and just ran. The path was not smooth like a race track, but we had to jump over logs and run down ravines. "All the boys appeared very jolly and happy in that excursion." Oh, leave behind all cares. "I will go there and touch Kṛṣṇa." Finally, we reach our hero and fall at His feet. "Kṛṣṇa! Kṛṣṇa! Kṛṣṇa! *He!*"

In the shack, I told Baladeva and Ananta what I felt while participating in the *līlā* as described by Śukadeva: a conviction to work for developing friendships in this world. Isn't that what the Kṛṣṇa consciousness movement is about? May a drop of the nectar of developing friendships and carefree absorption with Kṛṣṇa and His friends fall upon us. And let us work to earn it.

❦

There was once a cottage by the Yamunā that was covered by vines. Sages gathered with their leader, Śukadeva Gosvāmī. He is inviting us to join them and hear about Kṛṣṇa. Come down the *ghat* steps and leave behind your material identity.

Ten more devotees slip down. Now the stone *ghat* ends and there are more steps in the earth. Give up your cares and come down. You will sit in their company and hear. Walk down—Prabhupāda wants you to go.

This is why *Śrīmad-Bhāgavatam* was prepared, so we can also join that gathering. "Descriptions of the Lord are the right medicine for the conditioned soul undergoing repeated birth and death. Therefore, who will cease hearing such glorification of the Lord except a butcher or one who is killing his own self?" (*Bhāg.* 10.1.4).

❦

Ananta has been making the point that we should have friends—all of us—and open up, admitting our faults so we can help ourselves. He is discovering this for himself. Religion could be a crutch for some, he said. One joins the movement and takes shelter in a perfect philosophy and thinks, "Now I don't have to improve myself. I have a perfect philosophy to explain everything."

He said he likes to talk with very new devotees because they don't hide their problems. One says, "I have a girlfriend and I am tempted to go back and live with her." Another says, "When I go before the Deity I have doubts about whether this is God," or, "I don't know if I can stick it out in devotional service." But as we grow older and get some status, we may not openly admit anything wrong about ourselves. There is no one we talk with about our problems, and we ourselves tend to deny them. But they don't go away.

July 4th firecrackers and dog barking, gentle breeze on the forehead.

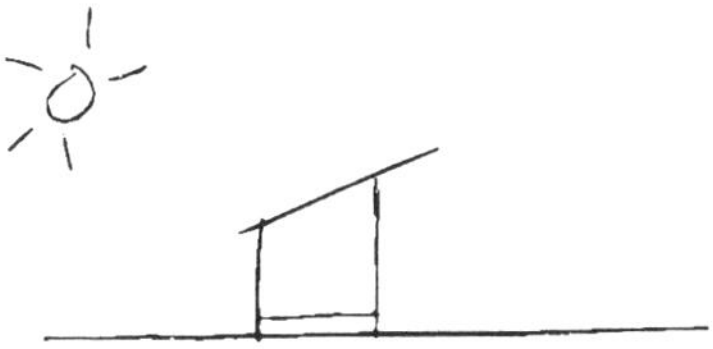

4:00 P.M.

The cowherd men met, and Nanda Mahārāja spoke up. "There are too many demons coming to Mahāvana," he said, and they all agreed that they should move to Vṛndāvana. They did so at once, loading up their possessions on the oxcarts.

Then as Kṛṣṇa grew older, He started going out with calves. They were frisky calves, and each boy took care of thousands. One day, Vatsāsura came into their midst. "There's a demon," said Kṛṣṇa, and He quietly approached him, then whirled him up into the tree. "Well done! Well done!" the boys cried. They liked to embrace Kṛṣṇa to their chests.

Those boys—complete freedom and bliss with their protector. They raced through the forest, stopped to grab flowers and fallen peacock feathers and red clay for marking their bodies. Then they entered the realm of animals—jumped into trees like monkeys, into streams like frogs, chased the shadows of birds, and raced to see who could be the first to touch Kṛṣṇa. They were ready for anything, so when the Agha demon appeared they were unafraid, even though they could not figure out what he was. "Even if he is a big serpent ready to swallow us, Kṛṣṇa will kill him just as He killed Baka."

By talking of Kṛṣṇa who killed Bakāsura, Nanda Mahārāja and the cowherd men "forgot the threefold miseries of material existence. This is the effect of Kṛṣṇa consciousness. What was enjoyed 5,000 years ago by Nanda Mahārāja can still be enjoyed by persons who are in Kṛṣṇa consciousness simply by talking about the transcendental pastimes of Kṛṣṇa and His associates" (*Kṛṣṇa,* Vol. 1, p. 79).

❦

I don't see the profit in the war between censor and creator—between left and right brain. These aspects are meant to work together in the service of Kṛṣṇa. It's embarrassing that all this inner fighting goes on, but this is how a devotee struggles to achieve proficiency in his service. Each has their own experience of that within their particular services.

Sorry folks, but I've got to keep writing. I promised myself this. Besides, I've got an editor now, so there's no problem in dealing with something not worth sharing. I've got to move on with this and talk on the page.

I'll tell Kṛṣṇa stories. It's like being in solitary confinement and talking to yourself to keep from going insane.

Kṛṣṇa stories. I have to walk around here and breathe. I can throw this page out.

The man next door: He is angry all day long. He is on holiday, but keeps yelling at his two big dogs, "Get out of here!" They try to come up on his deck. Why keep them if you don't want them? This is the man with the blue wooden duck on top of his house. Its wings revolve in the wind. One day, sudden death or some other disillusion will hit his family. The husband and wife will look at the blue painted duck and it will occur to them, "We have created this home with millions of details. We worked hard, spent hundreds of thousands of dollars to create it, and now it has ended—it is a dream world, topped with a blue duck whose wings revolve in the wind."

Will death and similar disillusion not strike this house too? Yes, in every house there will be lamentation. The season of happiness will give way to the season of unhappiness. But a devotee of the Lord will say, "Let us chant and hear of Lord Hari. This alone cannot be destroyed by time. Let us remember Him now and at the time of death." The house of a devotee cannot be defeated, despite inevitable loss, dwindling, and death.

Our house is packed with busy workers.

And the wood thrush sings.

My dear Lord Kṛṣṇa, You are the controller. I cannot get anywhere on my own. You determine everything. I have to leave this scene in a few years, just like everyone else; it never happens otherwise. And then another body.

("Get out of here!" That dog might have been his father in a previous life, and *his* son, four years old, is now the prince. He is their little "Kṛṣṇa," but he will disappoint them in the end.)

❦ ❦ ❦

July 5, 1:30 A.M. ◐

Your job is to praise. Like a musician who writes inspirational music, others should feel inspired by (and appreciative of) the upliftment coming through in your voice. Even if the musician doesn't name a particular Deity as the object of his praise, the praise should still be evident. If the theme is perfect, others will be able to listen repeatedly and be transported to their own inner sanctuary of love for Kṛṣṇa.

I also want to tell others how a musician makes praise of the Supreme and His creation, and how it effects the listener. There is a technique to weaving even chaotic, unhappy elements together until both musician and listener are left with a sense of God's immanence.

Although there are different levels of praise, it seems to require inner peace to both speak it and offer it. If there is too much pain and confusion, then it remains on the level of "humanistic" music—it evokes empathy in the listener, but does not draw either musician or listener into the transcendental realm. Praise is a religious experience.

All glories to the Supreme Lord who lives in the spiritual world, which is inaccessible by all methods of worldly endeavor, but which is revealed to us by the Lord. We simply have to hear submissively.

All glories to those who remind us of Kṛṣṇa by painting accurate pictures of the walls of the spiritual palaces and who enter the nature of the Supreme Lord's majesty and dominion and glory. All glories to those who live in this realization through their relationships with the pure devotee.

Glories to the best song-praises made by those who know Kṛṣṇa in His intimate feature in Goloka. These praises describe His yellow garments, His flute playing, His consort Rādhārāṇī, His parents, and the boys who run with Kṛṣṇa. These are the best songs of praise.

❦

In our *Kṛṣṇa* book sessions, we spend five to ten minutes preparing ourselves. Without that, the reading of *Kṛṣṇa* book would go past us almost unnoticed in its many details, and we would fail to *feel* it. I am bashful to share with any but an intimate group, the simple methods of physical relaxation we use to prepare ourselves to read *Śrīmad-Bhāgavatam.* The reading can be a deep group meditation as we try to visualize our own participation in the pastime being described. It is a lot better than the drowsy, inattentive heads who often attend the *Śrīmad-Bhāgavatam* class. As our elementary school teacher used to say, "You are present in body, but not in spirit."

All glories to Śukadeva's group who can sit up and listen.

❦

This is a book about writing in devotional service. I like to think of it as a book *for* writers, helping them to see the process of writing and to recognize the challenges writers face. Those who are not writers can apply these principles to their own attempts in devotional service.

When I began writing at seventeen, writing was a wonderful discovery—not just something *I* should do, but everyone. I proselytized on behalf of the writing craft. I told people they should write vignettes and stories and poems of their life experiences . . . Of course, not many people took me seriously, but those of us who did write would read to each other regularly and gently advise each other, responding to each other's writing. Our main emphasis was to encourage each other to continue.

Gradually, I learned that just because *I* loved to write didn't mean others had to. Perhaps I even began to prefer people not write; I didn't need too much competition. But that early sharing among friends was nice. We were not professional writers, but I especially looked forward to hearing a friend read his latest piece. We wrote from the heart about how we saw life, and it was very refreshing and personal. Then we talked and wrote more. Sometimes we even wrote in each other's company.

It would be nice to share like this in Kṛṣṇa consciousness. When I was seventeen, I felt like a lone trail-blazer, but I had the audacity of youth. Now we are uptight adults worrying if someone doesn't like our poems, or afraid to be honest when discussing another's writing.

In the spiritual world, genuine praises of Kṛṣṇa are appreciated "by those who are thoroughly honest":

> . . . That literature which is full of description of the transcendental glories of the name, fame, forms, pastimes, etc., of the unlimited Supreme Lord is a different creation, full of transcendental words directed toward bringing about a revolution in the impious

lives of the world's misdirected civilization. Such transcendental literatures, *even though imperfectly composed, are heard, sung, and accepted by those purified men who are thoroughly honest.*

—*Bhāg.* 1.5.11 [emphasis added]

Another point: Sometimes we cannot directly repeat the pastimes of the Lord and His devotees because we have to speak of other realities we are faced with in our struggles. We still have to bring our writing into transcendental focus. All works, especially those in the fields of education and research, should culminate in poetry describing the glories of the Lord. It is a preaching service: "Those who are not so well-situated due to material attachment, should be shown the ways of transcendental realization, by your goodness, through descriptions of the transcendental activities of the Supreme Lord" *(Bhāg.* 1.5.16).

Let us be engaged in this as much as possible. "It is personally experienced by me that those who are always full of cares and anxieties due to contact of the senses with their objects can cross the ocean of nescience on a most suitable boat—by *constant* chanting of the transcendental activities of the Personality of Godhead" *(Bhāg.* 1.6.34).

❦

We want to be accepted as we are.

❦

Thank You, Lord, for allowing me to rise and write. I didn't feel much like doing it when I began—felt indifference and distaste for existence (like the stuff we scrape off our tongue when we get up in the morning). But You told me to get up anyway, and then You delivered me. I wrote about praise. Now I beg you to allow me to be a praise-maker. I know one has to earn it. One has to tell it as one's own desire to praise; not as a professional blesser. The Salvation Army Band and the street *harināma* party have to feel joyful when they play and sing, "Glories to the Lord! Join us in praise!"

So I require you to mold me into a praise-maker. That *will* include singing some blues and chaos—getting out of chaos, rising up, "I saw the light! I was in darkness and my spiritual master saved me." The world is suffering, and praise of You is the remedy:

> Please, therefore, describe the Almighty Lord's activities which you have learned by your vast knowledge of the *Vedas,* for that will satisfy the hankerings of great learned men, and, at the same time, mitigate the miseries of the masses of common people who are always suffering from material pangs. Indeed, there is no other way to get out of such miseries.
>
> —*Bhāg.* 1.5.40

As I said, this book is about my experience with writing. Please, if you are not a writer, translate this into meaningful action for you. As Śrīla Prabhupāda states, "One *should work* only for Kṛṣṇa. It *does not matter in what kind* of work one engages, but that work should be done only for Kṛṣṇa" *(Bg.*12.6-7, purport).

I struggle; I rip up efforts and start new ones. Is this the sign of an unhappy man? No, I am very fortunate, and I have a duty to share the fortune. The "ripping up" doesn't mean I am unfortunate.

Recently I read a book, *No More Second-Hand Art,* by Peter London. The author is an artist and an art teacher, and some things he said can be applied to the arts of devotional service. London talks about "getting lost" as one of the aspects of creative art. He says that sometimes an artist reaches a stage where he becomes competent in a certain form, but then has nothing to look forward to in developing himself. Then he cuts himself off from creativity by not going forward more. He describes how in his own art development, he decided to try to get to the very roots of his creativity and again ask questions as if asking them for the first time: *"What is art? What does it look like? How do you make it? What does it mean?"*

> Starting off a creative process with the belief that we can predict and control the eventual outcome is, similarly, to squeeze out of the creative process its inherent evolutionary character and invite frustration. *Not to allow the hand, eye, and spirit to learn from moment to moment throughout the creative process is to deny us access to an enormous quantity of new data that becomes uncovered, but is quickly covered over again by the veil of our own expectation.* To constrain and deny what is natural and universal is to pit ourselves against the universe. And guess what? We lose. . . . *Instead of asking, is the work right and am I right, we could ask, "How honest was I in disclosing what I know and feel? How deep did I allow myself to go? What range of new territory have I explored? How close to the center of my sense of self do I dare go?* What really resonates within me as true in the work, what is false, tinny?"
>
> —Peter London, *No More Second-Hand Art,* pg. 36, 57
> [emphasis added]

6:30 A.M..
Shack in rain, dark but happy

A devotee-friend read *Memory in the Service of Kṛṣṇa* and was surprised that I spoke about my childhood. He said he thought the "standard" was not to talk about our pre-Kṛṣṇa conscious lives. I see his point, but the memories I allowed were fit into a preaching format.

It makes me think: Are we supposed to censor memories? Is it possible? Is that repression? And if so, what good will it accomplish? Of course, it is possible to indulge in it: "Hey, let's listen to 'Trane again. He's spiritual, right?" But to at least note one's memories, especially when they do come—and they *do* . . . the child walking in the woods . . . his father yelling at him . . . Ananta remembering his training as a boy in the British school system . . . How does it affect him now? We can leave our histories behind because we are spirit souls, but in another sense, we can use our pasts to heal the whole person—the child who still lives in you . . . the nail-biter . . . the guy who always gets angry (why?) . . . the lusty one who can never get enough . . . the overeater (or the under-eater) . . . Bring them all *with* you as you surrender and transform. You don't want to hear me indulging in my own *māyā* and I don't want to hear about your exploits as a football player. But I would like to hear how you are grateful to Prabhupāda for saving you from all that. And sometimes, since we are friends, if you feel like telling me, I will hear how you felt when you were lonely or ridiculous before your awakening in Kṛṣṇa consciousness. I won't hold it against you.

"Forget the past," says Bhaktivinoda Ṭhākura. Forget the past cheaters, the past loves. I have gone on to better things in God consciousness, and I hope you have too. Past lives, please know I am on the path of liberation now. There is no turning back. If I meet a familiar face in a crowd, now growing older past recognition, and he steps forward to me and says, "Remember?" I won't be afraid. Kṛṣṇa can save *all* souls, including my old high school friends, my college teachers, my Navy friends, dogs I used to know, dogs I used to be . . . Kṛṣṇa can save them all. So if I am giving a lecture on a houseboat in Hamburg, Germany, and someone comes up to me and says, "I knew you *when,* buddy," I will smile (not without a tremor), and hang in there as

Prabhupāda's man and say, "Well, this lecture is for you, too, and it is for me as you used to know me."

In 1979, at the restaurant of the 55th Street Hare Kṛṣṇa temple, Professor Thomas Hopkins said to me, "How do you feel now that you are supreme?" He meant now that you are one of The Only Eleven Gurus In The World. He smiled in a knowing way. I said, "I guess I am the same as I always was."

He laughed. "I thought you would say that."

Yes, I am the same person from Great Kills with the same inferiority complex. That carries over even into my life in the spiritual institution. I am the same rebel who felt crushed by my father's heavy-handed control. Unfortunately, that sometimes carries over in an uncalled-for rebellious streak toward my spiritual father. The old self isn't quite dead yet, but I know about him.

Yes, "forget the past," don't feed it anymore. Don't associate with nondevotees except to preach. But don't *deny* the past. Or are you a *nitya-siddha?* Was it only your *līlā* to be so degraded you almost died of want and madness? Better to remember: Śrīla Prabhupāda says, "Not only should one give up his past bad habits, but he must always regret his past sinful acts. This is the standard of pure devotion" *(Bhāg.* 6.2.27).

❦

Shack, speak to us.
Rain allow us to tap
into your memory,
muses, give yourselves to
divine utterances—
all nature fall at the
feet of Govinda.
Tiny self, adhere to His teachings.
Give all you can
be a generous saint—
do as your master did
traveling and taking the time
to tell people the truth—
we're gonna die soon,
the life we're leading will
throw us down to suffering,
so give it up and
serve the guru.

❦

Did you see the picture of the bulldozer excavating? Yes, it has to be followed up by other kinds of workers. It's just a crude example. But as for you, critics, you better watch out. This is a hard hat zone. Look out. I am a Prabhupāda man and I've got work to do. We are preparing a new world for devotees to live in. They have hired me too. So don't interfere. After me, the house builders will come. But we bulldozers have our own satisfaction, as we clear the rough land.

❦

Here is what happened—it was an action scene, doing a cluster on blood/flesh—I looked close at my hand without thinking. "Boy, I am seeing things up close," I thought, "this is good." I felt a pressure to *think—as a devotee should.* But I challenged it, "No, don't think. Keep going with this experiment."

Then I just *leaped* right out of the clustering rules of order—and without connecting one ball to another, I made a big Kṛṣṇa in a circle. It was like leap frog! It was exhilarating and radical (and yet somehow conservative). I want Kṛṣṇa, *bas!* The Kṛṣṇa circle was like an unconnected island. From it I started new connecting circles, circles that wandered around, and I had to try to connect them to the original cluster. I saw it as an enactment of the separation between body and spirit. I wanted to bring them together in Kṛṣṇa consciousness. I inched along without knowing *where* I would connect, but finally I did. It was a satisfying sense of completion. I connected the "Kṛṣṇa" chain with "Don't think." The two poles came together. Kṛṣṇa isn't merely intellectual or merely dogmatic, as opposed to free spirit and "don't think." It was nice.

❦

Downpour. Freedom to serve. "Regulated principles of freedom." Active all morning.

❦

Baladeva, Ananta and I sat in the shack in the rain. It reminded me of Kṛṣṇa and His friends sitting in a cave when it rains. Ananta said that *kṛṣṇa-kathā* makes him happy. He acknowledged that "it forces you to use your emotions."

I tried to imagine being there when Kṛṣṇa had lunch with His friends, but I was banned by my false ego. Then I thought, "You can attain it if you serve your guru actively and in complete surrender."

Did we serve like that more in the '70s? Nārāyaṇa Mahārāja told me no, now we are more surrendered. Now we are doing it in a mature way, a thorough way based on our own decisions. We are no longer like the small child who does his father's bidding only "because he is told."

Sit out this rain. This life dripping. Time running out. We are happy (in our mild way) hearing about Kṛṣṇa in Vṛndāvana.

❦

Poem on Harmonium as a Metaphor for My Body

He's dead, he's dead,
he can't play a note,
even if you pump him
'cause he don't know how.

O body, sweet soul-holder,
music divine from thee
under expert player.

Hey body, give us a tune,
old dead one, dying one,
broken stops, pearl keys,
from Calcutta Music Shop,
I love thee
I love thee
"But don't be attached."

I'm not attached to this
dead wooden object
but when he plays
"Bhaja Hure Mana"
or *"Jaya Vṛndāvana"*—
who can fail to cry tears!
Yeah, it's the body-soul.
I love thee
O eternity
and body,
you will
work to get us there.

So be dead, be *bhajana* player,
I have 2 minds about you,
and simply can't play you well.

Why I chose this metaphor
I'm not sure—
Wind down, stop pumping,
the song ends in grace.

Kṛṣṇa, please save me in
the silence after the last note.
I know we don't need
harmonium music to reach You.

4:30 P.M.

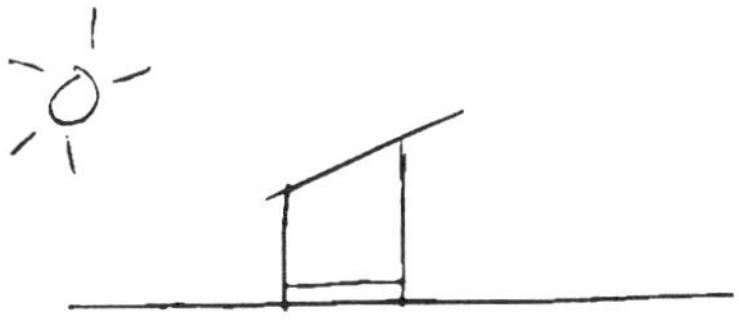

This schedule-follower is a humorous fellow, trotting around the clock.

Now Kṛṣṇa conscious reflections, not mine. Prabhupāda said that Lord Kṛṣṇa used His Vraja-*līlā* to show the external devotees (those who worship His greatness) that He is a submissive servant to His devotees' love.

❦

I want to talk freely. Free of myself, and free of the hang-up that "you have to be free of yourself."

❦

I am writing this before going in to our group hearing of *Kṛṣṇa* book—*brahmā-vimohana-līlā* tonight. "Puffed-up Lord Brahmā," we say, but he is our *sampradāya* head. Compared to him, what am I?

❦

It's just another day.
Yeah, another day less.
Don't make me less urgent
by your lulling "relax."
I want to serve.
But gently.
Heart of flesh
body of blood and muscle,
carry me where I must go . . .

Master I hear you every day,
forgive me
forgive me
my constant wrongs.
Find the good in me—it *is*
there.
You crash down the *mūḍhas*.

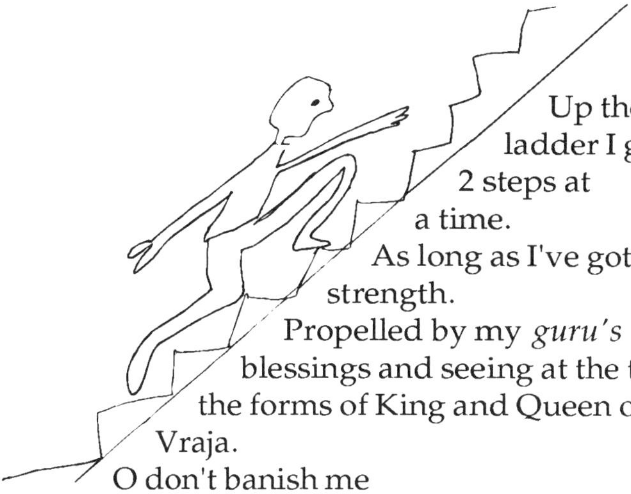

Up the *bhakti*
ladder I go,
2 steps at
a time.
As long as I've got
strength.
Propelled by my *guru's*
blessings and seeing at the top
the forms of King and Queen of
Vraja.
O don't banish me
entirely.

Sixteen more days.

This work is driven by a confidence that whatever I say will have lasting value. Kṛṣṇa conscious reflections are always worthwhile and I always have genuine Kṛṣṇa conscious reflections. Some may see this as pathetic because it's untrue. I listen to them, but I bulldoze ahead. I've got my work to do. And my faith. And I've got an editor. If she thinks something isn't valuable, then that's the editor's job. I work from early morning, take a few breaks during the day, and always want to get back here, to start up the engine. (It is a loud engine, and I can't hear much else while I drive.) I scrape away at the raw earth. I hope to dream of this work. And while I drive, my hands on the levers, I think of the pastimes of Kṛṣṇa (and other things) and I pray.

July 6, 1:30 A.M. ◐

We have been admitting there are many barriers that prevent us from entering the eternal pastimes of Kṛṣṇa in *śravaṇam.* But we have been surmounting those barriers. We are feeling positive about it, new gains. Barriers for me: (1) an intellectual skepticism toward the stories; (2) a familiarity with them through repeated hearing over the years; (3) a feeling that they have been treated sentimentally and superficially in paintings, dramatic skits, conversations, and in skim-through, out-loud readings—to the point where their depth seems lost to me. All these barriers and more, we are crossing over. We are also opening ourselves up emotionally. Yesterday, we heard of the tremendous increase in affection the parents and cows felt for their offspring during the year when Kṛṣṇa expanded into the forms of boys and calves. This pastime describes much flowing of breast milk and hugs and kisses and tears of love. But where is my milk of love for Kṛṣṇa? Why can't I be affectionate to Him and to His devotees? Nice session of opening up and at least beginning to receive the mercy of *kṛṣṇa-kathā.*

❦

Going slow this morning, why is that? Some blocks? I feel I don't have too much to say. Don't want to take up readers' time. Not convinced maybe of the urgency of writing, and unaware how I can tap into Kṛṣṇa consciousness through what I write.

The internal censors, like a pack of wolves, are always ready to move in on me. They say, "See? He admits he's pushing himself even when he has nothing to say. Heed us, heed us. We know what's best. Submit to us and write according to our Critical School of Writing. You are too cocky. We will take you down a few pegs."

Be humble in response. Be humble and keep working. Don't boast, "I'm a hardhat bulldozer driver." Let flow Kṛṣṇa topics. Pray for Kṛṣṇa's mercy.

❦

> It is said by Rūpa Gosvāmī that the attachment exhibited by pure devotees for Kṛṣṇa cannot possibly be perfected in the hearts of fruitive workers (*karmīs*) or mental speculators, because such attachment in pure Kṛṣṇa consciousness is very rare and not possible to achieve even for many liberated persons.
> —*Nectar of Devotion,* p. 139, Classics of India edition

You have to be liberated first. Even ordinary devotees cannot have such pure attachment for Kṛṣṇa.

❦

Observing our own movements—Rūpa Gosvāmī prays in that way too. He refers to himself as "a certain poor person in Vṛndāvana." He repeatedly calls out to Rādhā and Kṛṣṇa, "O King and Queen of Vṛndāvana, please give me mercy."

"Placing his face in his hands, this person cries in anguish: 'O King and Queen, please, please, give a small drop of Your mercy!'

"Crying, I, who am a great fool, beg in a piteous voice:

'O merciful King and Queen, please splash me with Your waves of mercy.'" Thus he writes in "A List of Requests," and "A Vine of Hopes."

"The most exalted devotee cannot attain in his heart even a small portion of Your glory. Yearning that You appear on the pathways of his eyes, this person has now swallowed his fear and shame.

"O King and Queen of Vṛndāvana, how sinful I am! Still, who will not become maddened by the sweetness of Your transcendental qualities?"

❦

"Movement to love"

(based on looking at a *Krsna* book painting of cows running down from the top of Govardhana Hill to join their calves)

It is a movement to love. My own movement to love is slow, but I am patient. Some people are cool and indifferent; maybe our institution has taught us coldness, but you can't just rush in and grab it. There are rules to follow. "Fools rush in," but they are *sahajiyās*.

Listen: Monks have to abstain from association with women. Lust is easily mistaken as love.

So what to do? Oh, in many lives from now, only then can you enter this pastime. Have hope, be patient, work hard. I have nothing new to say about love. At least I am thinking about it. It is the goal. It takes hard work.

"Only after many lives of accumulated pious devotional service, can the boys come to play with Kṛṣṇa as their friend."

The painting is before me. Let me see the essence. As cows run to calves, as men embrace their "Kṛṣṇa-sons," as young Kṛṣṇa and Balarāma look on: I stand afar, desiring to enter a movement to love.

❦

Our Kṛṣṇa consciousness movement seems small. A devotee who is the leader of the ISKCON center in Portugal wrote me that the Portugese nation is strongly Catholic. But even the Catholic religion is small in comparison to big business and the military . . . What can *we* hope to do?

We have the truth. We must speak the truth, even if it goes unheard; it is the answer to all dilemmas. Spirit souls need to follow God's law. This is a primary edict that, when neglected, spells disaster.

Devotees of Kṛṣṇa preach the truth and live lives of devotion. We may be little integers in the material society, subject to the whims of politicians. We may be physically and mentally pushed around by the hurricanes and upheavals of the material energy. Therefore, we must plead with the Lord to grant us the determination of will, and His mercy to keep us fixed in devotion at His feet. And we must keep speaking the truth.

Kṛṣṇa has already sent us his pure devotee, Śrīla Prabhupāda.

❦

Any response to a stimulus is valid if it is Kṛṣṇa conscious and leads to our improvement. Improve yourself and help others; that's our only purpose. Do it one way or another.

6:00 A.M.

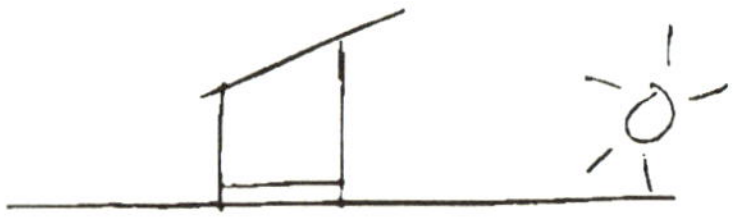

Coming back from my exercise walk. It rained all day yesterday and all night. The rain stopped just before dawn, and the trees are still dripping. The sky overhead is clear, but mist is rising from the ground.

Everyday I walk in a home development construction site called "The Woods." Three bulldozers are parked along the temporary gravel road. Coming back today, I was alone on a patch of Brislin Road, which looks like a tunnel covered by arching trees.

I walked down the yellow stripe in the middle of the road. The Macaddam raincoat was soaked through. I deliberately tried not to think too much while I was walking, but then I suddenly began thinking of a phone call I made to my mother a couple of years ago when I was in Dublin. It took a lot of thinking and talking with others to get the courage to do it. I hadn't spoken to her in twenty years.

I don't feel like talking about it right now, but I just want to say it was meaningful. My mother updated her rejection of me. She said, "As long as you're with them [the Hare Kṛṣṇa movement], we don't want anything to do with you." Today when I thought of this, I made the same shift I made twenty-five years ago after my original rejection by my parents: I mean, I turned myself over to my spiritual master.

Reading the mail. One lady writes to me that she is about to get married in a week but has cold feet because her husband isn't a good wage-earner. Another man writes me of his feeling restricted as a congregational member by the authorities in one of our temples. Every person's voice jumps off the page—unique, full of accent, tone.

The Kṛṣṇa conscious writing muse is unlimited. The process is unlimited. My present lifetime is very limited, along with my talents of expression, my ability to write, etc. Teresa of Avila said she wished she could write with both hands at once because she felt so overflowing with praises of God and things she wanted to reveal about the "inner castle." This is similar to Rūpa Gosvāmī's statement: "How much can I chant with only one tongue? If I had millions of tongues, then I could actually begin to satisfy myself in chanting the Holy Names of Kṛṣṇa."

This is a poem to my spiritual master.
His speech is sometimes gruff.
He's a general like Bhīṣma.
Cuts down false *avatāras.*
He hurt my false ego
when I too-casually said
"I forgot." He touched me.
Prabhupāda, forgive me.
You are too great for me to
try writing a poem about.
Some say you are so transcendental
we should not even see you as a human.
But I see your old age,
your missing teeth, your pain
as glorious sacrifice.
Let's see another old man
equal you. Can't be done.
You suffered and sacrificed
to manage Kṛṣṇa's movement.
I see you—far away.
Yet you touched me close too.
O commander of rough voice,
you stand among lances and arrows
—you had to be rough.

I want to see you,
O spiritual master
of many thousands.
You are impressive
beyond compare.
Let us read your books.
And please you,
personal guru,
unfathomable
pure devotee of Kṛṣṇa.

Wood thrush. Now the day is moving quicker —breakfast, rest, *Kṛṣṇa* book class . . . Submit. You have no choice.

❦

"I Know Better"

We read the chapter entitled, "The Bewildering of Lord Brahmā." At first I felt skeptical toward this pastime, which began today with Lord Brahmā coming back to see how his trick was working. But then my devotional side resisted the skepticism. The two forces rose in conflict. I let out an inner cry against the skeptical attitude, and then this line got exposed, "I know better." It is the self-assured arrogance of Western skepticism thoroughly saturating my limbs.

But you don't know better, you just think you do.

I released the tension and began to hear with improved attention. Intellectually, I am quite confident of personalism over impersonalism. I understand the error in the Māyāvādī's position. I regard him as offensive and I participate in the victory of the Vaiṣṇava philosophers over the *nirveśeṣa-śūnyavādi* people. So, intellectually, I am fit: my devotional forces have invaded and controlled that intellectual ground. But in my gut reaction, the skeptic occupies strategically important space.

I want to fight back. I want to cause a revolution to recapture my original emotions. I want to be simple and loving and capable of worshiping Govinda and His devotees. I want to soften my heart.

Bhaktivinoda Ṭhākura analyzes the *anartha* represented by Brahmā in the *"brahmā-vimohana-līlā,"* as cultivation of karma and *jñana,* "which ultimately leads to a skeptical mentality." There it is again: karma causes skepticism because one thinks he is better than a simple *bhakta* by virtue of his money or political position, his prestige. And a *jñanī* thinks he can spend his life in speculation and thus know more than a *vrajavāsī.*

Bhaktivinoda Ṭhākura goes on to say, "The pastime also reflects the offense of disrespecting the Lord's superior quality of transcendental sweetness (*mādhurya*) in favor of His inferior majestic opulences (*aiśvarya*)." Lord Brahmā does not appreciate the sweetness of little Kṛṣṇa enjoying lunch with His friends. This is my problem also when I doubt Kṛṣṇa's Yamunā pastimes. To prefer majestic Godhead is ultimately an offense. Brahmā will be rectified, and I hope to be rectified too. We have to be willing to go through the process of hearing these pastimes with depth and emotional participation. That is part of the rectification process.

❦

Do not commit the offense of favoring the majesty over the sweetness.

❦

Pearls of rain on the pine branch in the now-sunny, rain-refreshed forest. See Kṛṣṇa in that pearl.

4:00 P.M.

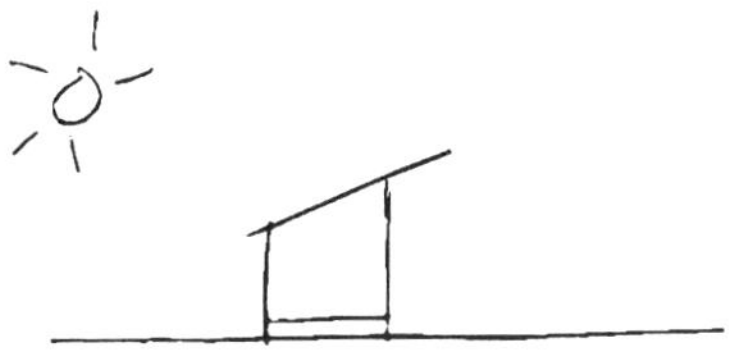

Visualize yourself walking out the side door into the warm breeze. A car approaches. As he passes, he can, if he likes, catch a glimpse of this saffron-dressed monk. Walk over the slate slabs and into the woods. Ahead you see the shack in the pine shadows, up on stilts, a screened-in room inviting you.

You walk in, sit, and start to write without hesitation. It is a successful piece. But here is the point—what is successful?

Does it refer to how it looks later? Is it a matter of how many times the word Kṛṣṇa occurs? Does successful writing mean you hold off your critics and inner censors?

Success means I keep writing. It can be decided later what will be saved from it or how it will be used. My success is absorption in Kṛṣṇa-thought. It is coming to grips with surrender—and lack of surrender. Work it out on the page. Success means to love and communicate the specific experiences and to help someone else feel it too.

It is hard for me to visualize success beforehand. I can picture the externals—a certain look of concentration, being oblivious to my surroundings, sitting straight, ink flowing, not too many pauses. But if I were to look over my shoulder, I would not be able to read it. I cannot know beforehand what part of my own inspiration will inspire others.

In *If You Want to Write,* Brenda Ueland says: "Only when you are playing *in* a thing do people listen and hear you and are moved. It is because *you* are moved, because a queer and wonderful experience has taken place and the music—Mozart or Bach or whatever it is—suddenly is yourself, *your* voice and your eloquence. The passionate and wonderful questions in the music are *your* questions. And with all the nobility and violence and wonderful sweetness of Beethoven, say, it is *you* talking to those who listen."

We may say this does not apply to spiritual writing. We want authors who are transparent via mediums. But what does that mean? "Transparent" does not mean "void." It does not mean a faceless head speaking with a flat, toneless voice.

If void is the medium, then void will be the message. Śrīla Prabhupāda did not do nothing—he convinced us. His voice sometimes cracked with the urgency of his message as he spoke. He was not selling himself, he was selling Kṛṣṇa. He had to present himself as one who was totally convinced and learned in Kṛṣṇa consciousness. He had to use all his wits to break through our preconceptions and lack of surrender. Therefore, he was a *medium,* the special person who carried the spiritual message. In his humility, he did not think of himself as special—but he *was* successful.

❦

After the Dodger game on T.V., broadcaster Vince Scully looked out at you and spoke some parting words for a Schaefer commercial, smiled, and then drank down almost a whole glass of beer.

The Ebbets Field baseball diamond was visible in the background. Then you turned off the television and faced the dread of your illusion in Great Kills.

I am very thankful not to be there anymore. Oh, I would deal with it busily—go to the fridge and get something, maybe a frozen chocolate pudding or a Coke—but no amount of looking out the backyard window could save me. Dad's corny, sad remarks spoken through cigar smoke haze didn't help, and neither did his attempts to dominate and shape the reality of our household.

I would go upstairs as a teenager and lead a life of "quiet desperation."

I don't go to the fridge now. I don't need any stopgap measures to carry me from moment to moment. Now God is my guide, and the guru shapes my life. My life is solid and sure, happy and sincere. And my sadness is of a different sort. It is based on failure to serve better, and the world not taking to *bhakti-yoga*.

6:30 P.M. 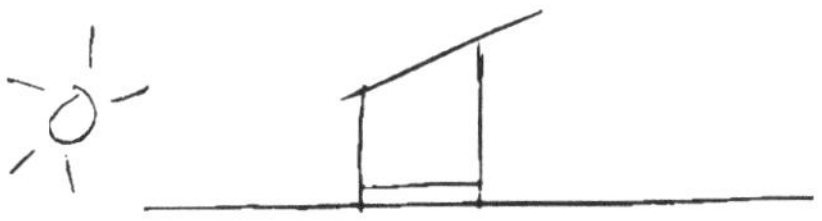

I made a stupid confession during our *Kṛṣṇa* book reading: I have trouble relating to descriptions of Lord Viṣṇu's ornaments, jewelry, anklebells, rings, etc. My comrades didn't say much to either relieve me of embarrassment or to help me. You cannot approach Kṛṣṇa or Viṣṇu with material conceptions.

July 7, 1:30 A.M.

Woke around 11:00 P.M. last night with my critical side taking the upper hand. He said, "Are you kidding about this kind of writing you are doing? You are writing this way in order to avoid more serious writing. You have done enough of this."

Here we go again. The left brain critic wants to start editing and put a stop to my creative efforts. He wants to start working on something else.

It may be too early for him to come in with his sword.

❦

I read in Peter London's *No More Second-Hand Art:*

> The thing just made is really new; it has never been seen before by anyone, including its author. The important thing—the *only* thing—to do now is to become acquainted with it . . . Too often we see our work as shallow, and all too often this is because we view our own work too quickly, too casually . . . Rather than rushing to obliterate "Mistakes," we might become interested in just what our "Mistakes" look like . . . why are we made uncomfortable with the products of our mind and hand? What powers do these marks contain that we will not or cannot use?

❦

Let me praise Kṛṣṇa in this present work with all honesty. Even if I say I cannot appreciate the descriptions of the Lord's dress and ornaments as given in the scripture, that is just my critical eye. A more submissive part of me *does* appreciate and desires to worship the personal form.

My distastes for those descriptions are crippling me and causing me to make offenses. Lord, please allow me to die to those perceptions of the world. You are not seen by material eyes, and I have little to go by in my material experience to know what You look like. When I see an actor dressed in a wig and wearing a red plastic necklace—and a wrist watch and eyeglasses—who looks like a ninety-pound weakling, certainly *that* is not Viṣṇu.

Praise to Lord Viṣṇu who is beyond my words and vision. Praise to sincere devotional service beginning with the tongue, which purifies us and enables us to one day see the Lord when He reveals Himself to us. Praise to working for the Lord in such a way that He sees us.

Praise to my spiritual master who taught us not to scorn pictures of Lord Viṣṇu as material:

> Hayagrīva commented that the religious art of the India prints was a bit garish, but Prabhupāda said the technique didn't matter. The important thing was that the pictures were of Kṛṣṇa and were executed according to Vedic descriptions. For the devotee, they were beautiful; they were non-different from Kṛṣṇa.
>
> —*Śrīla Prabhupāda-līlāmṛta,* Vol. 3, pp. 85-86

I desire to praise and overcome my prejudices against Kṛṣṇa's particular beauty. I realize that I am a ridiculous tiny ego who bases his ideas of dress and beauty on his American upbringing. I have not even seen spiritual ornaments—what does a pearl look like in the spiritual world? I want to purify myself. I know I can do it simply by continuing to hear of the form of child Kṛṣṇa. My true self does not want to scorn Kṛṣṇa's form or to worship only His impersonal form. Neither do I want to worship my material conceptions.

> That the Lord is not formless is experienced by Nārada Muni. But His form is completely different from all forms of our material experience. For the whole duration of our life we go see different forms in the material world, but none of them is just apt to satisfy the mind, nor can any of them vanquish all perturbance of the mind. These are the special features of the transcendental form of the Lord, and one who has once seen that form is not satisfied with anything else; no form in the material world can any longer satisfy the seer. That the Lord is formless or impersonal means that He has nothing like a material form and is not like any material personality.
>
> —*Bhāg*. 1.6.18, purport

❦

My voice is weak, cracked, impersonal. I will sing anyway. "It does not matter, I am child!" said Prahlāda.

Someone asks, "How can you pray to Kṛṣṇa, you are just a child?"

"It does not matter," said Prahlāda. "I can pray with my feeling, 'O my Lord.'"

And Prabhupāda says we too can pray by praising and bowing down.

6:30 A.M. 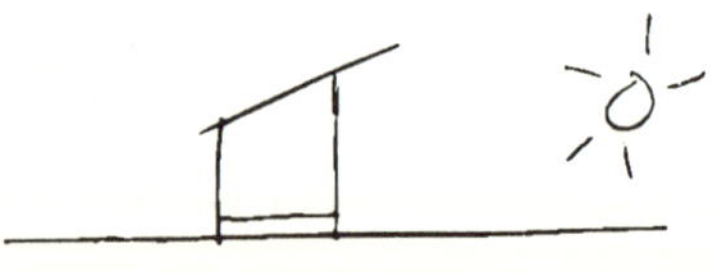

> This love of God is now in a dormant state in everyone's heart. And there, love of God is manifested in different ways, but it is contaminated by material

> association. Now the heart has to be purified of the material association, and that dormant, natural love for Kṛṣṇa has to be revived. That is the whole process.
>
> —*Bg.* 12.9, purport

Love of God takes the form of lust in the material realm. The cleansing process is the chanting and hearing of the name, form, teachings and pastimes of the Supreme Lord. Just apply yourself to *bhakti* and all contamination will be washed away. Extra counselling and discussion is only needed by "dysfunctional" persons, or by those who think they are dysfunctional. Only those persons who cannot obey the command, "Chant and don't worry" need special attention. And who is *not* in that category?

❦

"Write when you write. Stop battering yourself with guilt, accusations, and strong-arm threats." *(Writing Down the Bones,* by Natalie Goldberg).

❦

One bird has a single-note whistle. There was a bird just like her at Gītā-nāgarī. People still don't know why I listen to the birds. It's a fact they sing (according to the ornithologists) to attract a mate or to defend themselves.

Deeper we go into real summer. Ferns bright green on the forest floor, the carpet made of last year's dead leaves and the humus of many years.

I am mixed with mundane references, not a pure Vaiṣṇava. Maybe when I go to Vṛndāvana I can throw some of this off, but usually India just brings out more of my Westernness.

Noon

I told Baladeva about the commando raid last night by the critic of "Shack Notes." He suggested I let him speak fully. He also suggested I *use* his energy as a Tai Chi fighter would: receiving his enemy's attack and converting it to his own counterattack, instead of directly blocking his blows.

I have already sparred with this critic a number of times. I will let him speak again, but not at great length. He should just state his basic points and then let us get on with it.

Critic's Piece

You may be avoiding the serious task of writing Kṛṣṇa conscious literature. People will accept what you write, but it will be an inferior, lower class of writing than you are capable of. You will, in your own little way, degrade the standard of Vaiṣṇava literature.

I don't mean that you have to confine yourself to commenting on Vaiṣṇava literature (although that is also good engagement for you). I just think you should write with structure.

You have too much faith in *whatever* you do. It shows a lack of humility. It is self-centered.

I am not anti-writing. I am in favor of form, careful work, and patient writing craft. It is slow, hard work with little progress sometimes, but it is steady. You already know how to do it. When you were in between stories, you wrote yourself notes and even created dialogues between author and characters in search of a new start. You should become habituated to constructing these stories so that when you travel, you will have a structured writing project to work on.

This is a summary of my point.

My Response

You spoke mostly good advice, although I see some loopholes in your arguments. But even by accepting your conclusions to write good stories I don't have to fold up "Shack Notes." You are not seeing what is actually going on here, *but I am seeing it.* This is a written testimony to a period in my life, written in its own way, *in its own form.* (It is not formless. There is no such thing as "formless.") It also falls into the category of a recognizable, respectable genre—journal, confession, vignette collection, autobiography. Why object just because it is not "structured"?

I feel love in doing this—that *has* to be honored. Something important is at stake. My only problem is that I am not writing enough, not loosening up enough. If I wrote more, it would result in *some* of it being *strong,* and that is the point you overlook. By the writing method I employ in "Shack Notes, " stronger pieces may come than by coolly executed methods within prescribed boundaries. Rather than degrading my abilities, I am strengthening my basic convictions as a writer. I am living thoroughly in a writing project.

You lack faith in my intuitions; you never credit them as having any connection with Supersoul or with Prabhupāda's desires. I am trying to serve, trying to break new ground, trying to find fresh language and expression. I am also working out some of my hang-ups.

This is the story of an extremely quiet, protected, but brief period of my life, written "between books" at a writing retreat. This *is* a story with structure; you just don't see it.

The more I write, the closer I will be to exhausting all inferior motives, talking out all conflicts, and maybe catching Kṛṣṇa's attention (like the loud duck begging for bread).

4:00 P.M. 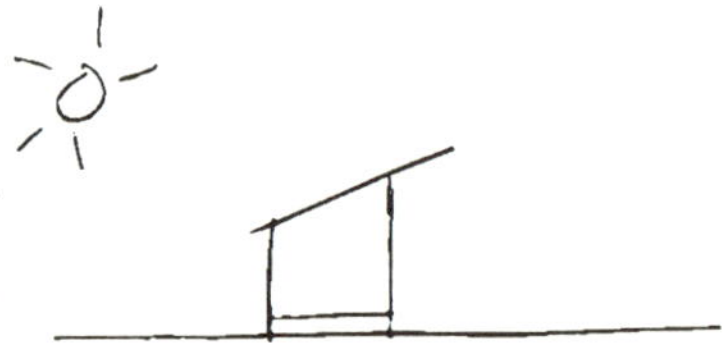

I dreamt that Prabhupāda was putting peanuts and other eatables into a big bowl and giving them to me. He said, "The devotees," indicating to me that I should distribute the *prasādam*.

I used to fill up notebooks with "junior" purports, imitating what Śrīla Prabhupāda does. It was just for me and was lots of fun. I sat in public libraries around the U.S. while traveling with the BBT library part, and I wrote them on Ṛṣabhadeva's teachings, Haṁsa-guhya prayers, etc. Just wanted to mention it.

Loud bees buzzing outside the screened shack. It has been a pleasant afternoon, stormy, and now sunny after the rain.

❦

Today, while I had my eyes shut and we were all hearing Baladeva reading "The Prayers of Lord Brahmā to Kṛṣṇa," it started thundering. Lightning flashed ominously. We continued reading and I didn't notice how dark it was getting. I said, "Brahmā's description of Kṛṣṇa at the beginning of this chapter is one of my all-time favorites. Yellow *dhotī* glittering like lightning, helmet with forest flowers, bodily hue like a fresh rain cloud, a morsel of food in one hand, a flute tucked in His belt, small lotus feet—and yet He is the inconceivable Personality of Godhead, the source of all."

Then it started to rain. Usually, you don't get wet in the shack, but this was a heavy downpour. We moved to a dry corner and continued. Brahmā's glorious speech resonated louder than the thunder. I imagined Lord Brahmā beginning to speak, his voice low and quaking, and then gathering volume as he said: *jñāne prayāsam udapāsya namanta eva.* I could hear the strength in his voice, see his chest filling out, his intelligence flowing. It is one of the *most* Kṛṣṇa-triumphant speeches ever made by any devotee in *Śrīmad-Bhāgavatam.* He does not just praise *God,* not just Viṣṇu, but specifically *Kṛṣṇa* as the source of all incarnations. And He describes His Vṛndāvana pastimes as the sweetest of all. We cheered Brahmā on, listening as best we could. He who had made a fool of himself before Kṛṣṇa was now used by Kṛṣṇa to speak wondrous and strong Kṛṣṇa conscious prayers.

> A person with a poor fund of knowledge may think that, because You are the son of Mahārāja Nanda, You are not the original person. . . . They are mistaken. . . . You are the original person, and there is no doubt about it. . . . You are the source of the original *brahmajyoti,* as well as the material luminaries. . . . When You place Yourself as subordinate to Your father and mother, Nanda and Yaśodā, You are not reduced in Your potency; this is an expression of Your loving attitude for Your devotees. There is no other competitor of second identity than Yourself. . . . You are the original *amṛta* (nectar of immortality), indestructible.
>
> —*Kṛṣṇa,* pp. 103-4

Winding up the first of three intended parts of "Shack Notes," I am happy to live for this. May I learn to face the truth—a fool again. O Lord Brahmā, how magnificently you teach us to rebound from mistakes and to become malleable in the hands of the Lord, to do His will. You teach us to aspire for a future birth free from passion, as a humble-as-grass servitor of the residents of Vṛndāvana. O Lord Brahmā, although you are not yourself a resident of Vraja, you have become the best philosopher and poet of Vraja-*līlā.* And Śukadeva concludes, "Ultimately, it is Kṛṣṇa who is pleasing and attractive. He is the Supersoul of everything. And in order to give us this information, Kṛṣṇa descends and tells us that the all-attractive center is He Himself. Without being an expansion of Kṛṣṇa, nothing can be attractive."

❦ ❦ ❦

Better
Sri Caitanya-candrodaya Act Two The Krsna Library Vol. 70
Sri Caitanya-candrodaya Act Three The Krsna Library Vol. 71
Sri Caitanya-candrodaya Act One The Krsna Library Vol. 69
BHAGAVAD-GITA

Week Two

July 8, 1:30 A.M.

Hearing the sound of trucks on the all-night highway. A summer moth excited by the light, bumps against the window screen. I am groggy when I first wake up. What incoherent dreams! I wash my face, polish my eyeglasses, and offer obeisances. Then I sit here, waiting. The pen feels good in my hand.

I placed a few "post-it" notes here last night. What to make of them now?

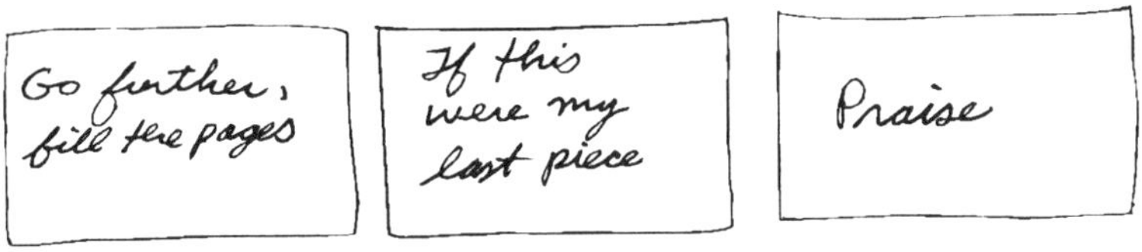
Go further, fill the pages
If this were my last piece
Praise

❦

This morning I awoke from a dream. I dreamt we were traveling together under the guidance of a Kṛṣṇa conscious leader. Most of us were flying. I could not keep up the flight and started to glide down, intending to continue traveling by floating in the stream. The Kṛṣṇa conscious leader approved and said, "Therefore, humbler than a blade of grass." Then the others joined me and we floated together in the stream. But then crocodiles started appearing in the water, swimming toward us from the opposite direction. At first they didn't bother us, but then there were a lot of them; so our Kṛṣṇa conscious guide led us out of the water.

I noticed among our group that a few were very devoted to him and chanted the *gāyatrī-mantra* with him with great concentration. Together they formed a secret understanding and I was an outsider. I couldn't keep up with them. The dream was full of frustration.

Earlier I dreamt I was walking in the park meditating on death and the next life. It occurred to me to be happy that I was improving myself spiritually in this life. I was aware that this life is ending and that I will have to suffer in the future. Suffering is for my rectification; therefore, I should regard it as good. This feeling of trying to prepare myself for inevitable sufferings came through strongly in the dream state.

Dreams shift like clouds and are gone. We have to face the waking moments and use them to get something done.

❦

When we hear Lord Brahmā's prayers to Kṛṣṇa, we visualize both Brahmā speaking 5,000 years ago, and Śrīla Prabhupāda dictating the *Kṛṣṇa* book in 1969. Because Prabhupāda speaks, we hear Brahmā speak. We can see, through Prabhupāda's description, Kṛṣṇa listening thoughtfully as the Supreme God.

❦

When we heard Lord Brahmā's prayers, the members of our little group had different main impressions. I spoke about Lord Brahmā's eloquence and how, once he got underway, he was full of intelligent praise of Kṛṣṇa. Baladeva saw Brahmā more as a puppet of Kṛṣṇa, and he saw that it was actually Kṛṣṇa speaking through Brahmā. Thus, Brahmā's speech is a continuation of Kṛṣṇa's dominance over Brahmā, which the Lord displayed in bewildering Lord Brahmā. Baladeva also felt intent on how Kṛṣṇa "melted down" Brahmā's false position.

This makes me think that I may have a meltdown ahead for myself. Just when I think I am ready to present a sophisticated piece of writing, Kṛṣṇa could extinguish my abilities, either physically, by making me paralytic or dumb, or mentally, by making me senile. Or He could reveal to me that everything I have done so far is infantile fool's work.

6:30 A.M.

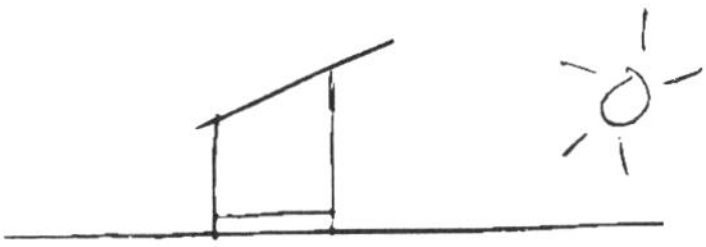

I just wrote a letter to a woman newly coming to Kṛṣṇa consciousness. She asked questions about how to approach a spiritual master. She thought she could get initiated right away, and that there were a group of initiating gurus to choose from who lived in different zones, as it used to be. At first, I felt myself becoming condescending, but then I realized that this person is one of that extremely rare group who has the fortune to inquire into Kṛṣṇa consciousness. How ridiculous and wrong of me to look down on her. I should cherish her interest and fan the spark of desire to serve Kṛṣṇa. Assure her that she *will* be initiated in due course. Impress upon her how serious initiation is. Give her encouragement to pursue it. And don't rattle off the philosophy, but present it as Prabhupāda would have done: with personal concern for that spirit soul.

It is so dark at 7:00 A.M. I can hardly see the yellow page in front of me.

I am too sleepy and superficial to see down deeper. One who is pure can see through all the superficialities and haze, like seeing to the bottom of a clear lake. I see only the agitated surface. But I am tired of speaking only truisms and second-hand knowledge. At least let me speak of the moment and be a devotee.

❦

I have only a few more letters to answer. Then, later today, a new batch of mail will arrive.

❦

The tree tops are blowing, and there is a feeling of rain in the air; but it is just the preface to rain.

❦

I will realize, at least at death, that this incoming mail is my chance to help others. In that sense, it is one of the best services I have in this life. There is no time to tell people what is on *my* mind. I immediately give out salutations and then respond to *their* points. But the letters are often official: "Congratulations," I say, "on getting the realization that you need to improve your chanting and that this is a very important function in your life. Actually, the chanting is the most important function."

I am trying to get rid of the falsity. Admitting it is a step forward. I really do want to be a friend, to be beside them. Kṛṣṇa is the center of all, and He came to reveal that; but as we sit in the circle around His lotus feet, we can help each other stay focused on the goal of all our lives.

10:00 A.M.

It is worth it to eke out some honesty here, even if it is not elevated. But your ordinary life? Be careful you don't claim, "Whatever I do is holy; when I enjoy, God enjoys." We should approach everything as sacred, and that means "accepting things favorable for devotional service *and* rejecting those things that are unfavorable."

The mail is here and I want to pause just five or ten minutes to sort it out. We couldn't do a full-fledged *Kṛṣṇa* book reading and discussion because I have a pain in the head. This by way of explanation.

❦

My God, I love You. I don't want physical pain, but the world is filled with it. When I get a little of my share, it can teach me a lot.

Kṛṣṇa, the King, I hear Your *līlā,* and I wish to always do so. When we do not see You—as Brahmā could not see You from the shore of the milk ocean, You reveal Yourself in our hearts. I desire that. My desire is weak, but I am trying to strengthen it.

My various strategies—walks, calisthenics, occasional forays into psychology—are all my ideas for strengthening myself to become a better devotee.

How come there wasn't any mention of me in the 25 year review of ISKCON in the I.W.R.?

O Vaiṣṇava Ṭhākura,
please be kind to me.
Please make me humble
like a blade of grass.
Even Lord Brahmā desires this,
and what am I in comparison to him?

Why does it irritate me when others get things I don't have? Why do I try to tear them down? What am I afraid of?

> O infallible Lord, kindly excuse my offenses. I have taken birth in the mode of passion and am therefore simply foolish, presuming myself a controller independent of Your Lordship. My eyes are blinded by the darkness of ignorance.... But please consider that I am Your servant and therefore worthy of Your compassion.
>
> —*Bhāg.* 10.14.10

Pain Song

Lie down, baby child,
you're all right.
It's the truth time again.
Prescribing methods, medicines
will not—

Start again:
Lie down, baby child,
it's truth time again.
Kṛṣṇa is your Friend,
and you have to *stop.*
Why? Oh, karma
and other reasons.
The eye and head are
filled with roads of pain.
You never should have come here.
Now ice cream won't help,
and your smooth flowing pen
can't write this one away.
You can sneak out a few sentences.
But when it's "Stop,"
then stop.
Lie down,
see the lessons unto death.
And take the time to
be with the One who never
deserts you.
Transcend,
lie down
and give it time
you can't control.
But blessings abound—
don't think they come only
when you're up.

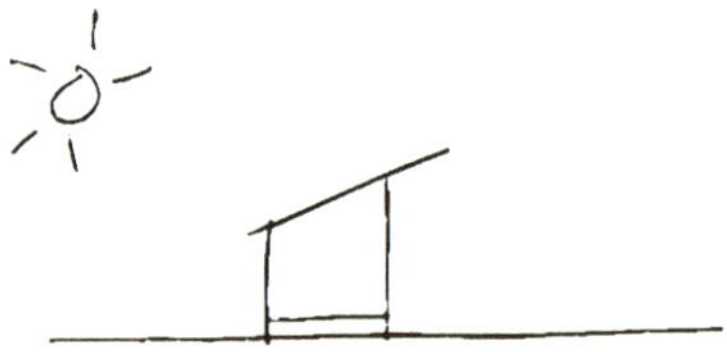

3:30 P.M.

The wood thrush's song is cheerful, melodious. He is absent this afternoon. Now I hear only the sad, pathetic *wheee* of the pewee. It is a one-note lamentation. The wood thrush has been cheering me on in my writing. With such full-bodied music accompanying me, how could I go wrong? If from the beginning, all I had was a pewee or crows . . .

Excuse the whimsy.

I have a bedroll in the shack now because I cannot work. I have a headache.

❦

O Kāna, please hear my call. I am in this world seeking to be with You. You know what it is like for all of us. I am one of a flock of sheep being herded by a most kind and capable herdsman. Now he wants me to grow up, transform, and become a herder of others. At least, he wants me to become some sort of helper and not a helpless dependent. But I should not mislead anyone.

O Kāna, is what I am doing a kind of misleading? You see the method in the madness, so please redeem me. Give it the magic touch.

❦

My head is clearing. Now if I could clear my intelligence, the soul could speak. Good news of Kṛṣṇa consciousness.

❦

It is hot out here today.

I want to be lined up with Kṛṣṇa and His devotees in my own unique way. I also want to help others do it in their unique ways.

A book just arrived in the mail, a best-seller called *Taming Your Gremlin: A Guide to Enjoying Yourself*. It is a self-help guide with good advice how to get rid of the "narrator in our head who keeps telling us who we are and interpreting our experience. Your gremlin wants you to feel bad, and he carries out this loathsome pursuit via sophisticated maneuvers . . . " Great stuff! Sure, I want to get rid of my gremlin, Mister Carson. Please tell me how.

But as I read on, there's quite a bit about successful orgasms and put-downs of religion ("Her gremlin wears a ministerial collar and engages her by preaching to her from the New Testament . . . she is unable to have an orgasm"). I can pick and choose through this to learn of my own gremlin, but why? Another and yet another self-help book.

These two weeks are supposed to be for me to be alone with a few valid tools—to let go *if I can* and write as honestly as I can toward opening up my Kṛṣṇa consciousness. I dropped the gremlin book in that box of books I will not be reading.

❦

Good guides protect me, but a humble servitor should be able—if he is liberated—to sing all day like the wood thrush. Does a wood thrush keep worrying, "Is this my false ego that makes me sing?"

If I have got the right thing and the way to the kingdom of God, why am I not happier? It is because I am stuck in the false self, the false concept of life. Can't *let go* in the absolute sense. Hanging on to last vestiges.

To be as honest as possible means putting on the page what is actually happening. As Robert Lowell wrote in a poem, "Why not tell what happened?" It would be good if in these weeks I could honestly report remarkable Kṛṣṇa conscious revelations, constant absorption and bliss in devotional service, getting in touch with spirit. The writing would *jump* off the page. But if that doesn't happen, my commitment is to go out to the shack and at least tell the truth. Write what comes, try to be happy, *and steer toward Kṛṣṇa.*

July 9, 1:30 A.M.

Yesterday we didn't have our afternoon *Kṛṣṇa* book session and I am sorry for that. A devotee has to be constantly filling up on nectar and instructions, or he dries up like a flower in the desert. He is left only with "old" instructions, things he may have lost touch with by the passage of time. At least that is what happens to me when I don't hear regularly. One day of illness prompts me to go eagerly forward today, on my knees, "Please Lord, regulator of all things, let me hear about You today in two full sessions. Let me participate fully."

The theme and plot of this book is "Time is running out." Two weeks remain in my attempts to realize this in writing.

Kṛṣṇa conscious realization is available at every moment. The amazing thing is that we keep forgetting it, or we don't believe it, or we water it down—we let it slip from our grasp.

The shack is a place to declare: "I am a devotee. I know the nectar is present within me at every moment, because Kṛṣṇa is the source and He resides in my heart." I have informed my "gremlins" to get lost. And the advice of the all-wise, condescending critic to "tighten up your work" is to be disregarded in favor of *loosen up.*

Kṛṣṇa, am I loose?
Is it not to surrender?
Let me work as a fool
persisting in admitting his foolishness.

The trucks roar and roar, so why not me too?
Kāna, let us all who know Prabhupāda work
together more lovingly.

❦

Now it is only two days until the gathering of hundreds of people in the tiny storefront at 26 Second Avenue. The event doesn't seem well-organized because ISKCON obtained the place very recently, and they have had little time or money to fix it up. Still, devotees are eager to go there. I probably will be given a chance to speak. I thought of saying, "This spot is very important. It reminds me of a verse in a Gosvāmī poem about Vṛndāvana where he says, 'In this place Kṛṣṇa killed the cart demon, in this place Kṛṣṇa did the *rāsa* dance, etc. ...' It is as good as a *tīrtha* in Vṛndāvana for us." But then what? Here it is in 1991 and the Lower East Side is much tougher now than it was in 1966. So it is a preaching center and not just a shrine. We must love this sacred ground together. We are so few. Lord, teach us the way to love each other—and to spread this message of Prabhupāda and Kṛṣṇa.

❦

No one—no writer—ever had the things to say in the West that we do. We are giddy and unprepared with our riches.

We *are* unqualified and unprepared and not fully practicing what we are preaching. But still, what urgency and what riches there are in the words of a Kṛṣṇa conscious representative. It's a shame that we sometimes bumble it so that no one really knows what we are talking about, or someone takes us for a cult or another institution—which we may be in some external ways.

❦

Kāna, help us. See this
crazy dance of fire,
dance over swords,
this swooning in Your arms,
this flailing to get away from You
and with compassion,
quiet us down and send us
in the right direction.
No one but You
knows best.

❦

Christ says something like, "Your left hand should not know what your right hand is doing." Give charity with anonymity. Be humble and religious. Race ahead of the self-conscious snob. Speak quietly the little we know. Don't be so complicated and worrisome. No one is perfect, and none of us should expect that in others.

❦

What gorgeous works the Vaiṣṇavas have created! Śrīla Prabhupāda writes that Vedic culture is the *most voluminous* and consistent of any religious culture. Raghunātha dāsa Gosvāmī, Rūpa Gosvāmī, Jīva Gosvāmī, Sanātana Gosvāmī—all of them wrote amazing books, poems, and metaphors to help us see the beautiful Lord they all worshiped. They wrote of the most beautiful forms—Rādhā and Kṛṣṇa—and others wrote of Their beautiful combined form—Lord Caitanya.

Let me relish their works with the patience required to read so many volumes. There are so many books to read, one who travels cannot keep them all. As I said, we are embarrassed by our spiritual riches.

❦

This book describes three weeks of my life. There is something very wonderful in trying to let go, in trying to quiet myself so Kṛṣṇa can come forward. I am not saying it so clearly, but I think you know what I mean. I have allowed myself to become congested in spirit, insipid, and afraid over the years. To acknowledge that and let those parts of myself go is a blessing.

This is an exercise in Kṛṣṇa conscious abandon, meant for one who doesn't know how to act with abandon in Kṛṣṇa consciousness. I worry too much what others think of me. Now my whole life is running out. Will I discover that I never lived it for myself—and that Kṛṣṇa *expected* me to live it to the full limit of self-surrender?

This is an exercise for one who confuses the body with the self. The body grows old and does not dance so nimbly anymore, but the self is as sportive as a new calf in spring grass.

This is an exercise for one who confuses the mind with the spirit, whose mind has taken ultimate authority and doesn't know the soul's simple realm.

I am just discovering that I *do* live, and I am scratching it down. I know these statements are oblique and indirect (at least they appear that way on paper), but this is all I can honestly do. I am so tied up in knots by what is happening to me that I cannot speak simple instructions or of love for Kṛṣṇa.

❦

I posted a big sign to the editor in myself:

Don't read it with your red pen out.
Don't mark passages "omit."
Not yet.

❦

Out Walking

The best part is that you meet no one.
And also best is the forest.
And a hawk *peeeping* his scary call
as he floats in the first light.
Best is to chant *japa* as I go.
It's my kingdom at 5 A.M., my bulldozers
where they left them yesterday.
So head into the place and begin to exercise.
I have nothing to tell you about it.

Sliver of moon . . .
you left behind most thinking . . .
but somewhere along the way you confide
to your *caitya-guru* that you intend to
do everything for His cause, and you feel sure
He understands you.
Eventually He will make it clear.

I'm back by sun-up, you can see daisies.
And into the house, past
up-all-night Baladeva snoring,
upstairs, here . . .

6:30 A.M.

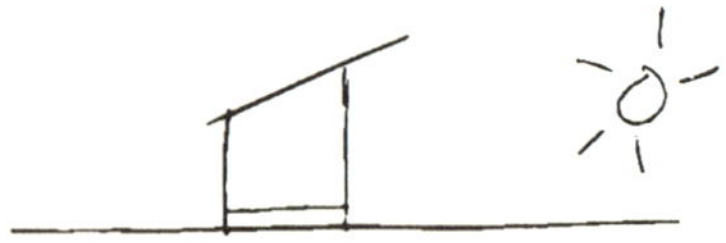

"Without relishing some sort of mellow or loving mood in one's activities, no one can continue to perform such activities. Similarly, in the transcendental life of Kṛṣṇa consciousness and devotional service, there must be some mellow, or specific taste, from the service. Generally, this mellow is experienced by chanting, hearing, worshiping in the temple, and being engaged in the service of the Lord. So, when a person feels transcendental bliss, that is called 'relishing the mellow'" (*Nectar of Devotion*, p. 152).

Śrīla Prabhupāda sometimes spoke of his disciples as experiencing advanced states of Kṛṣṇa consciousness by chanting and dancing and serving without fatigue or remuneration. "It is not material, it is not ordinary," he said. He especially liked to inform audiences in India about "these American and European boys and girls," who were fully absorbed in Kṛṣṇa consciousness. We should not reject this estimation, but live up to it.

I remember the bliss of reading literature. I discovered it in college. Partly, it was showing off that you had a brain and were an intellectual college student, that you were sensitive. But there was a real bliss in it, especially in writing. That bliss is pure and helpful and eternal in Kṛṣṇa conscious literature.

Evidence that you can use free-writing in Kṛṣṇa consciousness: It is the soul's nature to freely love God and freely give help (mercy) to others. If you don't give *freely,* it becomes charity in the mode of ignorance. When you discover that your duty includes transcendental bliss, then you are on the right track.

> Every living being is anxious for full freedom because that is his transcendental nature. . . . We can just imagine the extent and unlimitedness of his freedom, which is as good as that of the Supreme Lord. . . . Similarly, the transcendental system of devotional service is also free. . . . It may or may not develop in a person even after undergoing all the detailed formulas. Similarly, the association of the devotees is also free. One may be fortunate to have it, or one may not have it after thousands of endeavors. . . . Therefore, in all spheres of devotional service, freedom is the main pivot. Without freedom, there is no execution of devotional service.
>
> —*Bhāg.* 1.6.37, purport

The trees—how hard it is to believe they are souls being punished. It sounds like a Grimm fairy tale. But what do we know? As Prabhupāda said, we are "wet behind the ears." Life is hard to believe. It is inconceivable, beyond our grasp. Who can say what a tree is? It stands with many others, grows straight up to get its bit of sunlight. It is a mystery. And why do different birds sing the way they do?

Why is the sky blue on clear days? I don't want to hear the explanation scientists give about light refraction and gas and stratosphere. I want to know why it makes us happy to see the blue sky? Why do artists especially love Nature? Why are they moved to paint pictures and write music?

You ask what is a tree; then, what is a human? Once you start thinking about the wonder of things, then the Vedic explanations make good sense. They accommodate the fact that existence is wonderful, *acintya.* They explain it all within a context of ultimate knowledge. It solves all bewilderment. I can look at a tree and accept the Vedic conclusion—a tree is a soul with very low consciousness, with a thick, heavy bodily covering, waiting out its karma. You can chant to the trees and they will benefit.

❦

Kṛṣṇa consciousness is urgent—wake up and be a devotee as soon as you can. Shorten your stay in this world. Take a direct route. Surrender now. And be patient.

❦

I subscribe to the conviction that an individual contains the universal. Most descriptions of "humanity in general" are abstract. To me, a "pure devotee" is abstract, but Śrīla Prabhupāda is truth, and you can follow him. Therefore, appreciate his personality with its concrete individuality.

❦ ❦ ❦

11:00 A.M.

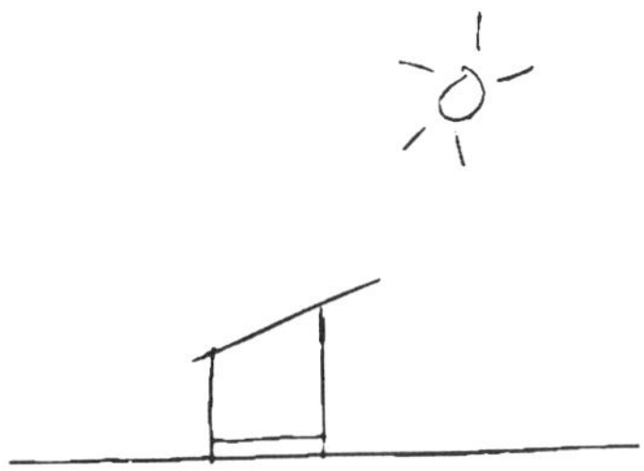

We heard cowherd boy pastimes. Kṛṣṇa shows Balarāma how all Vṛndāvana worships Him, trees bending down to offer their fruits. Kṛṣṇa made perfect imitations of the birds' songs. He vigorously imitated the dancing of the peacocks and made the boys laugh. Then He ran after the little animals, mimicking them in their fear of ferocious animals. Sometimes they took a break and rested in a nice spot. Balarāma lay down with a boy's legs as His pillow, and Kṛṣṇa massaged His feet.

We were not excluded. We are always invited. It is those "demoniac" voices in the head that tell us, "You are too dirty to enter here. Go away!" Prabhupāda doesn't say that! And other voices say, "Don't you have something better to do, Prabhu, than read *Kṛṣṇa* book in the middle of a busy day?" O Voices, be gone! We are hearing of the singing of the bees:

> Sometimes the honey bees in Vṛndāvana became so mad with ecstasy that they closed their eyes and began to sing. Lord Kṛṣṇa, moving along the forest path with His cowherd boyfriends and Baladeva would then respond to the bees by imitating their singing while His friends sang about His pastimes.
>
> —*Bhāg.* 10.15.10

When you come up from reading *Kṛṣṇa* book, you are Kṛṣṇa-ized. With Kṛṣṇa eyes.

❦

Just prior to this morning's hearing of *kṛṣṇa-līlā*, I wrote myself this note: "Quit posing or trying to make literature, why not write something to directly help yourself *become more Kṛṣṇa conscious?* If your writing can serve and if it has power, then use it for this: Help yourself, for example, to chant Hare Kṛṣṇa *japa* with attention and devotion."

Hearing the pastimes leaves us relaxed. But now that we have to get back to work, what shall we do? Write to improve *japa?* Make a speech to oneself? I cannot write about anything now: I am still thinking of the soft grass, of Kṛṣṇa's cows grazing, of Balarāma lying down, and of a young boy singing while others, "qualified by being free of all sin," expertly fan the Supreme Lord.

❦

Isn't this forest a little like Vṛndāvana? I know the highway is just outside (like Dhenukāsura in Tālavana), and it's me sittin' here in the shack. But if I think over what we heard . . . the words themselves . . . then hear these birds and consider those birds of Gokula . . . You see? I told you that listening to birds was okay. Kṛṣṇa does it Himself.

❦

In the Woods

Kṛṣṇa's woods and
the scary woods and
the sexy woods of teenage years,
and a place to race motorcycles,
"Fairyland," Great Kills woods.
Tight groves . . . deep and
lost! Panic of lost in a deep
Northern woods and
Indians with hatchets—
and a black bear,
a grizzly! A tiger!

Come back from the woods.
Go to Kṛṣṇa's woods with Him,
and if a hundred wild donkeys
charge, He'll kill them all.

I am lost in a woods.
No way out.
Calling to my Lord.
Save me.

❦

I say I will be honest here. That means even though I cannot write something great or inspire Kṛṣṇa conscious heroics, I will write anyway. But what if I could write anything I wanted? If I had a yogic *siddhi* or the power to say whatever I wanted, what would I say? Would it be different than this?

Oh, it would be.

I would like to write masterful, humble stories. That is why I was fascinated that a publisher had collected thirteen volumes of Chekhov's stories. Thirteen volumes! I would like to do stories (just like my friendly censor wants me to do).

My storytelling ability would start to improve and become like modern-day Kavi Karnapura quality, Rūpa Gosvāmī drama quality. It will probably never happen, but you asked me my writing aspirations, so I am telling you.

But why wish for such a thing? Why desire to get blessings for that? It would obviously take a lot of time and energy. Why not desire instead to convert a large segment of the U.S.A. to Kṛṣṇa consciousness and fulfill Śrīla Prabhupāda's desire?

Now this is turning into a fantasy. I cannot have my pick of impossible dreams. We started with a more modest supposition, "What would you like to write?" and I told you. If you want to ask me, "*Why* do you spend time writing?" that's a different question. Maybe I am compensating (a wonderful word from the world of psychology) for my obvious lacks in other areas. It seems hopeless that I could achieve much as a manager of temples, money, and people. I tried and failed. Didn't like it.

I love writing. Some of it works, helps people. It's right in the heart of our *paramparā* tradition. I was "hooked" into it before I even met Śrīla Prabhupāda, so why not use it in his service? And you, dear readers, why not do what comes naturally to you?

❦ ❦ ❦

4:00 P.M.

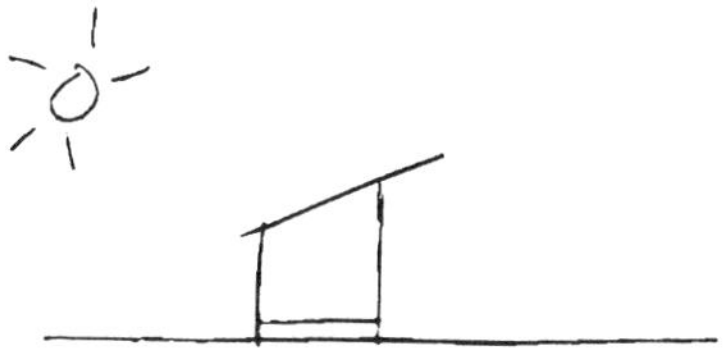

Get to the bottom of things. Can work in one area, like writing, help others the same as growing determined in chanting?

A big step forward in self-confidence is to trust that you can speak on philosophical issues without being way over your head or being pompous. Professional philosophers cut each other to pieces if a small mistake is made in rigorous logic. Literary writers have their own standards. So one is aware of this and fears looking foolish; one knows too well what will happen—it will be categorized, psychoanalyzed, and torn to shreds.

Mavericks go forward anyway. Damn the torpedoes, full speed ahead. But a devotee is in a different world. He speaks for the whole tradition, yet even within that tradition, according to time and place, there are many opinions.

What am I trying to get at here? The courage to speak for yourself—if you dare. If you must. Not to make a laughing stock of yourself.

❦

Both *BTG* and *IWR* covered 25 years of ISKCON for ISKCON's anniversary. *IWR* especially noted external media events as major happenings in the life of ISKCON. A mayor attending a ribbon-cutting ceremony for a homeless people's shelter to be run by ISKCON. Good publicity. But a year later it closed down. Never mind, it was good P.R., a mayor cut the ribbon. Besides, do you want inner events reported in the newspaper? Wouldn't it trivialize them? Yes, keep it out of the press. Keep it hidden. Pass it among interested persons only. Don't be dismayed. On with the revolution.

❦

Remember when someone dared to criticize us, and we would say, "Who are you? What have you done for Prabhupāda? How many devotees have you made? How many books have you distributed? How much property do you own? How many miles have you traveled?" We would wither them like that. The "good ol' days"—scorching opposition from the high seat.

Self-centered

The subject of self-centeredness generates a lot of energy. It appears to be split into two interpretations. The common meaning of "self-centered" makes me cry out, "Bad! Bad! Wrong! *Māyā!*" No one likes a self-centered, selfish brute. "Conceited," as we used to say as kids. So it's bad.

But you can't stop being "I" and speaking of "I." "I am a tiny servant of the Lord." "I only want Your causeless devotional service in my life, birth after birth." "Never was there a time when you did not exist." Self-annihilation is not possible. Spiritual suicide refers to separating yourself from Kṛṣṇa, but still you exist. So be Kṛṣṇa-centered. Be a speck of dust orbiting around the sun.

We should be happy in our tiny servant's capacity. We *must* swallow our pride. We must pray to be successful at this. We should do whatever is necessary to die to the false self. Do as much as you can, and then give the credit to Kṛṣṇa. *He* is the ability in man, in *us*. *Śrīmad-Bhāgavatam* tells us that only uninterrupted, unmotivated devotional service will bring satisfaction to the self (*yayātmā suprasīdati*).

A note to myself: when I push and strive with creative passion, it is *rājo-guṇa.* Learn how to work hard in goodness and with the greed of a servant to glorify the master. Then it is no longer *rājo-guṇa,* it is *kṛṣṇa-śakti.*

Here's a picture of me beating a drum for Kṛṣṇa.

"But why make it so small?"

Well, I wanted to show that I know I'm tiny.

"Yes, but the drum can be big—*bṛhat-mṛdaṅga.*"

Then how can I play it if I'm small?

"You just play it. It's not even 'your' drum."

Can I sing a song of my own composition? Can it be made out of my life?

"Yes, but be careful. Don't concoct. Don't be so bold. Follow the *mahājanas.*"

No original beats?

"No . . . it's hard to say. You have to follow, but you also have to use your own intelligence to serve Kṛṣṇa. Maybe I'm not the one to explain it. I'm just trying to say what your spiritual master wants."

Do you know what that is then?

"Sometimes. Śrīla Prabhupāda didn't like it when Pandu composed his own verses in praise of Lord Caitanya and printed them on the walls facing the street in Māyāpura. And there is that story of the painter who painted *kṛṣṇa-līlā,* but depicted something not specifically described in the scriptures."

What about this book I am writing?

"I can't judge."

I am *so* attached to my way. I hope I can become purified of this. If I had to just give it up and throw it all away . . .

"You were ready to do that once in 1966. Can you be sure what you write helps others? Is the philosophy correct? The *rasa* right?"

I think so. And I'm very wary of critics. Without examining the whole situation, they superficially dismiss it.

"'We' are also wary of you."

I'm willing to pay that price.

"Don't be *too* willing. The price may be to sacrifice attaining pure devotional service. You have to learn to listen."

To whom?

"Prabhupāda and Kṛṣṇa in your own heart, and to his devotees."

And if some of his devotees approve and others disapprove?

"Think about it. Pray to do His will and try to discern it. Pray every day for that."

Thank you, I will. In the meantime, I will work to improve what I am doing.

6:00 P.M. 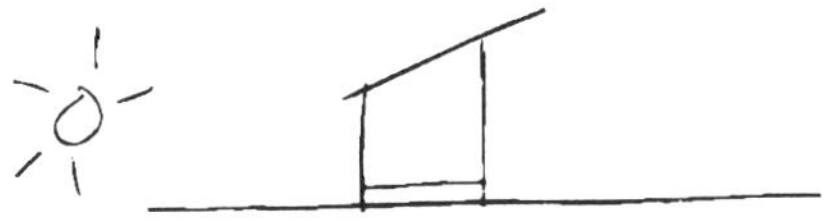

Tonight we heard about Kṛṣṇa and Balarāma killing the jackass demon. After that, Śukadeva describes how Kṛṣṇa comes home in the evening with all the boys and cows and how the *gopīs* and parents are so eager to see Them. We tried visualizing how the residents of Vṛndāvana waited for the first faint sound of a flute or a boy's distant shouting. Mother Yaśodā ran into the roadway repeatedly, looking in the direction of Kṛṣṇa's expected return, and strained her eyes to see the cloud of dust raised by the cows' hooves. Nanda went to the roof of the house to look for signs of their coming home. By now it was well known that demons regularly came to attack Kṛṣṇa, so there was always cause for worry (even though Kṛṣṇa always killed them).

In this chapter, we hear of the first stirrings of the *gopīs'* love for Kṛṣṇa. They are described as anxiously awaiting Him after a long day's separation. He never left their thoughts.

> All the *gopīs* in Vṛndāvana remained very morose on account of Kṛṣṇa's absence . . . when they saw Kṛṣṇa returning, all their anxieties were immediately relieved, and they began to look at His face the way drones hover over the honey of the lotus flower. When Kṛṣṇa entered the village, the young *gopīs* smiled and laughed. Kṛṣṇa, while playing the flute, enjoyed the beautiful smiling faces of the *gopīs.*
>
> —*Kṛṣṇa,* p. 152

7:45 P.M.

For many years, I identified the critical (left brain) side of myself as the Kṛṣṇa conscious person. He knows *paramparā* and he corrects all deviancy. He is always right; he represents Prabhupāda and Kṛṣṇa. He has absolute authority. He pretty much squelches playfulness and creativity, seeing them as *māyā.*

But this may have been a mistake. Someone may have an authoritarian air, while lacking compassion, intelligence, and the broad spirit of Kṛṣṇa consciousness.

In *Shack Notes,* my playful, creative side has been asserting itself and saying to the logical man, "You are not the only Kṛṣṇa conscious person within me. *Yes,* Kṛṣṇa consciousness is truth, and whatever is not Kṛṣṇa conscious is *māyā.* But you are not the sole judge of what that entails."

My critical side has been a stalwart guard for twenty-five years, but there is definitely a revolution brewing in me. I see the "logic is right" man as just one part of the whole self. Maybe it was right that for years he ruled with an iron will over the others, but they are growing up and feeling ready to express themselves in pure devotional service. Left-brain's barked command, "Stop the *māyā,*" just doesn't strike fear the way it used to. I've become more democratic.

Right brain is singing like the thrushes of Stroudsburg all day long. And left brain? He's as tough as ever. "I'll get him," he thinks. "Let him write as much as he wants. I will find a way to show him he's an egotistical madman."

❦ ❦ ❦

July 10, 1:30 A.M.

Often as the afternoon lengthens, a battle wages between my critical and my creative sides. *Shack Notes* favors both, but it needs the creative side in order to come into existence. In 1966, Śrīla Prabhupāda lectured repeatedly on "dovetailing your consciousness with the Supreme consciousness." Whatever you are doing, he said, whether you are a musician or artist or businessman or householder or student—*do it for Kṛṣṇa.* Kṛṣṇa consciousness is not difficult. Do what you are doing, but do it for Kṛṣṇa.

Even *raja*-creation can be purified. It must be purified. It cannot be repressed. So the critic is working against our best efforts when he tries to punch the creator into submission or tries to utterly destroy him. I have a creative drive. It is normal to have a creative drive. And Śrīla Prabhupāda said to the passionate American disciples, "Do something wonderful."

Dovetailing is a principle that must be firmly established as a fact of devotional life. We should preach it to newcomers. We should preach it to ourselves. Why should this make us feel dejected or impure? Do you feel joy in writing freely? Then, dovetail that in the service of the Supreme.

❦

Remember Prabhupāda's prayer, "Please accept my defective offering." This also means that the person offering the service must feel humble and contrite. The offering is made in knowledge of one's unworthiness. What makes the work acceptable to Kṛṣṇa is the *bhakti.* It is not our arrogant self-confidence that forces Kṛṣṇa to accept the offering. The devotee puts all he can into the offering, tears well up in his eyes, and he humbly places *himself* before the Lord, begging to be accepted, "Don't kick me away."

And the Lord is always free to correct us.

A Song of Humble Creativity

Please accept,
a song of love.
A Love Supreme.

Let us act as we sing,
for our cause it is just.
Please accept.

Please accept Lord,
because You are
mādhurya's essence,
You are great,
You are beautiful—
even *our* stingy hearts
are melted and we must sing
    Your glories.

We are not yet qualified to sing
for Your pleasure like the
cowherd boys "free of all sin"
who wave a peacock fan
as You rest in the forest and
the boy who sings in pure voice
free of sorrow, free of ego.

We sing at some distance,
in the streets and homes of this
material world,
among the fallen.
But no doubt about it,
we are Your men,
we are Prabhupādānugas.
This band plays for You.

We don't even say
You and Prabhupāda should hear us—
just be pleased by the results,
that we love You,
we are working full-time,
we *are* repeating Your pastimes,
we stick to the rules and regs
and recite Your *upadeśa*—
But it all comes out
loud and brassy 'cause that's
who we are.

Some folks here like it,
they dance and sway,
and use it in their lives
against the demons within,
and the demons against us
don't know why we're so cheerful.
We've got a song in our hearts
because of You.

So please accept us, Lord,
know our song is for You,
we're Your monkey-like servants,
brewing up a storm
preaching up a gale
feelin' fine,
because You're true,
You are the flowing nectar.

And if we mistake
a gaudy glitter for pure gold,
well, we've got to learn.
And You've got some heavy critics
posted here Lord,
so they're telling us.
But just the same,
please accept us.

Good deeds
follow our song.
Please accept.

Loosen up.
Tighten up.
Balance up.
Settle up.

May Kṛṣṇa, the Killer of Dhenuka, protect you and inspire you to kill within yourself the jackass demon of stubborn materialism. May you surrender your false claim over the Tālavana forest.

Instead of forbidding the Lord to come and letting the fruits rot (or eating them all yourself), may you sincerely invite the Lord and His devotees to come and partake.

May Kṛṣṇa, the Killer of Dhenuka, give you courage and please your heart. May you cheer as Balarāma twirls a big donkey around by its hind legs and throws it into the trees. Just see Kṛṣṇa's concentration and joy, the drops of perspiration on His face, as He whirls the fiend around! Don't be afraid. Tālavana will be free.

May Kṛṣṇa, who killed Dhenuka, be always in our thoughts. May we join with His *gopīs* and hear their spontaneously composed songs glorifying Kṛṣṇa. May we, too, make songs purely for the joy of exclaiming His merit, His prowess, the way He stood when He twisted them overhead!

May Kṛṣṇa, who killed a herd of demon donkeys by throwing them into treetops, be the object of our loving service. May we think of Him and thus purify the scope of our minds. He walked home before sunset, leading the cows and playing the flute. The *gopīs* could not take their eyes off such a vision. His body has the luster of lotus flowers. He is the beloved of Vraja, the Lord of the universe. May He be your Lord, and may you be guided by His devotees.

❦

Soon in our daily readings, we will be hearing of *mādhurya-rasa*. It already began in the Dhenuka chapter. Kṛṣṇa praised Lord Balarāma and said that all the trees and birds and all residents of Vṛndāvana were eager to receive Him. He said Balarāma had made the twigs glorious by touching them, that the grass was blessed by His step, and that the hills and rivers became glorious when He looked at them. "Above all, the damsels of Vraja, the *gopīs* attracted by Your beauty, are the most glorious, because You embrace them with Your strong arms."

After killing Dhenuka, when Kṛṣṇa created a blissful festival by His entrance into the village, the *gopīs* exchanged glances and pleased Him.

It will be a test to our newfound happiness of participating in *kṛṣṇa-līla,* whether we can hear of the *gopīs* without being disturbed and embarrassed. Prabhupāda will guide us. If we are not offensive, the *gopas* and *gopīs* will guide us. We will watch how they please Kṛṣṇa by their total dedication and their heart-throbbing appreciation of Him. Following the careful lead of Śukadeva Gosvāmī, we may speak further on what we hear. The best position to take is that of a blade of grass in Vṛndāvana, as aspired to by Lord Brahmā.

After the Walk

The pink sky . . .
puffs of pink. Every time you have to let
    yourself do it . . .
Our predicament
is a little different than the nondevotee's.
We are unworthy of the great topic,
and yet we don't want to talk about our
    false self.
It's not a handicap, but a fortune.
You have to forget a lot of things,
and remember who the sun is
as he blazes through the pine tops.

Now it's time to go to the shack
and the cold desk and the notes.
Look at your watch, delay . . .
Think of reasons why not to write:
"Only a classical master could describe
the pink in clouds over trees."
Finally you settle for less but
with desperate joy you
ride like a surfer on a wave,
discovering as you write it down,
another way of saying what Prabhupāda said.
And that's the truth.

6:30 A.M.

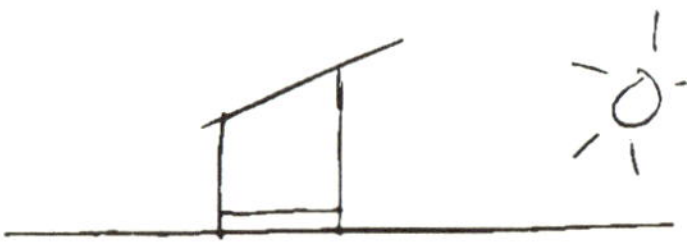

I sometimes sneak out of the house so no one will see me, but this morning I stumbled on a rock and almost fell.

Twelve days left. Set up shop: Put the picture of Rādhā-Dāmodara, Lalitā and Viśakhā on the desk. *Cādar* over shoulders and knees.

Note left in the shack to greet me for 6:30 A.M. session on July 10: Come here and write from the heart as best you can. Be contrite for your excesses and egoism. Dig the earth for purifying subject matter of *kṛṣṇa-kathā* and the sort of self-realization that will help others.

❦

All glories to Śrīla Prabhupāda for presenting the *Kṛṣṇa* book. Now we all know Kṛṣṇa who comes home to His village in the early evening.

May everyone be blessed and hear of Śrī Kṛṣṇa. Perhaps it is too much to hope for, to expect everyone to give favorable aural reception. We became attracted to Kṛṣṇa's pastimes, and we were no different than anyone else. May all people be blessed! A drunkard, an atheist, a puffed-up intellectual, a gangster, a tough guy, a girl of low morals, a Christian, a Jew, a junkie, an Air Force officer candidate —they all heard and have now become lovers of Kṛṣṇa. A man who tested weapons for Navy submarines is my best friend, and so is an ex-"skinhead" from Britain. So why not everybody? A computer salesman from Connecticut, his Catholic wife —why not anyone? Vedic knowledge is not so difficult to assimilate; there are no special problems to prevent our understanding. We just have to be serious.

Blessings

God, You bless us.
Gurus too.
No one else?
"Bless me Father for I
have sinned. It's been 25
years since my last confession."
Oh, I've blessed you, son,
but for penance say 10
Hail Marys and 25 good
rounds of Hare Kṛṣṇa mantra *japa.*

Bless. Bless best
Bessy the cow blesses
with her milk.
A grumpy *brahmacārī* blesses
me with a greeting short.
Bless me with a whack
on the side of the head.

Best blessings—are what?
To surrender and go back to Godhead.
No one can bless,
you can only serve, see?
No, I can bless too.
If I say the Name and
someone hears, if I
give out *prasādam,*
if I'm happy in Kṛṣṇa consciousness,
if he gives his wife a child,
if they bow down to Kṛṣṇa,
they bless the earth with their presence—
the devotees.

Bless us, Father,
for we have sinned, it
has been one whole week
since our last confession.
O, I will bless you, son,
but don't keep coming back;
it's a ludicrous proposal and
condemned in the *Nectar of Devotion.*

Oh bless us, and
let us bless.
Let's be blessed
and shower grace on ugly heads.
Give them mercy and
give us too—

Yes, yes, but what about
your act of contrition?
Say the prayer—
"Uh . . . I am sorry, very much,
and I fear the loss of heaven and
the pains of hell,
come to think of it
I'm scared of hell and I'm
sorry I let down God and guru."
All right son, go in peace,
your sins are forgiven.

Bless the country,
the mortgaged home,
the heavily mortgaged home,
the hucksters and the *śūdras,*
bless the Pentagon?
The White House?

Pray for us, pray for us,
the suffering and hell-bound cry,
and devotees do—
they bless,
they bless
with the nectar of immortality,
as they were deputed to do
by His Divine Grace.
He wants to see us active
in doing this blessing
as much as we can.

11:30 A.M. 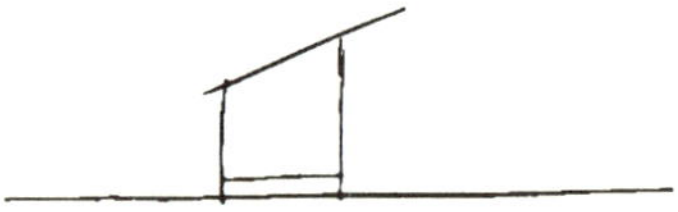

I spoke of evasiveness and indirectness. It is yet another form of mental clutter. It prevents us from getting at our dormant love of Kṛṣṇa.

Speaking of mental clutter, Ānanta just interrupted me in my shack to tell me he needed my passport. So I went back to the house to get it. I told him to wear it in a shoulder pouch and be very careful, because this passport is a replacement for a lost one. "Oh yes," he said, "if you lose a replacement, they don't like it. They think you are selling them. Ekātvam lost his, and they wouldn't give him a new one."

"What? His own country?"

"Yes."

"Oh . . . that's right. They don't have to. It's a privilege."

Then I thought out the "worst thing that could happen" if I lost my passport, as advised by Dale Carnegie in *Stop Worrying and Start Living.* He says to think of the worst, accept it, and then recoup your losses as much as possible. Lost passport . . . and the government won't give me a new one: No going to India, no going to Europe in the new van. At least I am still free to live here. I could spend more time in this shack or at Gītā-nāgarī. I could live with it. Get plenty of Kuśakratha's books, study Prabhupāda's books, develop relationships with devotees in this country. And I could travel the U.S.A.

What's worse than that? Death, inevitable death, the sure-fire worst scenario. It must also be a "best scenario" because it has to happen. No Europe, no U.S.A., no passport, no head, no hat—no books, no lunch, no rest in this body. No appeals, no reprieve.

But we are devotees, so surely something good will happen, even from death.

Tempus fugit. That is the theme of this book. The hands on the clock are visibly moving as we watch: 11:30 A.M., 11:45 A.M., Noon. Early summer, mid-summer . . . 25th Anniversary . . .

We have stopped time in a sense—or at least left our temporal concern for it—by meditation and prayer for submissive aural reception—in our group reading of *Kṛṣṇa* book.

I saw Kṛṣṇa swimming in the Kāliya lake. Ananta said, "I experience, at least a little, that

Kṛṣṇa is a person. In my prayers, since we have been reading, now I think of Him as a young boy."

"Yes," I said. "Or else he is just God."

He is swimming, and the serpent cannot help but admire His delicate body and His strong swimming strokes. His black hair is shining wet. It is a wonderful sport as He swims toward the demon, Kāliya.

I noted, "The pastimes are going by too quickly. This one especially seems to rush by. It contains a deep exchange. The Vṛndāvana residents are grief-stricken to see Kṛṣṇa in the serpent's coils. It goes by too quickly. And the entire Vṛndāvana pastimes are done in about two hundred pages. That is why the poets have dwelt on the pastimes in detail. This is just a tiny glimpse. On higher planets they hear more. But whatever we have . . . "

He danced on the head of the serpent. He didn't just smack down His heel to kill a snake. He danced with graceful movements of arms and head, dancing with unique steps. And the demigods knew, "Kṛṣṇa is dancing!" So they rushed to the scene to provide rhythm and tune.

A Query and Reply Regarding Experience

"But did you have any experience
when you heard of Kṛṣṇa swimming
in the Kāliya lake?
I just read a poem where the poet has
a deep tho' casual experience listening to the
jazz piano of Thelonious Monk.
So I know Kṛṣṇa is supposed to be greater,
but what about your experience?
Or do you say that's not even important?
But how could it be unimportant?
I mean, Kṛṣṇa is there in eternity (they say), and
His eternal devotees have deep experience,
but what about you?"

That's a good question, and
I'd like to answer.
Kṛṣṇa swimming eludes me,
and yet He is swimming in my mind,
maybe like a little fish.
Let me put it this way;
even if Kṛṣṇa swimming in me is just a little thing,
He's got something Monk is alluding to,
but can't give us as his song ends.
Monk is this world only. I know the feelings—
I remember listening to his "Getting Sentimental
Over You,"
with Charlie Rouse playing sax.
I felt it for years,
pain and beauty and Art, for sure.
Human genius, the gods, mysterious sounds.
What does your poet say?
" . . . Monk is playing
the warm dusk and everything within us
and beyond us
goes without saying."

If you don't know Kṛṣṇa at all
then there's no use my explaining
and if you know what He is, even a little bit,
then you'll know what I mean.
I'll take that little fish of Kṛṣṇa in
my mind,
instead of all the world's beauty, pain and love,
as summed up in any moment or
jazz song.

4:00 P.M. 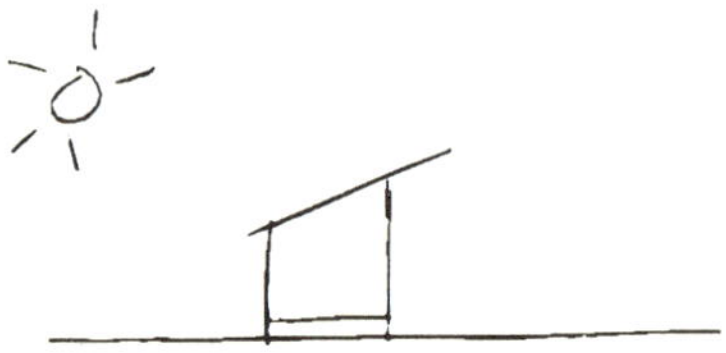

There is nothing to wait for. Begin writing. You cannot go on with this forever.

I just received a FAX that a good friend, Dr. Leonard Wilder, has suffered a ruptured hernia and the doctors say he has a 50/50 chance of survival. We are each on our own, but we pray that he and his family can remember Kṛṣṇa. He was doing so nicely, caring for devotees, living peacefully, conducting his dental practice and chanting Hare Kṛṣṇa, showing conservative British families that the Kṛṣṇa calling is for everyone.

Brace yourself friend, think of the Lord who calls us near in His own way. I remember how you told me about your one-engine airplane losing its propeller several thousand feet in the air. You glided down, just missing a church steeple, and landed in an empty field. As you climbed out of the plane, you heard a blackbird singing and it sounded like the most beautiful thing you had ever heard. You got down and kissed the ground.

You tell that story well, sitting with a guest like me who comes demanding free dental work or at least reduced devotee rates. You tolerate us cheerfully and accept it as service to Kṛṣṇa. Your wife and children are worried now. What can we do but chant His names and ask for either your safe delivery back to this world, where you can seriously develop your devotional life, or safe passage to the next—as Kṛṣṇa desires. Your prayer now is the one we all must make sincerely, "Wherever I go, let me remember You and serve with devotees. Please see, Lord, that I have no other desires."

Fear

I am afraid of many things. Fear is material. It is the most prominent of the four animal propensities.

The things I dream of—tigers, losing my I.D., becoming lost—perhaps they will never happen. The fears I consider—being thrown into jail, a sex falldown, torture by bullies, fear of losing my reputation—these things also may never happen.

And when what I fear does take place, the fear itself is often the worst part.

The remedy for fear: If the circumstance is not too bad, breathe deeply and chant Hare Kṛṣṇa. If it is really bad, then chant Hare Kṛṣṇa within and without.

Think of Kṛṣṇa. He tells us not to be afraid, and He says, "Surrender to Me." His devotees are fearless.

I am afraid of many things, real and illusory. Kṛṣṇa, please save me. The prayer made out of fear is not misplaced; it is a way to come close to He who vanquishes all fear.

Dear Leonard, don't be afraid; Kṛṣṇa is near.

❦

Don't wait around. Soon all your life's work will be tallied. "What did he do? Did he care for other people and help them in the spirit of Prahlāda Mahārāja?"

❦

If your selfishness is exposed, try to make an act of charity or sacrifice. Act in Kṛṣṇa consciousness.

❦

I have not bothered to notice the gorgeous, green, deep forest, and the shades and lights filtering all over in speckles and particles—falling beauty all around. I sit in the midst of a heavenly place. Note it and thank the creator. The secondary creator was inspired by the Primary Creator to create this world based on the beauty of the spiritual world. Thank them and praise their work even as it appears in this reflected earth world.

Leaves rustling, treetops in swaying motions. It is almost time to go back up again to hear *Kṛṣṇa* book. Hare Kṛṣṇa, Hare Kṛṣṇa, Kṛṣṇa Kṛṣṇa, Hare Hare/ Hare Rāma, Hare Rāma, Rāma Rāma, Hare Hare.

July 11, 1:30 A.M.

The shack is not just a wooden structure with screened walls in the backyard of Śamīka Ṛṣi's house; it is a way of writing. Maybe there is such a thing as a "mobile shack." That is what I am going to find out today; whether I can take the shack with me when I go to New York City.

❦

Break loose from inner critics, and say what is on your mind. It may not be so bad.

❦

After feeling almost euphoric in my plan to be a writing teacher, I am starting to have doubts. Why wish this life on others? What can you teach them except strategies of self-expression from nondevotee friends, like how to use the "hourglass" method of essay writing? Maybe writing isn't for everyone. It may be better service for you to teach *Kṛṣṇa* book pastimes.

And it is not that I can *teach* Kṛṣṇa's pastimes instead, but we can utilize our classroom time reviewing and recalling the *līlās*.

If anyone out there really wants to be a writer, they will figure it out themselves.

❦

I am feeling something I have not been able to enunciate. I was kept awake last night by a strong desire to express myself and to visualize something. I imagined I would be able to come out to this room and that after a little while, whatever it was would simply come out. Then we would both know what it was.

May I be able to travel, Lord, to one place or another, with or without a "shack," and speak Your teachings to help others. But may I also survive. And then when you see fit, off I go, another tiny spark—out of its present kernel, into space, and then into the next body.

Material nature is cruel. Because of our desire to dominate, we must take another body for suffering in delusion. The psychologists talk of becoming free, but freedom in this body isn't possible.

And this is the strong argument of my inner critic: He wants to know, *if this writing is still coming from the conditional self, then how will it help you or others?*

But the "free-self" advocates and replies—"If I am not free—and I agree I am not—then what good does it do me to repeat the Vedic truths *as if I were free?"*

Work together, selves. Stop the wrangling. That is what I want—whole effort, whole expression—everyone, body, mind, soul, child-self, adult-self pulling together. This particular work, *Shack Notes,* is a three-week effort for that.

❦

T.S. Eliot said, all literature is "making a raid on the inarticulate." We cannot say what we want; we are incoherent. We also suspect glib voices who know it all, who say it all, reading to us from chapter and verse. "Fellow strugglers, let me enlighten you . . ."

We *want* the chapter and verse, but from a friend, and at the right time.

❦

Sometimes it doesn't work out well. Just to be confused isn't good. We don't want to write mere ramblings and confusions. I am basically all right and functioning. Today I will make a little speech about preaching, and the occasion will force me to be sober and to the point.

I remember Brahmānanda saying in '66—when we had each maybe given one or two lectures on our own—he said, "You don't just speak according to how you feel at the moment. [You speak what Kṛṣṇa says in the *Gītā*.]" Years later, Brahmānanda Swami said, "Privacy is sense gratification." But . . . we are imperfect, confused, and want to speak what we feel at the time we are speaking. And we want privacy. Brahmānanda wants it and I want it. There is a time and place for it.

We want someone compassionate to love us and say, "It is all right. You are being misunderstood and mistreated sometimes. You are doing what you can, but try more. Don't give up your spiritual practices. Find time to chant your sixteen rounds. I do mine mostly in the early morning."

❦

I cannot speak for you. This is my raid on the inarticulate.

I may not be coherent enough to share this morning, but I have faith that the process of writing is helpful in itself.

❦

Prabhupāda, today we will observe the 25th Anniversary. I am with you and your followers. Bless us with strength—we especially need to be kind and understanding among ourselves. This is the department in which I want to work. You told me once that preaching to devotees was more important than preaching to nondevotees. You meant we have to train the people we have. That was in '72, and you were stressing that we should sit and hear *Śrīmad-Bhāgavatam* class. We still need that stressed for us, and now we also need care and decent human exchanges. We, as a movement, may have neglected your compassionate side. I mean, we haven't developed it among ourselves.

We criticize each other. I criticize someone as too strict, and he criticizes me as too loose.

Help us, Śrīla Prabhupāda, to go ahead. We are a small religious movement in this world. We note our successes as advancement. We note our failures also. We are still small after twenty-five years, but not doing so badly considering it is Kali-yuga, and considering what it takes to make a world religious movement. We are surviving. I suppose my area of work is to ask: Yes, we have an institution, but does it have the kind of spiritual life one can pursue for a whole life duration, while sharing it with many kinds of people?

I am trying to find my own place. And trying to help others.

Your mercy is on us.

Mercy

Who can give mercy? He who has truth. God is the ultimate source of mercy. We turn to Him with our petitions. Mercy is from God and His representatives. Perfect shelter is in Him. Those who take shelter want to extend it to others.

But the preacher has to be careful in what he is doing. He cannot become overwhelmed by the chaos of lost souls who clamor for their needs in the world, and who sometimes devour "do-gooders." Also, he has to give the right medicine and shelter. He has to protect himself from drunkards and exploiters, or he too will be lost. Yet, the challenge is to work with everyone and to rescue them from the chaos.

We ask for relief from pain. Can You please make it easier? Allow us to enter Goloka. We seek Your mercy.

We seek the way. We seek mercy, and even the seeker can be merciful to his followers. Be like God and guru, be merciful and please the Lord who will then be merciful to you. Kṛṣṇa says, "He for whom no one is put into difficulty and who is not disturbed by anyone . . . who is not envious, but is a friend to all living entities—is very dear to Me."

Walking

"Today ISKCON is 25 years old."
Save that for later when you have an audience.

One bird calls the same over and over
from way in the past,
seems to say, "Go out and play baseball."
Kṛṣṇa consciousness is nice because you get to chant
on your beads when you go for a walk.
No one else knows that.
You stride, wear sweatpants, but
in your two hands you hold the strand
    of *tulasī* beads,
breathing in dawn freshness,
exhaling soft Hare Kṛṣṇa mantras, as you
go quietly in the dark past their houses,
walk into the new development site,
all to your own, chanting loudly now.

6:30 A.M.

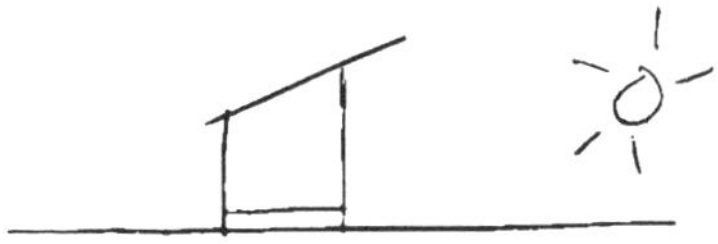

Go for it. Don't reject thoughts. Turn to Kṛṣṇa, His world. We hear *Kṛṣṇa* book and try to point ourselves there. Want to make sense of this place we live in. The explanation given to us by *śāstra* is clear enough—it is all *māyā,* the three modes combined. The longing to live and enjoy is our original love, but it is covered by illusion now.

Keep that *śāstra-cakṣuṣaḥ* vision clear, like keeping your windshield clean. Don't allow yourself to drift mindlessly in the present. Don't set up your own domain, a false castle.

Allen Ginsberg thought that Śrīla Prabhupāda was confining him when he said, "Write poems about Kṛṣṇa."

"Just one image?" asked Ginsberg. He didn't know that everything is His energy and He has jurisdiction everywhere.

Blue jay and thrush and gray cool forest. Kṛṣṇa, please save us. Let us pray and chant Your glories. Let us remember Your unlimited pastimes.

I remember hearing the Kāliya pastime. Be like a child. I like the way Kṛṣṇa dances on the heads of the serpent. It is nice when you live in a room with a good painting of the pastime. You live with it, and gradually the pastime speaks to you in your own life. Sometimes while dealing with business, you glance at Kāliya-Kṛṣṇa. You chant *japa* and see Him dancing. You think something unworthy, and He is there. You see Him even when you don't notice.

❦

Salinger writes how one of his fictional children thinks that "Awake!" is the best line in the Bible. But he is thinking of some non-theistic *awake* probably. They mostly are. Christ didn't mean that. He meant you may die at any moment, and you don't know when, so stay awake. Don't sin. Remember God: *man-manā bhava mad-bhakto.* Awake in Kṛṣṇa.

❦

You've got a long way to go. You already know the answers.

❦

My Own Writing

I have doubts about my writing because I have doubts about myself. My writing is me.

I can stop the false ego utterances by purifying them. I want to write in a purified voice. There is not much encouragement for self-expression around, but I am allowing myself the audacity to try to use my personality in Kṛṣṇa's service. I *can* improve myself.

In India, the temple domes are sometimes golden. They are made as an offering to Kṛṣṇa. Writing is another kind of offering, like a temple *cakra,* a temple foundation, decorative Deity doors, the black and white design on the marble floors—all the workmanship and labor that goes into constructing a glorious temple is also there in writing.

❦

It is work time at "The Woods." I hear the bulldozers, and something that sounds like a pile driver is pounding the earth. Cars rush to offices. I bend my back here all day, searching for the combination of honesty and pure *paramparā.*

❦

Let me turn my attention to today's plan. After breakfast, Ananta and I will hop in the car and head for the city. I hope to be able to write on the way down there. I doubt there will be time to write while actually in the storefront with the other two hundred devotees. I want to look for images to express the essence of the day. What is the 25th Anniversary of ISKCON, and what was 1966 like at this place? I feel like a journalist or poet on assignment, and I am hoping to get back with minimum expense and damage, to tell you how it went.

❦

I am madly attached to writing. Can't give up my way of doing it or trying to learn how to improve it. Plenty of Kṛṣṇa and plenty of open truth—that's the aim. I am surrendered to my spiritual master. Please let me serve him. He has protected us all these years. There is no one but him.

I am doing a crazy dance and calling it "practice."

Prabhupāda, I dance so I can write in my own words, so that Kṛṣṇa will use it to wake people up, so they will take to the philosophy.

It is also a way to cope with life.

As Kṛṣṇa desires, please make these things happen. Please accept my offering.

Kṛṣṇa subdued Kāliya snake, and He is free to do with me as He desires. I want to rid myself of poison and be Kṛṣṇa's helper. I want to do that by helping Śrīla Prabhupāda preach. I want to help by writing.

❦

Dear Prabhupāda,

Please accept my humble obeisances. All glories to your lotus feet.

Thank you for *Kṛṣṇa* book. Thank you for keeping us together in ISKCON despite our break-apart tendencies. Today is ISKCON's birthday. We are having a get-together at your first temple. You already know about it. Please forgive us. Give us the *śakti* to work together. Some are ready to distribute your books, some are living in your temples, some are living at home—in all *āśramas,* we have everything except unity and love in our purpose of *sādhu-saṅga.*

I want to help in my own way, and as you wish me to. I am not the temple president of Boston anymore, or on the GBC, but I am serving alongside your other disciples. We need to try harder at coming together. Merely renting 26 Second Avenue isn't such a great feat—but coming together there, caring for each other, working together for your mission, and chanting Hare Kṛṣṇa together—these are great achievements.

Dear Baladeva,

There is a daring involved in this project. And a trust. I would like to live up to it.

Our working premise is that I have "paid my dues" by completing *Prabhupāda Meditations,* Volume 3, and I am in good standing, at least in a minimum sense, in the society of devotees.

Now for my own sake, and for the sake of "my art"—let me explore the possibilities of going beyond routine forms, of reaching for more honest expression, with more trust in the basic urge to create and express oneself in Kṛṣṇa conscious writing.

The premise is that I should "write my head off," so to speak, and then see later what can be edited and what can be deemed as successful for sharing. In other words, it is not a time to play it safe. I have to write faster and with less looking over my own shoulder to see whether it is coming out as it should. What I have done so far seems all right, much of it, and is more mild than wild. I take up much space debating whether to do it at all.

You are assisting me. So help me in these last ten days to write more freely than before. This means more trust in the free expression—and more trust that editing will come later. (The chaos and messiness won't be passed off as perfect or publishable.)

And more trust that, although this is an experiment, it is conducted sincerely in Kṛṣṇa consciousness.

Each time I put pen to paper, let me try to do the best I can. Churn the ocean and expect odd things to come up.

Yours in the service of Prabhupāda,
Satsvarūpa dāsa Goswami

P.S. I am thinking there should be less dialogue with the editors and more permissive writing without fear, "What if I make a crazy mess?" At worst—the last section of the book would have to be thrown away, and I would have learned something (I hope).

9:30 A.M. 

Shack Mobile Unit (Śamīka Ṛṣi's LTD station wagon en route New York City, bumpy Interstate 80 East):

They are fixing the highway. Your thoughts are bumpity, but Kṛṣṇa consciousness is deep.

How do I feel about nondevotees seeing me dressed as a devotee? I used to be bolder. I know how I look in their eyes; I can see how they look at me. And I know how they appear to me. There is a frustrated love affair between me and all the people of the world. We misunderstand each other. We are worlds apart. Some see me as a cultist, a weirdo; I see them as two-legged animals. But we are all spirit souls. Once in awhile, one of the *mūḍhās* gets to know one of the crazy Kṛṣṇas, and we find out each other is not so bad.

❦

The highway under repair bumps, but this pen is smooth.

Pray. Remember Dr. Wilder and his wife. She gave me a blanket for my legs when we had to drive north in a snowstorm. They have two cats in their house . . . I can't help them now. They will want to know how Kṛṣṇa and His devotees can help them when it is 50/50 between life and death. I am sure devotees are there with them.

George Washington Bridge ahead. A summer day. Hare Kṛṣṇa, Hare Kṛṣṇa, Kṛṣṇa Kṛṣṇa, Hare Hare.

We are going to 26 Second Avenue. I was already there this morning while I took breakfast, listening to Śrīla Prabhupāda lecture on *Caitanya-caritāmṛta*. I doubt I can get more intimate than that. He said, "Chant Hare Kṛṣṇa mantra wherever you are in the world, and keep a picture of Lord Caitanya dancing, as we have here in our window." He made several references to the activities of his fledgling movement, speaking to us in the early morning. He was speaking about the *manvantāras* and asked the audience to figure out the mathematics of "four thousand, three hundred plus eight zeroes." So many Manus in a day of Brahmā, and the whole life of Brahmā lasts the time it takes Mahā-Viṣṇu to exhale and inhale once.

Because of Prabhupāda, I am living the way I am, grateful for his all-round protection. My social security number is dormant or dead. I have accumulated very little karma since I met him. I only regret, as he knows, my inability . . .

These are notes en route to the grand reopening of 26 Second Avenue. America still reigns. We are still breathing, though we have changed our young bodies for aging ones. Everything takes place in one breath of God's expansion.

And God beyond God is playing in Vṛndāvana.

The police are stopping cars.

❦

We see the city skyline in morning smog. The Empire State building looks like a mirage.

Life is hard reality. I have it a little easier because people take care of my material needs. My needs are renounced: no sex, tobacco, drugs, house, etc. But I am no St. Francis kissing his greatest fear—a leper—and becoming transformed and strong. But let me write. I have received the matchless gift. Even if I completely fumble it, I can still pass it on.

❦

Now the highway has improved. We are closer to the city. Writing makes you firm. When you don't write, things feel nebulous, as when you first wake up. Writing is a way of giving.

My previous identity no longer matters. I am here now, in saffron, in the back seat, on a summer sunny day. I used to live near the George Washington Bridge, but that is just a sad story now. I hope I don't get a headache. I want at least to be able to tell the devotees today that I am thankful Śrīla Prabhupāda came here. I am really able to mean it.

That's a preacher's problem! He has to speak constantly on elaborate topics and it's not always easy to mean what he says. He *means* it, but it is routine delivery. He learns by practice how to deliver even when he is not thinking deeply about what he is saying.

The shack is helping me come to terms with this—even if it is not clear—to at least talk each bit as I feel it.

❦

The fierce city. I catch a glimpse of the West Shore and the Hudson River all the way south.

I want to serve the people who come to me. They are my own congregation, a group within ISKCON, a ministry.

The Hudson is filled to the brim like a big tub. Kṛṣṇa's hand is everywhere. If He tilts something or moves the sun a jot for just a moment, we are all screaming, "The end of the world." Some of us turn to Kṛṣṇa's names, even now, while it seems okay.

10:00 A.M., West 79th Street

Put on your *sannyāsa* top piece. Start to get ready. It is not going to be a quiet *tīrtha* visit. It is Manhattan and a grand reopening. But I too want to pay my respects to the sacred ground. May my inner man note what is happening even while the social man goes on.

❦

Devotees bow down in the street.

❦

I showed Ananta where I used to live on First Street. "It must have been different then," he says. Tough, low-down street. I'm so different now, used to more delicate treatment. We walked past a soup kitchen. Culture shock for me. People talking to themselves out loud.

"Hey, can I join the Hare Kṛṣṇas?"

Not a bad idea.

We are on time, but the program hasn't begun yet. Haṁsaduta is leading *kīrtana.* I don't go in, but come over here to sit in a car and wait and breathe easy. At this point, all I want is to put in some respectable appearance and then go. I am just hoping my head will cooperate.

People hanging around, looking in the window at 26 Second Avenue. "But it's so different now," I think. Maybe it's me who is different. The neighborhood seems raunchier, tougher, more dangerous, and probably is. But I was quicker on my feet when I lived here, used to walking into the slum apartments of my welfare clients, used to living in my own slum apartment and glazing things over with marijuana.

1:10 P.M.

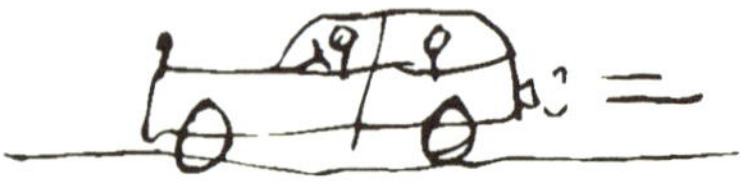

Heading uptown with a full-fledged headache (sorry, but I have to say it) after participation in the sweet, grand reopening of 26 Second Avenue. Mukunda Mahārāja spoke, and I spoke, and many others who also joined at this place. The room was packed. Now my body hurts. I was almost trembling in there. I wanted to be understood and forgiven for having to leave early. All glories to Prabhupāda.

Now we head back to my bed to recover overnight. Ten more days of *Shack Notes*. I am preaching, Prabhupāda, as you told us. I am keeping memories alive. I am one of us, all devotees, blessed, special persons.

❦ ❦ ❦

July 12, 2:00 A.M.

Ten days left.

❦

In his speech yesterday, Jayādvaita Swami recalled that he joined ISKCON at a time when everyone was surcharged with Prabhupāda consciousness. He told how letters came from Śrīla Prabhupāda and how everyone was intent on pleasing him. The first time he saw Śrīla Prabhupāda was on television. I nodded in agreement at different points in his talk, although, by that time, my head was aching, and I was waiting for him to finish so I could leave.

In my own short talk, I emphasized Śrīla Prabhupāda's compassion. He took the trouble to come and save rough Lower East Side characters. I was a bit evasive because my message was political. I was trying to say, "ISKCON is in danger of pushing on the external goals of propagation, but neglecting its own members. Let's remember how Śrīla Prabhupāda loved us with such personal warmth in the beginning. He didn't mind that we were fallen or had rude behavior. Let's be like that with each other."

I call that a "political" message because it levies criticism at the way things are managed now. I don't like those messages when I hear them either. A speaker shouldn't take advantage of a gathering who have come to share Prabhupāda nectar to get his own messages across. Anyway, I tried to avoid having too much of a didactic tone, and instead tried to turn my talk into a plea that we all become compassionate by some kind of preaching.

The gathering was a success. The little storefront is now reopened and off to a flying start.

❦

*I*f you want to be daring, then preach. Why are you hesitant to preach?

I fear being too preachy or being rejected by those I preach to. I myself am tired of heavy evangelism. But I know there is a thin line between disgust with poor preaching and disgust with all strong preaching. I don't want to flinch every time someone calls out *"Haribol!"*

The dictionary gives several definitions for the verb "to preach": "To exhort in an officious or tiresome manner." (That's exactly the definition I am trying to avoid.) Another definition: "To advocate earnestly." (That is Śrīla Prabhupāda at 26 Second Avenue.) "To deliver a sermon." (Prabhupāda always did that; we all like to do it.) "To urge acceptance or abandonment of an idea or cause of action." (This is what Lord Caitanya wants us to do.)

It is the "tedious or unwelcome" speeches, the too obvious "moral exhortations," that we want to be spared from. Give us the divine spark to preach like Lord Caitanya did, like Prabhupāda followers.

Prabhupāda led the way in ideal preaching behavior. He didn't care for *vox populi.* He had the standards of the Vaiṣṇava *ācāryas* in mind. He didn't care for any other opinion, and he infused us with that boldness, although he taught us to preach with careful discrimination. He knew victory: He preached with love because he was empowered by Kṛṣṇa. He spoke fearlessly and with complete faith in the Vedic scriptures. And he made good sense.

Images of the Day

The *sannyāsī* and I who didn't greet each other. I was waiting for him to reach out to me, but he waited for me. Who knows why, but we both lacked the energy to reach out. Then when I lectured, he looked up from a deep place.

❦

Yesterday, a few devotees lectured while glancing at notes. Another said, "My head was spinning trying to think of what I would say that could convey the essence of 26 Second Avenue. But I decided *everything* was essential, so I will just speak what comes from my mind and heart."

The best speeches were brief, I thought. It's so hard to sit all packed in a room.

6:00 A.M. 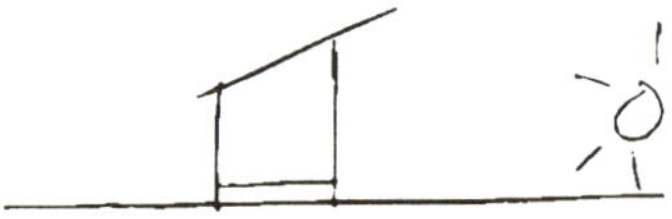

What do I want to say? Kṛṣṇa, please help me. Honesty and Kṛṣṇa consciousness, how can I combine them?

❦

From This Window

"Speak to us about the old days with Prabhupāda."
From this window I see the entrance to the woods,
a deep and rich portal.
Kṛṣṇa consciousness is in books.
No more headache—You take
painless bliss for granted as if it's
your right, as if you deserve
mangos and ice cream.

"Speak to us about the old days with Prabhupāda."
He was kind, he picked us up;
we will soon be dead, and you too,
O young-faced girl smiling
as you look in the back windows
of 26 Second Avenue.

King Akbar asked, "How long does sex desire last?"
His minister replied, "Till the fag end of life—
and I will prove it." You know the story—
he took Akbar into a room where a man
was on his deathbed.
"Now watch his eyes," said the minister.
And as Emperor Akbar and his young daughter entered,
the dying man looked
to the daughter and not to the king.

I am happy without that,
hungry to write, hungry to dig,
hungry to find gold and to eat soft food.
And hungry to become greedy
for that love which will make me
give up everything else.

6:30 A.M.

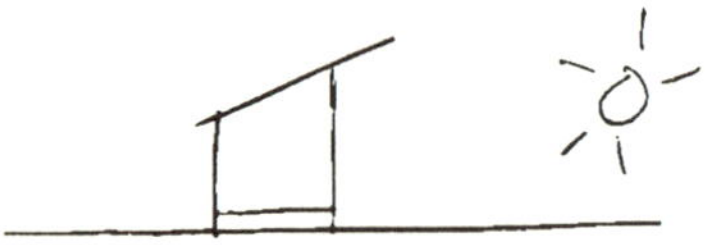

Don't look now, but they just stamped your passport for a six month stay in India. What could you do with that time? (I saw a raunchy poster yesterday in Manhattan, "Let's Waste Quality Time." An ad for a rock group?) Oh, give me a few blessed months or years, please, in the right association—and maybe I can turn a new corner in my life and head into real *bhakti.*

It only takes a minute.

Everyone else seems to be struggling more or less, how can I expect any different?

You know the phenomena where you think the grass is greener somewhere else? So here I am in the shack, daydreaming of Vṛndāvana—Vṛndāvana in your mind doesn't usually tally with the real Vṛndāvana in India.

The shack writing is for coming to terms with the moment. Is summer really fading so fast? Yes, it is true, the daisies are withered on their stalks.

This is a poem about my spiritual master
who I have failed to follow thousands of times,
who takes me back again,
smiling or tolerating
when I make my rhetoric
praising him to elevate myself
in the eyes of his devotees.
I can say worse things, but why bother?
He took care of me and brought me
to spiritual life and even my
whipping myself for failing him
is eased by the kind words of a devotee like
Trivikrama Swami and others whose glances say,
"Don't fret so much about it. You are not the worst
or best.
We are all mostly mediocre, but let's remember him.
See the feast his devotees have cooked?
Here, take his garland and put it around his neck.
Let's talk about the work for him."
It's true we are a family
as Prabhupāda said—
"I have so many transcendental children
and without the botheration of a wife."

In the storefront there's a *mūrti*
of Prabhupāda, but he wears
gold stud buttons on his *kūrta*
and the *dhotī* is silk.
It's a legend. The stories I tell
about Prabhupāda also have little
infringements on the truth,
legendary additions and transmissions which change
as a story passes on.
But sometimes I
remember him straight.

He loved Kṛṣṇa, believed fully in Kṛṣṇa,
and preached more effectively than anyone.
The best is true of Prabhupāda
and I want to be a witness:
O Spiritual Master,
your fame is sung all over the three worlds—
thank you for coming to New York City,
thank you for being who you are.

❦

Thank you for this day and the chance to write, this day to hear Kṛṣṇa stories. Thank you for faith and for planting the *bhakti-latā-bīja* in our hearts. Thank you for taking our hands in yours and directing us how to pour water from the watering can onto our devotional plant.

Thank you for this day of sober Kṛṣṇa consciousness, regulated senses, a little rest, the ability to pray to Kṛṣṇa for help, and the sport of writing Kṛṣṇa consciousness, the big *mṛdaṅga.*

You fooled us, Śrīla Prabhupāda, into giving up material life. You charmed us. How could we have given up our mad, scared lives, but for the spell you cast over us with gravity and humor?

How different I am now from the day I first met you. I am still a little pathetic, even twenty-five years later, but I am still your son, and still serving with so many of your other sons and daughters. All glories to you.

❦

I am waiting for the moment to surface.

Our *Kṛṣṇa* book group spoke about entering different dimensions of consciousness when we read. Here we are, absorbed in the story of Kṛṣṇa defeating the serpent Kāliya, and suddenly Mahārāja Parīkṣit asks Śukadeva Gosvāmī a question: "Why did Kāliya leave his island home, and why was Garuḍa so antagonistic toward him?" This question didn't abruptly break our trance on Kṛṣṇa's pastimes. We flowed with it, with Mahārāja Parīkṣit and Śukadeva. We are following Śukadeva, who is guiding us through the whole spiritual journey. When Śukadeva speaks of Kṛṣṇa in Vṛndāvana, we are there; and when he speaks of Kāliya fighting Garuḍa, we are there.

I joked that it would be nice if after our reading, we stayed stuck in the trance on Kṛṣṇa's pastimes and became forgetful of ordinary reality. Unfortunately, there is no real danger of that, but I wouldn't mind being able to forget sleep once in a while (or a few meals) due to absorption in *kṛṣṇa-līlā*. "The world is too much with us; late and soon,/Getting and spending, we lay waste our powers."

Now I am here in the shack relating the scene. Ananta, Baladeva, and Rāma-rāya have vanished back into the house, the *Kṛṣṇa* book is closed, and I am making bird tracks on the page.

❦

I want my VIHE course on Lord Kṛṣṇa's Vṛndāvana pastimes to take my students on a "journey." We should alter our consciousness, enter the pastimes. I have to make it more than just another scholarly review. I think I should prepare myself in advance, and then let go when the class begins. Someone can read a passage aloud. As soon as something impresses me, I can speak about it and invite others to participate.

❦

Kṛṣṇa, it would be nice to know Your fierce Garuḍa. How we have been mortally afflicted by skepticism in this lifetime! But Sarvabhauma Bhaṭṭācārya used to be like an iron bar, and he became a soft-hearted devotee of Lord Caitanya. We can be converted.

May I have such a conversion one day. May inner life—the life of Kṛṣṇa's pastimes and names and teachings, drive me to distraction.

I am so intent on a regulated life that I find even the concept of being "distracted" by love of Kṛṣṇa a disturbing one. I wouldn't want to lose sleep over *anything.* I would hate to miss my hot rice, *dāl,* and *capātīs.*

Although it is admirable to become fixed in following rules and regulations, is it possible that I am really petrified at heart? Why don't I ever cry? Why does my heart throb only when I perceive danger to my body or an attack on my false ego? Where is my heart? Where has my original love gone? It is lost. As Thomas Wolfe said, "O, lost!"

❦

I hear a siren, and kids are playing nearby.

Today, when we started to read *Kṛṣṇa* book, I suddenly fixed on the moment when I was sitting in the battered Toyota with Baladeva, a block from 26

Second Avenue. Instead of entering Kṛṣṇa's pastimes, my mind fixated on that moment as if it was the most important thing that had happened to me in the last two days. Was it because I had my legal pad out and was writing that it made such an impression? Whatever the reason, now let it go. I am not bound there forever. I did that in New York City. Let it go. It slides away and I go down to the Kāliya lake with my friends.

At the time of death, you will have to let go of everything.

❦

Rāma-rāya has joined our group here. (I hope my hosts aren't feeling burdened by so many people in their house.) There is a helicopter overhead. I have lost my train of thought.

How long can you expect to sustain this free-flowing absorption in topics leading to Kṛṣṇa consciousness? I don't want to insist the writing has to take place. Being too insistent for peak expression leads nondevotees to stimulants like liquor and drugs, something to give them "inspiration." I would never do that of course, but in a subtle way, I might become restless to the point of *inventing* inspiration, or I might try to push myself against immovable forces. Lao-tzu said, "Notice the natural order of things. Work with it rather than against it, for to try to change what is so will only set up resistance." Relax.

❦

Things to be thankful for:

1. Sense of fulfillment, as I noted in prayer log book.

2. Gift of the holy name, although I mistreat it. Thankful for it.

3. Thankful I have the best spiritual master. His mercy on us.

4. Thankful to follow God's laws and be free of worst reactions.

5. Thankful to make progress in this life in *bhakti*.

6. Thankful not to be a Māyāvādī.

7. To have food, clothing, and shelter, no worry.

8. No material anxieties, compared to most.

9. To be alive.

10. To know the meaning of death and to have good preparation for it.

11. To know about Vṛndāvana.

12. To have devotee friends and disciples who care about me.

13. To have a service in caring for them by writing letters, books.

14. Thankful for all the big things in life and many little things.

15. To at least know about gratefulness and to value it.

16. To know enough to check my bad habits when they arise.

17. To have been given direction by Śrīla Prabhupāda.

18. To have been given strength to follow the four rules.

3:45 P.M. 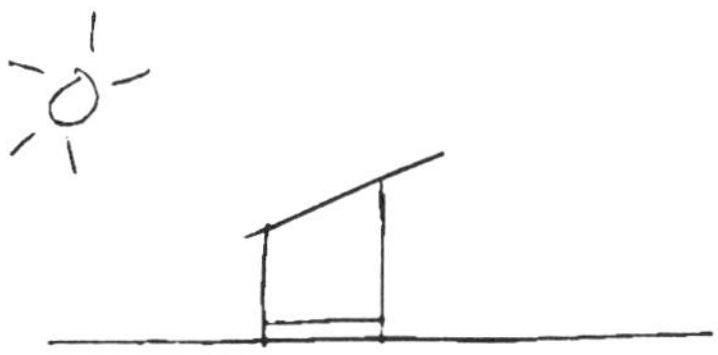

Sleeping on the floor, drifting away. O Lord, O energy of the Lord, please engage me in Your service.

I woke up and instantly forgot my dream. Something was there.

Be yourself, a boy who has heard his teacher's words and who repeats them.

Some essay topics for discourse:

1. There are three aspects to the Absolute Truth: Brahman, Paramātmā, and Bhagavān. They may be compared to the sunshine, the sun disc, and the sun god. Explain the analogy.

2. Write an essay summarizing the seventh chapter of *Bhagavad-gītā.*

3. Describe the five conclusions that Rāmānanda Rāya spoke to Lord Caitanya in answer to the question: "What is the perfection of religion?" Why did Lord Caitanya reject these conclusions? Which conclusions did He finally accept?"

6:15 P.M. 

Shack Notes means spending three weeks in a wholehearted attempt to live entirely occupied by writing. The writing is centered on repeated attempts to evoke Kṛṣṇa consciousness. Each attempt must start from scratch. I accumulate markings, some direct hits, sometimes a feeling of going nowhere . . . but, gradually, I am gathering a growing conviction that writing itself is *bhajana.*

If you ask a devotee who spends his time chanting or singing *bhajanas,* "What do you get out of this? What tangible result does it produce?" He may reply (as Śrīla Prabhupāda did) that "chanting produces chanting." One sings to sing. He builds stamina to sing for longer periods of time. He improves. He stops measuring one session against another, one attempt to surmount his mind against another. He sings to sing, and he knows there is no other way *but* to sing. In this way, writing produces writing.

Tonight we heard of Kṛṣṇa's playing in Vṛndāvana in the summer season. It wasn't uncomfortably hot there. The waterfall sent droplets of water into the air, cooling the bodies of Kṛṣṇa and His devotees. The lotus pollen wafted in the breeze. Kṛṣṇa blew His flute, and everyone was fixed in love of Kṛṣṇa.

We spoke about Vṛndāvana and the apparent difference between the Vṛndāvana we find today and the Vṛndāvana described in the *Kṛṣṇa* book. I am trying to fix just a tiny particle of our talk, which is just an infinitesimal particle of Goloka Vṛndāvana, on Kṛṣṇa, so that someone may read these lines and think of Him.

❦

Praise

I praise Kṛṣṇa according to the Vedic description of the Supreme Person. If it is actual praise, I do more than repeat the words of scripture. The dictionary gives us a definition: "To glorify [a god or saint]." I both praise God and offer my thankfulness. In this act, I hope to lose my false self, my sense of hunger, in the process of devotional service. I want to be engaged in a worthy pursuit.

❦

Kṛṣṇa, I heard how You came out of the water of the Yamunā wearing a beautiful garland and the golden ornaments given to You by the serpent Kāliya. The residents of Vṛndāvana were so happy to see You, it was like getting back their lives. Please accept my small appreciation. Help me to remove old associations so that I can see You clearly.

❦ ❦ ❦

July 13, 1:30 A.M.

I speak of the Lord as He appears in my mind. But His presence seems faint there, so I turn to the Vaiṣṇava *ācāryas.* I must convince my mind to be submissive and receive Kṛṣṇa consciousness in full force from the poetry and prayer of scripture. The mind can be the best friend in this endeavor, or it can be the worst enemy.

Writing can be a way to train the mind. One can write down *ślokas* that absorb the mind. When the mind demands something more, one can either ignore it, or express the problem in writing and seek the solution—"My dear mind, why are you not a Vaiṣṇava?"

One wants to rise early to write Vaiṣṇava *smṛti.* I recall Śrīla Prabhupāda's devotional labors in *Śrīmad-Bhāgavatam.* We want to do something like that. His work is ideal, and like small children, we rise early and write as we saw our master do.

This is what he wrote one night in Hawaii, just after completing the Seventh Canto of *Śrīmad-Bhāgavatam* and beginning the Eighth:

> First of all, let me offer my humble, respectful obeisances unto the lotus feet of my spiritual master, His Divine Grace Śrī Śrīmad Bhaktisiddhānta Sarasvatī Gosvāmī Prabhupāda. . . . He personally told me that publishing books is more important than constructing temples. . . . I am continuously trying to publish books, as suggested by my spiritual master. . . . On this occasion, therefore, I am praying to my spiritual master to give me strength to finish this work. I am neither a great scholar nor a great devotee . . .

No need to repeat my own lackings. I've got no Sanskrit, no power, not much of anything. But I have a desire to go to the gathering of Vaiṣṇava sages and report something I have heard.

❦

If we chant Hare Kṛṣṇa, then Kṛṣṇa, the Holy Presence, will be present on our tongues. Let us chant always, you and I. It is the only way to escape the demands of the world—the mental influence, the life threats, the constant disturbances. We are preoccupied with struggling for survival, but chanting helps us through to the more important goal.

Anxiety arises when we work hard to stave off material miseries, something we can never achieve. Therefore, the sages advise us to keep our lives and efforts simple, reduce pain in that way, and take to chanting and hearing as the only recourse. Never say, "I am too busy," or, "I have no taste"—just chant.

And I tell myself, writing can bring me closer to the chanting. Therefore, just write.

❦

Morning considerations: How to purify my thoughts and direct my hand? How will I spend today in Kṛṣṇa's service? Is there a way to salvage the duties we must perform and transform them into acceptable *yajña?* Can we find time to directly bathe in the hearing and chanting of Kṛṣṇa's names and pastimes? And can we exert our will to be kind to others?

Kṛṣṇa is kind to allow me to chant His name. He invites everyone. When Lord Caitanya performed a drama in Ācāryaratna's courtyard, He played the part of Rādhā, while Advaita took the role of the Supreme Lord. Only a few qualified persons were permitted to attend. But the Lord invites everyone to chant Hare Kṛṣṇa, Hare Kṛṣṇa, Kṛṣṇa Kṛṣṇa, Hare Hare/Hare Rāma, Hare Rāma, Rāma Rāma, Hare Hare. And by chanting, we will gain entry into *all* the Lord's pastimes.

I must chant. This page is in the *kīrtana.*

❦

When I met a humble *sannyāsī* Godbrother who sometimes writes books, I asked, "Are you writing?" He replied, "I have no propensity. I am reading." I took that to mean, "I do not have the ability or desire to write in Kṛṣṇa consciousness, so I am imbibing great masters of Vaiṣṇava literature." It was a humble statement. It left me thinking, "Why, why do I insist on writing? What *is* this propensity?"

The propensity is the need to communicate. Let it be purified in Kṛṣṇa consciousness.

❦

O Lord, O Energy of the Lord, please engage me in Your service.

❦

"The ocean of Lord Nityānanda's glory is infinite and unfathomable. Only by His mercy can I touch even a drop of it. Please listen to another glory of His mercy. He made a fallen living entity climb to the highest limit" *(Cc. Ādi,* 5.157–58).

Try to be smaller and holier. Try to be more honest. Become quieter without becoming completely silent. Take us on your morning walk. Share your thoughts from your prison cell. Write down quotes from the *śāstra.* Live in Kṛṣṇa through the process of *bhakti* and share that.

6:00 A.M.

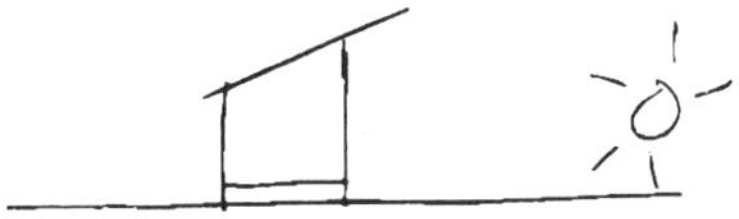

I have faith in my "original mind" as a friend in my writing. It is not my *true* original mind, but my battered and concerned mind; at least it's something. The full charge of Prabhupāda's mercy has hit me. Maybe a little of it bounced off my false exterior, maybe I have accumulated some new dust, but the process of enlightenment continues by practicing my guru's instructions.

So I will write from my original mind—not that center of the senses telling me I am too hot or dictating what I feel like eating. It is my deeper mind-self that wants to speak. It is the lover of Kṛṣṇa in me, the pure soul. It is that part of me that wants to see the words "Kṛṣṇa" and "Caitanya" grace every page and which gives me hope.

6:30 A.M.

This "post-it" note to myself: "Kṛṣṇa is more interesting than I am. I should not be self-centered, but Kṛṣṇa-centered." Good.

❦

Why don't I know Kṛṣṇa better? Why can't I record what He is doing right now in His relationships with everyone, especially me? I am covered by *māyā*. I think I am the doer, the center. But I can be changed. I can be converted.

One way to know Kṛṣṇa is to learn about Him from authorized sources and then to repeat it feelingly, in writing. But we don't want to merely write "about" Kṛṣṇa, as if He were a subject in Hindu religion.

We can also see Him in this world. But *look* for Him. Don't just talk on the *concept* of Kṛṣṇa when you see a leaf wet with rain. See Him in His nature: "inconceivable and always a person."

❦

Rain on the roof. Kṛṣṇa is in His name. Bow down to Him. Be a happy servant of His pure devotee. Be happy playing on a small "flute" and dancing before Lord Kṛṣṇa in my mind. My spiritual master approves this and tells me to go on.

❦

I look at the great poet Kavi Karnapura's drama of Lord Caitanya's pastimes. This is true art. I am standing outside the door of His transcendental theater and begging with my bowl.

❦

Our wits need to be recovered from the garbage heap where they were thrown by misuse and bad association.

❦

So dark I can't see, although it's almost time
for breakfast.
I thank You, real Lord, for allowing me
more time to write
and little bursts of sincerity.
I have some mad attachment to say "I love You"
in a way that sounds right to me.
You employ me, and my spiritual master
encourages a sort of writing, as long as one
has permission from guru and the Lord
in the heart.
Taking that permission, he may write.
Śrīla Prabhupāda says, "Poetry or prose."

Touching life,
hear the rain drops on this roof
Kṛṣṇa, Kṛṣṇa, Kṛṣṇa,
I want to serve Kṛṣṇa
(in this life and the next).
Let's help each other;
follow what he says.

When I end this life, I'll go for another,
but where, I don't know;
it depends on my deeds,
it depends what I think of at the end.
So here I'm trying
to impress on myself
Kṛṣṇa, Kṛṣṇa, Kṛṣṇa,
writing down
and hearing the rain as Kṛṣṇa too,
and savoring and thanking him
for this routine, worshiping my Lord.

❦

If I try to meditate on Kṛṣṇa too much, quietly, with my eyes closed, I simply doze off. Writing keeps me awake in my meditation.

Tell a stranger about Kṛṣṇa. Even a little faith can help tremendously.

Live with friends. Share *kṛṣṇa-kathā.*

❦

Lord, I am running out of time. It is thundering and raining. I want to praise You.

❦

Thought I might write even while tired, as another way to escape inner censors and slip a true word from my imprisoned self to the outside world. Let them know at least that you are still alive and your spirits are up. You are not sure how long you can keep up like this—you hope they send help soon.

Kṛṣṇa, save us, Kṛṣṇa *he.*

11:00 A.M. 

Kṛṣṇa's pastimes are perfect, but my hearing is not. I am sometimes beset with doubts and distractions and my lack of love. But does that mean I should stop hearing? No, I have to proceed into the forest with the *gopas* and Kṛṣṇa and Balarāma.

Today we heard about Balarāma's killing of the Pralambha demon and Kṛṣṇa's pastime of swallowing the forest fire. I like to participate with full emotion and visualization, but if some emotions are still closed to me, then at least I can go ahead with faithful, intellectual discussion. I see it like limping, or continuing to work even with a slight headache.

And I can relate this imperfect hearing to my imperfect writing. Go on, be assured, this process of *bhakti* will deal with the demons. Bhaktivinoda Ṭhākura compares the forest fire to the antagonistic or atheistic philosophies that disrupt religious people. And Pralamba is a symbol of sexual lust.

Dear Lord Kṛṣṇa, player of the Vṛndāvana sports, You are present in my heart in Your expanded form of Supersoul. You see my crippled condition. Allow me to praise You even though I am like a car with two flat tires. Let me repair myself and continue. You accept sincere service. Part of me is sincere and wishes to expand that sincerity within myself. I don't want to burn in the forest fire. I don't want Pralamba to carry me off.

And so in tune with today's muggy weather, dark sky and rain, I feel somewhat dispirited that I cannot fully run and romp with the *gopas* due to my skeptical, dried-up emotions. Yet my unhappiness is also a spiritual symptom. And my companions are not as depressed as I am. Give me more of this. The more I hear, the further in I will be able to enter.

I love to write. That is why I keep doing it. It is awkward, tainted, flawed, I know, but it is love, and a love that helps others. I can learn to sing better, to compose more expertly.

In terms of time (or as Baladeva says, time-wise), *Shack Notes* is already on its way to the end. A little more than eight days left. If it were a dramatic piece, I would be heading for the grand climax, full force, all suspense devices clicking away . . . or if this were by a person who went into a Walden-type retreat, I would be saying how I have changed and how I won't ever see the world again in quite the same way as when I began. But that's not happening.

Each day I make the same attempt, the same capturing of the moment, the same hoping to find Kṛṣṇa there. It is writing *sādhana,* and I'm glad to be doing it.

The truth is, I am unqualified to write *kṛṣṇa-kathā.* I should in no way venture on my own in this sublime topic. But I cannot be still. What does Prabhupāda say? He says, "Write your realizations." He says do something to spread Kṛṣṇa consciousness. He says it is a *sannyāsī's* first duty to write. He says write to save the crippled humanity. Kṛṣṇa will be pleased, even as a father is pleased by the broken speech of his little child. Speak of Him.

My dear Lord Kṛṣṇa, I read of Your pastimes in Prabhupāda's books. I am desiring to enter them more. But You have also expanded Your energies to create all reality. Therefore, I also want to feel Your presence in ordinary life.

I want to obey your guides. I want to serve You. And one day, I want my faulty and self-conscious "I" to melt away and be replaced by a pure consciousness, a consciousness knowing only You.

❦

I am trying to use words to find a way past the deadness, the spaced-out forgetfulness of You. Even these apparent meanderings, as soon as I begin them, give me hope that I am on the trail that leads to You.

❦

My failure is not allowing myself to love Kṛṣṇa. I seem to know that.

My knowledge is shaky because everything about me is ultimately shaky. As Śrīla Prabhupāda says, "We are on a tottering platform." At any moment, we may fall off and die. This life is like a drop of water on a lotus petal.

❦ ❦ ❦

4:15 P.M. 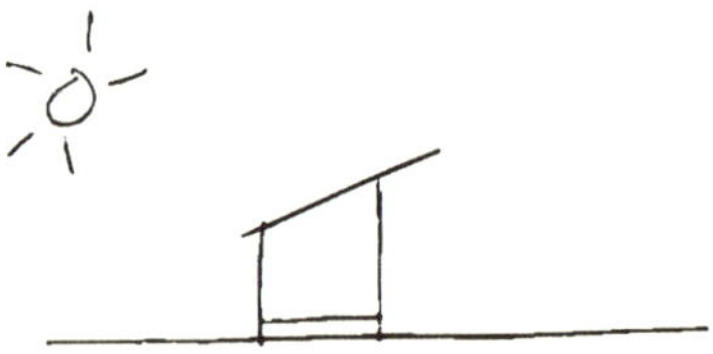

Writing is your devotional service, so manifest it. Say what you want to say, and don't let the censors stop you.

My purpose is apparent. (Do I feel pride? Accumulating pride is like Kāliya accumulating poison. Kṛṣṇa will have to kick it out of me since I am His devotee.)

❦

Kṛṣṇa, directly Kṛṣṇa. It is worth proclaiming the smallest affirmation of His presence.

We are all looking forward to the next *Kṛṣṇa* book session. We will soon be reading of His love for the *gopīs.* He is a rogue, at least in social terms. And this is the same person who as a boy was such a trickster, so daring and sportive. I suddenly got a tiny grasp of His character in Vṛndāvana. Knowing of His life prior to the *kaiśora* age helps one to understand His behavior with the *gopīs.*

Faith, pure faith. Live a life to attain it.

❦

Rāma-rāya and Ananta sit with me. Sometimes I confess skepticism, but they don't respond to that. Then I ask them, "What are your impressions?" They always answer with something positive.

❦

"He thinks with his heart," said a Lower East Side hippie *paṇḍita* when he saw a photo of Śrīla Prabhupāda on the record album. Thinks with his heart?—I wasn't sure I liked that. Then one day a welfare worker looked at one of Prabhupāda's books. He said he particularly liked the phrase, "All living beings from the insignificant ant up to the greatest demigod . . ." He said, "This devotion is a beautiful gem—*but it is not truth.*" A professor who bought Śrīla Prabhupāda's *Śrīmad-Bhāgavatam* from me saw the dedication, "On the disappearance day of my spiritual master," and he smiled. "That's beautiful," he said. He meant, "What a cool, cute, far-out Hindu way to say my spiritual master died on this day." They have no faith.

My own skeptic is sometimes screaming inside when we read *Kṛṣṇa* book. It is good for me, provided something comes of it. Skepticism is like sex desire. Is it a permanent curse? Sex desire, envy, will they ever go away? You tend to think, "*Next* life. Probably, in the next life you will be born and raised by pious people."

But then when I become a teenager, will I meet a hip friend who will turn me on to the latest drugs, and who will blow away my faith? I remember one guy in our group of hip Brooklyn College friends. He had red hair and freckles. They called him "the Barry Goldwater of the hippies" because he was more well-bred than most of us. Anyway, this "Barry Goldwater" once told me that his father was a God-fearing Christian minister and that he had been raised to see God's will in all things. "Now I am painstakingly removing God from everything in my life," he said. He gave me the impression that he thought he was suffering from a severe handicap by being raised in God consciousness. These were the kind of people I counted among my friends.

Alan Shiffman, another classmate, was a philosophy major. He knew the Logical Positivists well. I didn't know them, but was intimidated to think they were absolute sages. Alan said, "According to Wittgenstein, the question of God's existence cannot even be raised. It is a useless question." When God was mentioned by my milder Staten Island friends, usually while we were drinking beer, I said, "We can't talk about that. Alan Shiffman said it's a profitless topic. Those who know, exclude all mention of God."

Win Burgraff, another minister's son, didn't like my bullying him with that. He said, "Just because Alan Shiffman says so, now no one can talk of God?"

I said, "You can talk if you want, but it doesn't make any sense." (I tried to impress him that we at Brooklyn College knew things he would never hear about at his Calvinist Bible College in Hope, Michigan.)

I am bringing this up to help me see why I scream with skepticism inside. A devotee said recently, "If garbage goes in, then garbage will come out."

But I am hopeful.

A bum can become a devotee.

A thief can become a devotee.

Their faces will shine with the luster of *brahmacarya*. They will be armed with the weapons of knowledge and logic. And sometimes they will have bad dreams. When they relax and go to hear how Balarāma killed the demon Pralambha, they will have to endure the sneers and sniggers of Alan Shiffman and his breed.

❦

Now I have used most of my time. It's muggy.

❦

Time to go up to listen to Śukadeva Gosvāmī. Dear Kṛṣṇa, that sportive hero who saves the residents of Vṛndāvana from the forest fire, is going to be into something else, and I want to go there and see what He is doing. May I hear and spit at bad thoughts. I want to love the Lord. Lord Brahmā prayed he would be very grateful to be born next life as a blade of grass in Vṛndāvana. I pray like that too.

6:00 P.M. 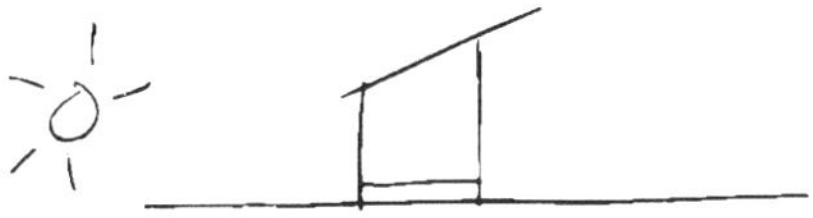

We listened to passages from "The Autumn Season in Vṛndāvana." I especially liked the descriptions of Kṛṣṇa and the boys sheltering inside the cave on Govardhana during a sudden rain. When the rain stops, they come out, sit on a rock, and eat their lunch, surrounded by cows resting in the fresh grass. The cows are tired from carrying their heavy milk bags, but when they hear Kṛṣṇa calling their names, they become joyful and go to Him.

In the next chapter, "The *Gopīs* Attracted by the Flute," there is a statement by Prabhupada endorsing our practice of full participation and visualization of *kṛṣṇa-līlā*.

> Persons who are constantly engaged in the transcendental meditation of seeing Kṛṣṇa, internally and externally, by thinking of Him playing the flute, and entering the Vṛndāvana forest, have really attained the perfection of *samādhi*. *Samādhi* (trance) means absorption of all the activities of the senses in a particular object, and the *gopīs* indicate that the pastimes of Kṛṣṇa are the perfection of all meditation and *samādhi*. It is also confirmed in the *Bhagavad-gītā* that anyone who is always absorbed in thought of Kṛṣṇa is the topmost of all *yogīs*.
>
> —*Kṛṣṇa*, Vol. 1, p. 147-48

"Let's always do this," I said. I want to live with at least a few like-minded friends and everyday have this kind of meeting where there is love and trust to talk about our feelings for Kṛṣṇa. We have to feel free to say, "I felt my old skepticism tonight." Or, "Usually I hold back, but tonight I tried placing myself beside Kṛṣṇa in the pastime." We don't criticize or judge what others say. We can discuss that later, if necessary. Let there be a sacred time to share visualized impressions. Kṛṣṇa, Prabhupāda, may I do this? And if something isn't proper, will you correct me?

We are invited to think of the person Kṛṣṇa in His most lovable form in Vṛndāvana. We have heard how His parents love Him and see Him, and how the *gopas* play with Him. Now we are hearing how the *gopīs* are disturbed and distracted into loving madness when they hear Kṛṣṇa's flute.

In the chapter on autumn, we get a picture of how a person is cleared of dirty consciousness. I will need that in order to hear of Kṛṣṇa with the *gopīs*. Prabhupāda writes,

> When the sky is clear of all clouds, the stars at night shine very beautifully; similarly, when a person is actually situated in Kṛṣṇa consciousness, he is cleared of all dirty things, and he becomes as beautiful as the stars in the autumn sky . . . Therefore, the clean heart exhibited by a devotee in Kṛṣṇa consciousness can be compared to the clear sky of the autumn season.
>
> —*Kṛṣṇa,* Vol. 1, p. 144

❦

Rāma-rāya said that cloudy, misty days like today seem to be mystical. One senses a presence. He said that he now knows that the mystical-something of a hazy day is the presence of Kṛṣṇa. As he said this, thunder rumbled overhead.

❦ ❦ ❦

July 14, 1:30 A.M.

I am after self-improvement in Kṛṣṇa consciousness. I will be able to write better letters. Just imagine if every letter I wrote could have so much Kṛṣṇa conscious presence that the receiver would actually *want* to apply it. If I was empowered, I might write to someone and tell them about tolerance or patience or humility in Kṛṣṇa consciousness, or prayer or hope or faith. I would be able to describe these things in such a way that they would be treasured in the letter, and be read again and again—a prayer or mantra emblazoned on the mind.

He who makes writing his *bhajana* may seem odd to others. He beats his own type of "drum" and plays his own style of "harmonium."

One devotee wrote me asking if I thought it is all right that he go to Bangladesh in order to learn the art of expert *mṛdaṅga* and harmonium playing. I thought, "He plays well enough already. Why does he want to be better?" But from a devotee-musician point of view, there is a difference. There is something wonderful to be achieved by studying under those who know the esoteric traditions. This is just an example of someone wanting to improve his art. With better skill and more absorption, he may actually be able to lift people's hearts in *kīrtana* to feelings of love of God. But an outsider thinks, "Why go to Bangladesh? Why improve on *mṛdaṅga?* It's just sense gratification." And by voicing this, the desire is killed.

Write your books. At least you will be satisfied you tried. What is that line in Walden? "I went to the woods because I wished to live deliberately, to front only the essential facts of life, and see if I could not learn what it had to teach, and not, when I came to die, discover that I had not lived."

But what does this have to do with my salvation? And what is salvation? What do you mean, "Act out your desires, write the book *you* want, the way *you* want, and become the best drum player possible, so you can give joy to others"?

Liberation in Kṛṣṇa consciousness means pleasing guru and Kṛṣṇa in such a way that they free you of all material desires, and then fully engage you in their devotional service. This becomes your last life in the material world. You go back to Godhead and enter Kṛṣṇa's *līlā:* "He does not, upon leaving the body, take his birth again in this material world, but attains my eternal abode, O Arjuna."

Or, if Kṛṣṇa desires, you return to this world and, as soon as possible, again contribute to the ongoing *saṅkīrtana* movement. Such a devotee is very rare, says Śrī Kṛṣṇa; such a devotee is very dear to Me. That is the result of self-improvement.

But what is the connection between this liberation and the acting out of one's *desires* for self-improvement? I am not sure. I am just timidly testing the waters. But as far as I *can* see, there is great value in fulfilling your inner desires and making something strong and beautiful for Kṛṣṇa's service.

I just heard a car pull up. Maybe Baladeva is back and will slide something under my door. Something new to divert me, to keep me going, and yet I am self-contained if I only knew it. How much more external input do I need? Haven't I heard enough and lived enough to draw my own conclusions? What am I waiting for?

Where is the source of the outpouring of Kṛṣṇa *bhakti* for the 21st Century? Should I go to Russia to taste it? Do I need to learn something in Bangladesh? Do I have to go back to the streets of Boston to learn what I avoided learning? Why did I miss my chance in Amherst? Will everything have to be done over? If so, how will I become successful the second time around and not repeat the same mistakes? *How will I succeed this time in surrendering to Lord Caitanya's* saṅkīrtana *movement?*

I went to the door, but there was nothing there, not yet. The traffic is roaring like the surf at Jagannātha Purī. The summer produces ease. Sit at your desk and write.

Baladeva wrote me a humorous note, comparing me to a person in a jail cell with bars made of four regulations, sixteen rounds, *Kṛṣṇa* book and Prabhupāda's instructions. I cannot get away; I cannot get beyond these "boundaries."

He says, "You can't hurt anyone . . . What jailer could be so cruel as to not let you write? They slide a few note pads under your door. We are all interested in what the prisoner has to say." In other words, I am free to write any damn thing to my heart's content, and it will all be within the scope of Kṛṣṇa consciousness. Fair enough. I am happy with that. Supply me the note pads (and a little *prasādam*). Leave me alone, mostly. Lend me your attention.

❦

What is needed is for everyone to find a place in this movement to work. Be satisfied with simple preaching work. Distribute the knowledge of Kṛṣṇa consciousness in whatever ways are open to you. Bhaktisiddhānta Sarasvatī Mahārāja said, "When you go to preach, even if no one attends, you can speak to the walls." You can speak to the four directions and to the moon and the sun. Tell everyone you meet about Kṛṣṇa.

But to do this we must be hearing. Otherwise, it becomes a farce. Hear and desire to hear, and then, one day, Kṛṣṇa may appear within us an overwhelming truth—the only Truth. There are already so many books written in pure Kṛṣṇa consciousness—why read anything else? Make Him your sole truth.

A devotee confessed to me, "I have been working for Kṛṣṇa for ten years, but I have no realization at all of His personal existence." I know what that's like. Twenty-five years of *no* realization? We mean *very little* realization. We do mean emptiness void of love. When we look within, we see pictures from television, billboards, material stuff. We don't see Kṛṣṇa, and it makes us sorry. But we go on serving anyway. We are afraid that if Kṛṣṇa would storm our hearts, we would become so proud that we would ruin it in a minute. We are not fit for love of Kṛṣṇa. This devotee who confessed said, "I think I need to practice more austerity."

❦

Today is a special day because we will be starting on the chapter, "The Gopīs Attracted by The Flute." Rāma-rāya suddenly began reading that chapter aloud last night. I stopped him and asked, "Are we ready for this?" Then I made a speech about how to hear *mādhurya-rasa* without misunderstanding. It is all explained by Prabhupāda and Śukadeva Gosvāmī in the *rāsa* dance chapter. We "know" it already. We have carefully read all the previous chapters beginning with Kṛṣṇa's appearance, and before that the nine cantos of *Śrīmad-Bhāgavatam* and *Bhagavad-gītā.* We are masters of none of these cantos, but Śrīla Prabhupāda has kindly given us the Tenth Canto. So let us hear. "We have not taken a vow to boycott the *gopīs.*"

There is a nice description of Śrī Kṛṣṇa.

The *gopīs* are talking to relieve their disturbed minds when they don't see Kṛṣṇa. The boys go to the pasturing grounds with Him all day, but the girls must stay home. They spend their day thinking of Kṛṣṇa and waiting for Him to return in the evening. We have been hearing about the different kinds of love expressed by Mother Yaśodā and Nanda Mahārāja, and the love of the boys. (When He and Balarāma kill a demon, the boys cheer in ecstasy, "Excellent!" and they rush to embrace Kṛṣṇa and Balarāma as if their lives had returned to them.) And we have heard how the cows come forward when Kṛṣṇa calls their names, and they give Him their milk. We have also heard of the ecstatic love of the twigs, hills, and lakes, due to their being blessed by the touch of Balarāma. But of all the residents of Vṛndāvana, the *gopīs* are the best. Their love is unexcelled.

What can *I* understand about love for Kṛṣṇa? My storehouse of affection is empty. I have nothing to offer. My love has been stolen by the rats of bad association and rapacious material desires, by speculation, by skepticism.

But the "bars" on my life are strong. Śrīla Prabhupāda has thrown me into this cage of Kṛṣṇa consciousness. He orders me, "Read *Kṛṣṇa* book whenever you find time. Read as much as possible." So how can I refuse? Prabhupāda says, "*Kṛṣṇa* book is written like ordinary stories, but they are not ordinary things. They deliver us from repetition of birth and death. We will understand what is Kṛṣṇa. Kṛṣṇa is very kind, and, as soon as you begin reading *Kṛṣṇa* book with a little faith . . . Kṛṣṇa is in your heart . . . He understands, 'Now he is serious to understand Me.'"

Kṛṣṇa, kindly give me the understanding by which I can come to You.

6:30 A.M.

To be away from this writing for a few hours seems to threaten the whole concentration.

❦

Canon Typestar

Canon Typestar, be my way to praise Kṛṣṇa.
This fool peers into the typewriter,
hoping he said something nice.
Thrushes dramatic,
they don't imitate the same song,
but talk back and forth.

Early this morning was good.
So much has passed since then. I have read
  a few letters—
One said: "You said I phoned
  but I never phoned,
Maybe it was a crazy person here
  who used my name"—
I can't even recall what I wrote two hours ago.
And so it should be. "Stay fluid behind those
  black and white
words. They were a great moment going
  through you.
A moment you were awake enough
to write down and capture."

Kṛṣṇa book that's
the main way. Anything else?
Nothing—I can barely keep my attention span
long enough to say, "Kṛṣṇa, please accept
  this *prasādam.*"
I could write a whole book complaining
  about my *japa.*
I just say, "Forget it,"
and go on chanting, writing.

❦

Much More Important

Keep going my friend,
play your folk songs.
And you keep carping, editors.
I want to praise Kṛṣṇa,
not speak a private language
like Gary Snyder.

But he has true feelings sometimes,
what about you?
What is your equivalent of his, "Four Poems
  for Robin"?
There is no equivalent.
We all love so many things,
we leave them behind, remember them
  when we sleep.
He says, "We had what the others
all crave and seek for.
We left it behind at nineteen."
I don't say I'm better, but
let's kick off old *māyā,* Gary.
I'm out here with the pines and
I like it. Much more important is
the chance to behave as a servant
of a bona fide guru:
worship the one God by whatever you do.

And please stop biting your fingernails.

We have got a good team for hearing and discussing *kṛṣṇa-kathā.* It is like a ball team or a band playing together. We share a mutual respect for each other, which includes an absence of judgement. Share what little we know among ourselves and make our disclaimers, "We are rascals." Everybody agrees.

Lord Caitanya took *sannyāsa* at a young age. His mother suspected it. She asked Him, "Why did You offer respects to Keśava Bharati Swami? What are you talking to him about? Nimāi, where are you going?"

He said, "It is all right, mother. I may just take a little trip to try to find my brother." Then He had a big *kīrtana* dancing at night at Śrīvāsa's house with the best devotees. Gaṅga dāsa watched it from outside. Everyone fell asleep just before dawn, and when they awoke, they couldn't find Viśvambhara. A man approached Gaṅga dāsa, "Is He at your house?" Other men sent by Śacī approached people in the street, "Is He at your house?" Then they started to realize that the independent, Supreme Lord has gone somewhere else. This is written about in the *Caitanya-candrodayā.*

From William Stafford in *A Way of Writing:*

> Along with initial receptivity, there is another readiness: I must be willing to fail . . . I am not thinking about such matters as social significance, positive

> values, consistency, etc. I resolutely disregard those. Something better, greater is happening. I am following a process that leads so wildly and originally into new territory that no judgement can at the moment be made about values, significance, and so on. I am making something new. Something that has not been judged before. Later, others—and maybe I myself—will make judgements. Now I am headlong to discover. Any distraction may harm the creating.

This *does* apply to Kṛṣṇa consciousness. We don't always have to know what we are going to say. Kṛṣṇa likes spontaneous play. It is already decided whatever I do must be service to guru and Kṛṣṇa. I cannot go wrong in that way, or if it is wrong, I will either correct myself or be corrected by my spiritual master. Even Lord Brahmā, in his creation of the universe, had only a general order. He had to figure things out as he went along.

Someone says, "I heard that if you are attached to creating something nice for Kṛṣṇa, this will bar you from entrance to Goloka. Creators stay in the material world because they are fascinated by their God-given power. If they are pious, they offer their works to Kṛṣṇa, but it is *rājo-guṇa.*"

But can't you create in pure spirit? Is there not creative play in the offerings to Kṛṣṇa in the spiritual world? Yes, there is. That is the meaning of spontaneous in contrast to regulative. The creativity of the *gopīs* is different from the creativity of *rajo-guṇa.* Vṛndā-devī creates an arrangement for Rādhā and Kṛṣṇa to enjoy. The spark of creativity is used to make something pleasing to the Lord—something for the Lord's enjoyment.

My present writing may be tinged (smeared) with *rajo-guṇa,* but I have faith that this is the cleansing process. And there is a *bhakti* school of pure creativity. Artists are not banned from Goloka. Geniuses serve Him—Madhumaṅgala creates jokes, Rādhā creates hundreds of bewildering situations to please Kṛṣṇa. Everyone is thinking how to please Him. But it is not the feverish, artistic madness that drives people to alcohol and cigarettes and suicide, as in the material world.

11:15 A.M.

The *gopīs* are attracted to Kṛṣṇa's flute. Today's reading raised discussion of how one has to be very discriminating in hearing of Kṛṣṇa and the *gopīs.* Rāma-rāya, Ananta and I saw two extremes neophyte devotees may take. One is to say, "This is too advanced; it is not for us. We don't want to hear it." That seems incongruent because the same person, when preaching, proclaims, "Kṛṣṇa consciousness teaches the highest form of love of God. Other religions have only a vague idea of love of God, but Lord Caitanya teaches us the perfection of religion in Rādhā-Kṛṣṇa's pastimes." If we preach that way, why do we refuse to participate in it or inquire about it? The other extreme is the well known *prākṛta-sahajiyā,* espoused by those who take things cheaply, imagine they are *gopīs,* or imagine they are Kṛṣṇa.

We will situate ourselves as hearers of the Tenth Canto from the mouth of Śukadeva Gosvāmī and Śrīla Prabhupāda. They will guide us. When they tell us how the *gopīs* were jealous of the flute because it touched Kṛṣṇa's lips, we will try to empathize with that sentiment. Whatever Prabhupāda describes, we will try to enter and follow. We will not create our own imaginings here.

Hearing of the *gopīs* changes the mood of our session. We are like puzzled travelers coming to an exciting but difficult passage. We are speaking more among ourselves, "What do we do next?" and referring to what the guides have said. There is a science of *rasa* and a technology of Sanskrit terms to describe the relations of Kṛṣṇa and the *gopīs,* but none of us are expert in it. We are dwarfs trying to catch the moon. But we are not tourists, not outsiders. We have been serving Śrīla Prabhupāda. We have been preaching. Rāma-rāya and Ananta have been distributing Prabhupāda's books, worshiping Rādhā-Gopīvallabha, and practicing the regulations of *brahmacarya*. We are not on a casual "day trip" into the land of Kṛṣṇa's pastimes. But, more than ever, we have to be guided at every step. We are speaking more what we have heard rather than what we feel. Taking cues from Śukadeva Gosvāmī and Śrīla Prabhupāda, we will try to appreciate that attractive power of Kṛṣṇa's flute.

> Another *gopī* said to her friends, "My dear friends, the cows are also charmed as soon as they hear the transcendental sound of the flute of Kṛṣṇa. It sounds to them like the pouring of nectar, and they immediately spread their long ears just to catch the liquid nectar of the flute. As for the calves, they are seen with the nipples of their mothers pressed in their mouths,

but they cannot suck the milk. They remain struck with devotion, and tears glide down their eyes, illustrating vividly how they are embracing Kṛṣṇa heart to heart." These phenomena indicate that even the cows and calves in Vṛndāvana knew how to cry for Kṛṣṇa and embrace Him heart to heart. Actually, Kṛṣṇa conscious affection can be culminated in shedding tears from the eyes.

—*Kṛṣṇa,* Vol. 1, p. 149

Even this place is holy. The breeze rustles the trees which are chock full of leaves. There are annoyances and disturbances, but Prabhupāda's *vāṇī* is here. I am in a good place, in the shack, completing a twenty-one day *vrata.*

Vāco vegaṁ—I can speak controlled words. *Vacāṁsi vaikuṇṭha guṇānuvarṇane*—Mahārāja Ambarīṣa engaged his words in talking of the glories of the Lord.

Sunlight descends to the floor of the forest, blessing lowly ferns.

❦

Now I have to leave the safe abode of reading *Kṛṣṇa* book and return to the shack. I have to write what comes, anything, left only with the aura of the *Kṛṣṇa* book reading. I have to return to my original premise for this twenty-one days, that I will write quickly and worship Kṛṣṇa by what comes—and that I will try to improve myself.

I am after readable things that are worth sharing, but I cannot insist on it now. I have faith in this process of writing as *bhajana.*

Come to the page. The smell of ink, the scratching, flowing marks . . . Offer mental obeisances and lean forward with your whole body.

Never mind the belches. Never mind the critics.

❦

I want to take myself to a secluded place in the woods and ask myself, "Who are you, and what do you know? How can we improve?" We want to praise Kṛṣṇa and serve Him, so sometimes this means asking ourselves (a self made of parts?), "Who am I?" Not, "What do the books say of the *ātmā*—the six working senses, the six knowledge acquiring senses, and beyond that, the soul?" But, "What do you know of it so far?"

Recognize yourself. Hear your heart. Know you are mortal, but for now, alive. You have come to a particular body: human, male, of an age, and yet you are different from the body. Can you sense this? It will be to your advntage if you can grasp some of this first-hand.

Do you love yourself? How can you help yourself? Become a humble, hard-working devotee, and then go further into the woods.

❦

Śrīla Prabhupāda told us that he didn't create our Kṛṣṇa consciousness: it was our eternal nature. He invoked it. But I was so totally covered over—I *have* to say that the invoker created my good fortune. What good is dormant spiritual nature if you remain unholy and confused? You bang your head against the walls, bang around writing unhappy books, reading unhappy mentors like Kafka, with friends who cannot love you as you need to be loved, who cannot respect you—and then you roll off the edge. But by Prabhupāda's grace, that didn't happen. He has invoked my spirit soul. Now I can sense holiness in my life, purity in the food I eat, and obedience to the teachings of the *Vedas*.

4:00 P.M.

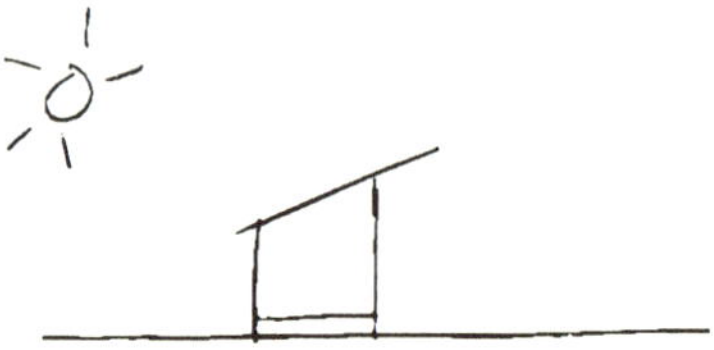

The breeze is up. Kṛṣṇa seems far away. I know He is a young boy, but sometimes He is God, the oldest. He seems so far away. I guess it's because I don't work hard enough to reach Him, don't pray enough.

Dear Kṛṣṇa, will You come closer and be my best friend? I am lazy and, therefore, not worthy of Your association. I am sulky and don't even want to be better. I think this means I have been stung into a coma by *māyā*. But if You could release me from this coma, it would be fun to run and play with You.

Writers work hard, but people find it uninteresting. A writer has to work, therefore, because he wants to and because it helps him, not because he wants people to admire his book.

And that's when I get stuck. I am trying to think of something good enough to share, rather than putting down what I think and care about right now. I have this note out here, taped to the wall: "You have to ask yourself where is your love? Where is your interest?" Love—such a big emotion. I *want* to love God. And *interest*—do I have any right now? It is embarrassing. *Shack Notes* is an act—of love? Of humanity at least. And I like to think it is an act of surrender in the devotional service of writing—to admit my homely truth.

I love, but maybe not right now. Love is dedication to Prabhupāda's order—that is ongoing. I get hung up with "love" as something big and awesome, like swooning ecstasy. I have a little love. I am not completely dead to it. I do *like* running along with a sentence, *like* walking in the morning. I like it when the sentences take on the quality of immediacy. I like it when the reader gets a nice vision of Kṛṣṇa.

Let me take up that question again: *What do I love? What interests me?* Write about whatever comes.

❦ ❦ ❦

6:15 P.M. 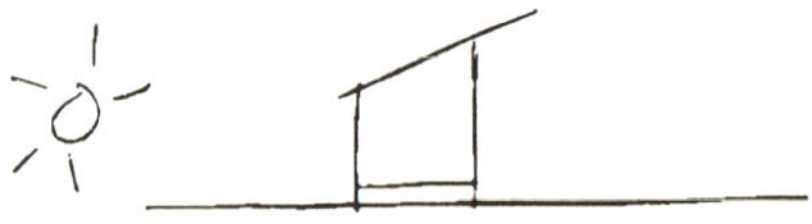

Tonight we read of Lord Kṛṣṇa stealing the garments of the *gopīs*. When the Lord completed that pastime, He walked along the bank of the Yamunā and began praising the beauty and welfare activity of the trees. At this point, Śrīla Prabhupāda writes a strong request for everyone to join in the topmost welfare of spreading Kṛṣṇa consciousness. Rāmarāya and I commented how we can enter the *līlā* of Kṛṣṇa by performing the *saṅkīrtana-yajña*. The *gopīs* also performed *yajña* to Kātyāyanī in order to get Kṛṣṇa as their husband. We cannot just float into *kṛṣṇa-līlā* by "wishing"—we have to carry out the orders of the spiritual master. For us, that means working in ISKCON temples, putting up with austerities and tribulations—and especially, "everyone should be prepared to propagate this movement."

Ananta said he appreciated the simplicity of this pastime and other Vṛndāvana pastimes. Everything is done to evoke love of Kṛṣṇa. Ananta also admitted the pastime brought out his self-centeredeness, something that was uncomfortable to see. I am grateful when a devotee shares with me his "little" perceptions and his painful admissions.

My admission is this: I slept through the main part when Kṛṣṇa joked and took the *gopīs'* clothes. Maybe I am not getting enough sleep at night. Maybe I am so dull that Kṛṣṇa doesn't want me to hear His intimate pastimes.

I have heard it before, so when I woke up, I joined the discussion. I like the vision of Kṛṣṇa walking, touching the leaves, fruits, and flowers, and saying, "Just look at these fortunate trees of Vṛndāvana."

❦ ❦ ❦

KRSNA
BHAGAVAD-GITA AS IT IS
SRIMAD BHAGAVATAM
VOL. III

Week Three

July 15, 1:30 A.M.

Seven days left.

I had a dream that Prabhupāda was present at a big international gathering of devotees. He was sitting on a *vyāsāsana* and singing, but he seemed distant. He didn't appear to be reciprocating with anyone individually. Everyone was competing for his attention. How could he be expected to reciprocate with everyone? Is it always like that, with so many devotees trying to maneuver themselves into a position to be seen by Prabhupāda? No, this was a particular dream signifying my own feelings.

In spiritual reality, we experience exchanges between the Supreme Lord and all His devotees, or between the pure devotee and His followers, but each exchange is entirely and uniquely individual. When Lord Caitanya went to Advaita Ācārya's house three days after taking *sannyāsa,* many thousands of people went to see Him. He stood on a balcony and "millions of joyful people on the other shore gaze[d] at the Lord to their hearts' content, and the Lord also glance[d] on them with great mercy" *(Caitanya-candrodayā,* Act 5, verse 94).

At that time, each person described their great fortune in seeing Lord Caitanya:

> Now we have crossed the ocean of repeated birth and death. The gate to Yama's kingdom is now closed to us. Now we have attained the ripened fruit of this human birth. Now we have attained the results of all penances and austerities. We have attained all this by seeing the sweet, merciful sidelong glance of the Lord.

There is a similar description of Lord Kṛṣṇa's mixing with all the living beings in Vṛndāvana: "Another *gopī* said that everything appeared wonderful when Kṛṣṇa and Balarāma traveled in the forest of Vṛndāvana playing Their flutes and making intimate friendships with all kinds of moving and nonmoving living creatures" (*Kṛṣṇa,* Vol. 1, p. 191).

❦

Write here whatever will best help you become Kṛṣṇa conscious. Give relevant instructions. Don't remain in the vaguely dissatisfied mood of that dream where Śrīla Prabhupāda seemed distant.

❦

Humility and full engagement in devotional service is our goal. Let us take up bona fide work and execute it, not expecting honor or distinction or profit from it. Just to work is sufficient, provided it is work recognized by the guru in disciplic succession. Śrīla Prabhupāda writes, "As instructed by Lord Caitanya, one should be humbler than the grass on the ground and more tolerant than the tree. The toleration of the tree is explained by Lord Kṛṣṇa Himself, and those engaged in the preaching of Kṛṣṇa consciousness should learn lessons from the teachings of Lord Kṛṣṇa and Lord Caitanya through Their disciplic succession" (*Kṛṣṇa,* p. 198).

Just serve with love to your best ability.

❦

Now in my last week of *Shack Notes,* I want to remain true to the process of writing what comes honestly. But it is up to me to prove that this can produce Kṛṣṇa conscious writing. Otherwise, it simply adds up to a string of zeroes. I may insist that what I am writing is worth something, but others may not agree. So what am I actually achieving? I have to know. Let me be immersed in striving for Kṛṣṇa consciousness.

I don't want to be stubborn or illusioned, but fixed in the right way. I want to find the best expression and give to it with my whole self.

Any topic that comes immediately to mind can be a first sure step to Kṛṣṇa consciousness. One doesn't have to wait for a Kṛṣṇa conscious thought per se—anything at hand can be directed toward the realm of Kṛṣṇa consciousness. As soon as one enters that realm, he can find his best subject and put his whole self into it. Then it will be successful.

Another way to write is to write letters. Some of them may be official, but many letters draw me out to address another's life situation and to infuse a person with relevant instructions. There is power in such words. Śrīla Prabhupāda's letters directed my life. His letters were like *śāstra* written specifically for one's particular circumstance: "Preach to college students in Boston." "Whenever you get a chance, read my books, or how will you preach?" Prabhupāda's example can be followed. Take the letter-writing as service.

The highway roars on. Truck drivers are driven by their internal forces and desires. I am also driven. I have to write. I have a compulsion to serve Lord Kṛṣṇa as a writer. Śrīla Prabhupāda states in the *Nectar of Devotion:*

> One should feelingly pray and become eager to render his particular type of service to the Lord. This is the teaching of all great devotees, especially Lord Caitanya. In other words, one should learn how to cry for the Lord. One should learn this small technique, and he should be very eager and actually try to become engaged in some particular type of service. This is called *laulyam,* and such tears are the price for the highest perfection. The only price for such entrance is this *laulyam lālasāmayī* or desire and great eagerness.
>
> —*Nectar of Devotion,* p. 83

So much is there. Thank you, Śrīla Prabhupāda.

Find your drum and beat it. Learn to play pleasingly in the company of devotees. Study with the masters. And when you get a deep taste for it, consider yourself fortunate. Then play it day and night.

The scriptures give us the example of the arrowsmith. He was so absorbed in his work that he didn't notice the king's grand procession passing right in front of him on the road. *Śrīmad-Bhāgavatam* offers this as a favorable example of how to perform devotional service in this world. Don't look up from your work. Stay as focused as possible.

And don't be whimsical. Do things the way Kṛṣṇa wants you to do them, not just according to your own idea. There is a statement in the *Nectar of Devotion* describing submission to Kṛṣṇa accompanied by the desire for perfection. The devotee says, "My dear Lord, when shall that day come when You will ask me to fan Your body, and according to Your pleasure, You will say, 'You just fan Me in this way'?" (*Nectar of Devotion*, p. 82).

❦

When one is always scratching the surface, there is no question of doing too much.

❦

A Godbrother wrote to me after reading *Harināma-cintāmaṇi* to tell me that he is convinced he should dedicate his life to *japa.* Bhaktivinoda Ṭhākura's books "[have] had, or promise to have, a profound effect on me. Already, my chanting has improved immensely . . . I am more determined now to live like a *sādhu,* making chanting and hearing my main focus. Unless I am purified of *anarthas* and seriously approaching pure chanting, what great good and happiness will come of all my hard endeavors?"

This seems to me to be a valid realization after reading *Harināma-cintāmaṇi.* Śrīla Prabhupāda also stresses chanting and hearing. The test is whether this devotee (or any of us) can actually do it. In other words, *the desire or concept to chant constantly is not whimsical in itself. It only becomes whimsical in the half-hearted or motivated attempt.*

❦

Thank you Lord, for allowing me to find service in writing. I want to reach the stage where I actually write without attachment for results and allow Śrīla Prabhupāda's teachings to flow out according to time and place. If writing is my way to preach, let me address my audience and do the best I can. It is a confidential, deep method of speaking to people. Assume *someone* hears. Serve as best you can. Don't worry too much about anything else.

6:30 A.M. 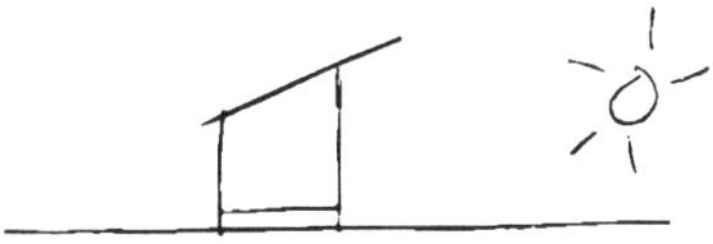

What Do You Want?

You sit facing the forest,
what do you want?
Something to put into my book.
You mean like a stuffing
for a *samosā?*
No, I mean a plain, tender *capātī.*

What do you want?
Or Prabhupāda said, "What do you want *more?*"
You have God's holy names, the best philosophy,
best food and friendship, what do you want more?
I'm satisfied, I just want to live
some more
and maybe go to India a few times more
and be able to see Kṛṣṇa
and Him see me.
I just want to please my spiritual master
with a life's work. Can't ask for
world peace, world revolution, or
presidents of countries all becoming Vaiṣṇavas,
and ISKCON members all saints.

I'd like to go on making *samosās* and *capātīs*
and on Sundays sweet rice
and *halavā* for the *brahmacārīs.*
The world-wide revolution
of chanting the pure Name!

❦

Mādhvācārya passed away from this world while writing commentary on Vedic scriptures. Viśvanātha Cakravartī wrote and wrote, and near the end of his life, he recorded that a rat had just carried away his last written purport. He thought that maybe the rat was Ganeśa's messenger and had taken the commentary to his master. Writing until the end was also the example Śrīla Prabhupāda gave us. Do these great writers pick it up again in the next world?

A successful devotional writer probably gives up his ink pen and becomes a cowherd boy with a stick and flute.

❦

I cannot always write about Kṛṣṇa directly, but at least before I write again, we will be reading *Kṛṣṇa* book. People like me, who reflect whatever they are held next to (like crystal glass), ought to stay as close as possible to devotees, devotional service, and *kṛṣṇa-kathā.* Dip me into the holy *dhāma* so I can talk of peacocks and *parikramas* and *sādhus* and temples. Take me out of Londons and Manhattans and bookstores and such. How about you?

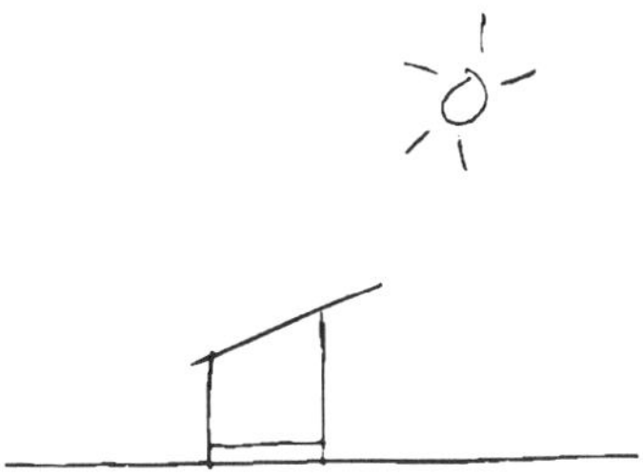

11:15 A.M.

Dear Friends,

You have allowed me to talk freely, and you have listened to me as a guide. I wish, therefore, that I had more qualification and could lead you further. At least I have the solace of knowing that no one can make spiritual advancement for you—you have to do it yourselves.

We are followers of His Divine Grace A.C. Bhaktivedanta Swami Prabhupāda. I am writing for his followers and for those who are aspiring to be his followers, and I am trying to encourage everyone to seek their spiritual nourishment from Prabhupāda's books.

Here we are, following Prabhupāda. We have come a certain distance—I picture us on an outing in a Vṛndāvana wood—and we intend to go further. We are friends, confiding and desiring to help one another.

What is this an introduction to? A little confession? Although I am acting as your guide, I fell asleep again today, the third time in a row, during the *Kṛṣṇa* book reading. I am getting up earlier in the night and not napping much in the day, and this could be the cause. But it is ironic. Today I dozed during the description of the "Stealing of the Gopīs' Clothes by Kṛṣṇa." We read each *līlā* twice, once in *Kṛṣṇa* book and once in *Śrīmad-Bhāgavatam.* I dozed twice during the same pastime.

Now I am awake, looking around at the bright trees of the forest. I feel a pleasant breeze.

Rāma-rāya and I read from the *Kṛṣṇa* book. Afterwards, we talked about whether a devotee who still has material desire in his heart can appreciate *at all* the pastimes of Kṛṣṇa and the *gopīs.* We are assured by Prabhupāda that any *kṛṣṇa-līlā* he gives us is the "right medicine." But I admitted that when we were talking about the parents' concern for baby Kṛṣṇa, we all felt freer to empathize with the parents and to imagine Kṛṣṇa's antics and the village situation. Similarly, we felt even more access to the *gopas* pastimes and we related our own boyhood adventures and tried to see how they exist in pure, original friendship with Gopa-kumāra. But the love affairs of Kṛṣṇa and the cowherd girls of His village evoke a conflicting emotion.

Sometimes it is less difficult. I *did* hear (before dozing) how the *gopīs* ate unspiced *kitri* for a month while performing a *vrata* for goddess Kātyāyanī. They wanted to attain Kṛṣṇa as their husband. I thought, "I would like to eat unspiced *kitri* for a month like those *gopīs*—with attraction to Kṛṣṇa as the goal." And I got a tiny glimpse into the simplicity of their worship. They did not fast completely like *yogīs* would have; they simply restricted themselves to unspiced *kitri.* But their austerity was more potent than any *yogī's.*

We also read the mantra that they chanted to the goddess. They bathed at dawn, worshiped an earthen deity of Durgā on the river bank, and chanted the following mantra:

kātyāyani mahā-māye
mahā-yoginy adhīśvari
nanda gopa-sutaṁ devi
patiṁ me kuru te namaḥ

It reminded me of groups of ladies I have seen at the Yamunā—country people—doing special observances, singing together with their childlike voices. And it occurred to me that this mantra to Goddess Durgā must have been privately manufactured by the young girls to include the line, "Please make the Son of Nanda Mahārāja my husband." People do not normally worship Durgā to ask for Kṛṣṇa as their husband. This must have been done secretly too. It was a bold religious adaptation. Seeing it in print and visualizing the *gopīs* seriously praying like this touched something in me.

So there is some access to these pastimes. One doesn't have to pretend to "be" a *gopī,* which is a dangerous folly. Neither does one have to be completely free of all vestiges of material desire—on the liberated stage—in order to feel some love and attraction for the true stories of Kṛṣṇa with the *gopīs.* Thus Śrīla Prabhupāda informs us later in *Kṛṣṇa* book, that hearing of Kṛṣṇa and the *gopīs* will in fact replace our lust with love.

We tend to be more scholarly in our talk now that we have reached these *gopī* chapters. We do not take the liberty of visualizing ourselves in the scene. But if we are charmed by the *gopīs'* Durgā mantra, and if we like to think of their month of unspiced *kitri,* there is no harm.

❦

Not me,
then who? Kṛṣṇa, the Supreme.
For Him, go inside,
bathe and pray and eat and sleep.
As His servants take a nap,
listen to a nonsense dream and record it—
how is that for Him?
After nap chant, grind it out,
Prabhupāda on *japa* tape. He's the link.
Get ready for 5 P.M. *Kṛṣṇa* reading.
Stay awake this time, but relax,
hearing and discussing for an hour,
evening fading—all day you closely
  watch the time,
but the last hour at night is loose,
maybe read a little,
notes for the morning.

Then last things in a hurry,
while Prabhupāda *bhajana* tape is playing
put things out:
sweatshirt, socks, cup of water,
tissues, eye glass wiper,
pens in a box, legal pad,
no doubt about it I'll be here.
Deities to rest, each in Their bed
with sheet only, but blanket if They need it,
lights out. Lay awake thinking
of dreams and sleep and what comes next.

Cicadas. We won't be here for the deep summer when the whole forest is filled with their electric buzzing. You know how it can get—hot, with locusts and gnats and yearning and memories of other summers . . . We will be in Europe by then, shack abandoned, not used by another.

Now a large black butterfly hovers around the trunk of a shaggy oak.

4:00 P.M.

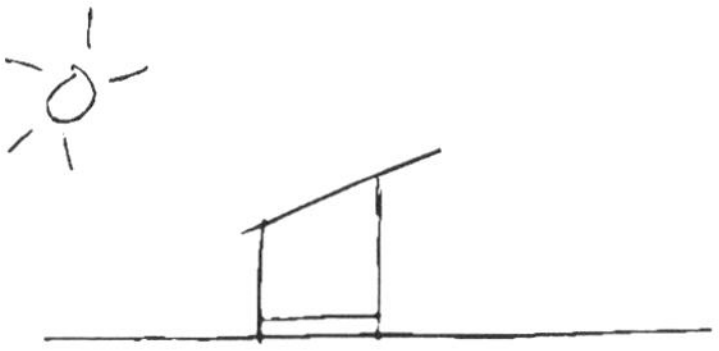

The sun comes in at an angle.

❦

Come out and admit a tiny truth: "I like to sit in a private shack in a little forest, where it is peaceful. I can sit here by the hour listening to forest sounds and feel at ease." To justify this, I write "madly." My critical mind prods me to do something worthwhile.

❦

The artist and his critic: an internal drama in twenty-one acts.

Dear diary, dear somebody, I thought I found freedom, but find myself confined to a way of expression. There is no freedom in this world.

I too am under the grips of the tyrannical mind and senses. Occasionally, I may wriggle free from their grip, and repeat with conviction what my gurus speak. *They* speak with conviction.

I play the role of someone entitled to give advice to others. I don't even know if *I* am entangled or free. Nothing is certain.

I keep wanting to create the right effect, to speak with grace, to enter and exit artistically.

One can subdue all this, regard it as nonsense. But one needs commiseration.

❦

Hare Kṛṣṇa, Hare Kṛṣṇa, Kṛṣṇa Kṛṣṇa, Hare Hare.

Dear Madhumaṅgala, you have been spending your days well, as I read in your FAX, constructing the van for travel and living on the road. Your days are filled with figuring out how to cut wood, how to make electrical connections, how to save and raise money, and so on. You may feel harried with so much work, but don't doubt the work's value. As for me, I don't know if I have been spending my time as well as you. I did solid work in compiling *Prabhupāda Meditations,* Volume 3, and then somehow drifted into this . . .

I don't want people to misunderstand. They say, "He is admitting it is a waste of time." They want to send me to work in the kitchen or on *harināma* where I belong. I don't want to admit defeat to them. It is up to me to see it honestly for what it is. A friend can say it is okay, and a stern leader can say it is a waste of time, and I can listen to one or the other as I choose. Ultimately though, I have to make my own peace with guru and Kṛṣṇa.

Kṛṣṇa spends time in the forest. One time, His friends felt hungry, and they asked Kṛṣṇa to provide them with food. He had an interesting pastime in mind. He told the *gopas* to approach some *brāhmaṇas* who were nearby performing a sacrifice and to ask them for food. The boys went to the *brāhmaṇas,* but the *brāhmaṇas* ignored them, even though the boys said, "We have come on behalf of Kṛṣṇa and Balarāma, who you know well."

The boys went back and reported this to Kṛṣṇa. He smiled and told them that this kind of rejection happens in begging. Then He told them to approach the wives of those same *brāhmaṇas* and ask *them* for food. Kṛṣṇa knew these wives were His great devotees and they were hankering to serve Him directly. Sure enough, when the *gopas* asked the wives, they were joyful and immediately prepared a feast. They carried it into the forest and personally offered it to Kṛṣṇa. Not only did they give the feast to the Supreme Lord, but they offered Him prayers and requested that He let them stay always in His direct association. Lord Kṛṣṇa was very pleased with them, but asked them to continue their religious duties as wives of *brāhmaṇas.* It would be better for their Kṛṣṇa consciousness if they left Kṛṣṇa's presence in the forest and instead, always thought of Him while prosecuting their duties in the world. That is the best for some devotees; Kṛṣṇa knows best.

We will read this pastime tonight. I am just recalling it from past readings. There is a particularly nice description when the wives first catch sight of Kṛṣṇa in the forest "putting on a golden garment." I will try to hear it nicely, notice things, and then tell you something about it.

6:00 P.M.

Thank God, I stayed awake and alert for our reading of Kṛṣṇa taking a feast from the wives of the *brāhmaṇas.* We read the same passages in the morning, but I spaced out completely. Tonight I was able to visualize it. The *gopas* were so spritely and strong and confident as they strode into the religious arena and begged food from the *brāhmaṇas* for Kṛṣṇa and Balarāma. "Lord Viṣṇu as Kṛṣṇa and Balarāma are standing nearby," they said.

I felt like talking, but then asked Rāma-rāya to speak. Just because we feel inspired to speak doesn't mean we should make others listen to us exclusively. He spoke well. I slowed down and heard his insights.

When Kṛṣṇa sent the boys to the wives of the *brāhmaṇas,* Śrīla Prabhupāda said that the women were sitting inside their houses. By this simple phrase, I began to think of them quietly in their houses. Then we heard they were always meditating on Kṛṣṇa. So they were overjoyed that the boys "broke" their meditation by coming to ask for food for Kṛṣṇa and Balarāma.

Hearing in a new way means being receptive to particular words and allowing them to open up within you. Kṛṣṇa appeared "exactly like a dancing actor on a stage." That one delighted me and I broke through my old aversion to descriptions of necklaces, ornaments, turbans, ankle bells, armlets, etc. I thought, "Yes, Kṛṣṇa is a particular person and He likes to dress up for His friends. He is already beautiful, but His friends take pleasure when they see

Kṛṣṇa exhibit the height of artistic creation in His dress. He likes to do it." I thought of how family members take pleasure and pride when they see their daughter or son or father or mother dressed up beautifully in their best clothes. That tendency is perfected in seeing beloved Kṛṣṇa like a dancing actor. We do this in Deity worship, partake in Kṛṣṇa's desire to dress up.

Then we read how the wives saw Kṛṣṇa in the forest with His peacock feather and beautiful form, with one hand on the shoulder of a friend and a lotus in His hand. They embraced Him with their eyes and took Him into their hearts. This description is not merely a sentimental metaphor—it is a specific mystical act of love. One may embrace the Lord in one's arms, but one may also embrace Him with one's eyes, and this can only be known by a lover who does it, by Kṛṣṇa's grace.

Śrīla Prabhupāda writes, "When Kṛṣṇa entered into the wives' hearts and when they embraced him and felt the transcendental bliss of being merged with Him, the Supreme Lord Kṛṣṇa did not lose His identity, nor did the wives lose theirs . . . When a lover submits to his lover without any pinch of personal consideration, that is called oneness" (*Kṛṣṇa*, p. 204).

We discussed this oneness. It is the long-desired freedom from false ego. At last, the self-centered concept vanishes. You love Kṛṣṇa, and the old self is gone. When *that* happens to me, *then* I can write, free of this mental back and forth, this dwelling on myself.

July 16, 1:30 A.M.

Yesterday Ananta went to New York City to get a visa. While he was at the embassy, his car was towed. He had to borrow $150 to get it back. The police would not even let him get into the car to get the registration papers to prove it was his! So devotees had to go back to the used car dealer in Pennsylvania, get a copy of the papers, and FAX them to Ananta, who was still waiting in New York City. The day became a nightmare for him, and, as of this writing, he still hasn't returned.

I am not going to feel guilty that I am spared from that or that I don't have any major theme to write on. I am going to use my last six days peacefully writing about Kṛṣṇa. And because I have chosen this method of "go to the page and be open," I will have to go through the "whoozies"* like I did yesterday. That is my version of getting the car towed away. And I do have a major theme—the return to Kṛṣṇa consciousness.

❦

Bhaktisiddhānta Sarasvatī said that a spiritual newspaper could be written every moment. I have been attempting to do a daily edition, but I have been avoiding the many journalistic devices for filling up space. Newspaper writers don't talk much about themselves or examine their motives for writing. They bat out their assignments one after the other. I have my assignment too.

---

* I call my inability to break through to a strong topic the "whoozies."

Editorial Comment

A Godbrother wrote me yesterday, commenting on B. dāsa who has been insisting on talking about his problems, his attempt at self-discovery, etc. This Godbrother said that B. dāsa is seeking psychological rather than spiritual solutions to his problems. I agreed that this is not good, and since B. dāsa is in my charge, I agreed to try and straighten him out. But now I am thinking, what is the strict division between psychological and spiritual? I know what we mean—we mean that the answer to our problems comes by rendering devotional service, by chanting and hearing. It doesn't come by nondevotee psychoanalysis or "sentimental" talks. But everything has a psychological dimension. People have to be given time and deliberate attention—a real hearing—about what they think they need. A counselor may want to tell them something relative he thinks will help them in their growth toward self-realization. Just as psychological treatment for a devotee can degrade into "too much attention to relative problems," so the "all-spiritual approach to devotional service" can become impersonal and mechanical.

In any case, we are all people, and we will only be satisfied by caring relationships and not otherwise.

(Editorials advocating a particular approach while criticizing another approach are fine, but there is something "loaded" about them. You want to win your delicate argument, so you make it in your favor. Oh well, a fellow's got to fill up his newspaper.)

My newspaper has a lonely hearts page and a Kṛṣṇa pastime feature (which I regard as the mainstay of *Shack Notes,* just as Śrīla Prabhupāda regarded his monthly *Bhāgavatam* supplement as the heart of *BTG*). We have letters to the editor, a few cartoons, devotee profiles, ISKCON news, literary allusions, book reviews . . .

❦

The heart of this process is accumulating pages while looking at the clock. I am not sure "who" is supervising, demanding this output, but I gladly submit to the control. Keep the hand moving, keep me employed. I don't want to be regarded as unemployed, just because I don't work for a cigarette factory or insurance company.

❦

News-in-Review

"Tell us about the early days." What a set-up. There we are, just as you always imagined it—ISKCON's re-opening of 26 Second Avenue—a preaching center and shrine. It occurs on the 25th Anniversary of ISKCON. The storefront is packed with over a hundred people, and people are standing outside looking in the windows, straining to hear every word. These are not ordinary people, but devotees, including *sannyāsīs,* very senior Godbrothers and Godsisters . . . but . . . each has only five minutes to speak. I have a headache (others may too, in such tight quarters).

It was almost too momentous. I mean the external event was "too perfect," too keyed-up, too crowded with video lights and microphones and a tight time schedule—too much happening for ease of meditation on Swamijī. But it is glorious that ISKCON has this place again. I am grateful. One of the most important Kṛṣṇa conscious *tīrthas* in the world has been rescued from the nondevotees. Go there, friends, and sit and think and read and hear about His Divine Grace who came to America to start Lord Caitanya's *saṅkīrtana* as ISKCON. It is "too momentous" for me to fully appreciate, but I want to be there in spirit and in memory with Prabhupāda. Everyone can go there. So what if I "blew it" on the Grand Opening day? The place is open, Matchless Gifts, in the original tough city, giving out mercy today to "da people" and to ISKCON pilgrims everywhere.

—Sign off . . . News-in-Review

The basic foundation is writing practice (an embarrassing term) by which I try with my pen to say what I mean and what I want. William Stafford calls it, "the value of an unafraid, face-down, flailing and speedy process in using the language." That is similar to conversations in which we have to forgive each other our mistakes.

> We must accustom ourselves to talking without orating, and to writing without achieving "Paradise Lost" . . . We must abjure the "I wrote it last night and it looked good, but today I see it is terrible" stance. When you write, simply tell me something. Maybe you can tell me how we should live.
>
> —*Writing the Australian Crawl,* William Stafford

As with many materially sound ideas and methods, this writing attitude seems best in the hands of those who can represent Kṛṣṇa consciousness, who can tell us "how we should live." We don't have to tie ourselves in knots before a writing assignment and finally go away from it with the task undone because we "couldn't think of what to say," or we felt "too fallen," or we "couldn't make it come out right," or we think, "I'm not a writer."

What is a writer? A person who writes. And who has something worth saying if not a follower of Lord Caitanya?

I am starting to read Act Seven of *Śrī Caitanya-candrodayā,* by Kavi Karnapura. Śrīla Prabhupāda told us that there is so much Kṛṣṇa conscious literature, we couldn't complete it if we read twenty-four hours a day. I didn't know what he meant when I first heard him say that, but now I can see it is true—we are a writing and reading *sampradāya.* We have utmost respect for the written word. Scripture is the "breathing of Lord Nārāyaṇa." Works written in pursuance of the Vedic literatures are also *smṛti. Smṛti* is like hearing your sister repeat and enlarge upon what your mother has said.

I am grateful and happy to be in this *sampradāya,* by the mercy of Śrīla Prabhupāda. I remember shortly before he found me, I was writing and smoking, producing "pipe dreams" on the page. I wrote a line, "I sit on the bench in the park and judge." I was ironic, aware of defeat, aware of absurdity, aware of painful hunger and lack of love. I sat on that park bench on the Lower East Side, hungry, with few people interested in what I wrote, facing chaos. "I am like the judge in court on his bench, but my 'court' is a slum park, and nobody cares about my opinion or dissent."

One could argue that the world *still* does not care about what I say, although I am deputized as a preacher on behalf of Śrīla Prabhupāda. But some devotees hear, some new people hear, and writing Kṛṣṇa consciousness is within the river of our *sampradāya*. This writing purifies both me as the writer, and those who read it. Therefore, I want to give more direct Kṛṣṇa consciousness, and I want to be more detached about it.

❦

Kṛṣṇe ratiḥ kṛṣṇe matiḥ: "May you love Kṛṣṇa, may you think of Kṛṣṇa" (*Caitanya-candrodayā,* Act 6, verse 116).

❦

Coming Back from a Walk

Bright bough summer leaves
engines revving up, on
highway 80, out of sight.
Baladeva's clothing and gear on rail outside.
He's about to go for three days,
    got new sales territory
in Canada. He jokes, "You've got a 20th
    Century *bhajana-kutir*"—
the woods surrounded by highway rumbles.
Me: "When you come back
    I'll have something
for you to read."
"*Jai.*"

Spider strand 20 feet long,
first morning sunlight thru tops of trees.
The entrance to the forest is dark.
Woodpecker tapping. It's time for me
    to go there—
hope I'll remember something
when I get there
so my studies are not wasted.
All these years some must have entered
within the bloodstream, deep memory banks,
and into the *prāṇa.*

In the shack I'll
reach out for what's closest,
repeated obeisances, calling out names
in the cool morning.

6:30 A.M. 

You mean you don't physically bow down before you write? I think you should do it. You pay obeisances when you offer your food, why not do it when writing? It doesn't *have* to be mechanical. Try it.

It makes you feel happy and helps to remind your brain who you are and what you are doing.

Samīka Ṛṣi gets free memo pads and Post-its from medical companies advertising their products. Most of it is indecipherable: "180 mg Calan SR Verapmil HC." But one, obviously a drug, says,

"Keep them under the rainbow." A memo pad with printed heading: "Another Bright Idea . . . " After awhile you don't notice the ads. On a "Bright Idea" note pad, this line to greet me here this morning, "One should not be disturbed by the activities of the modes of nature; instead of putting his consciousness into such activities, he may transfer his consciousness to Kṛṣṇa activities" (*Bg.* 14.26).

Does this suggest we should retire from the world in order to be free from disturbance? Should we chant and hear, and in that way "transfer" the consciousness? Śrīla Prabhupāda writes, "Kṛṣṇa activities are known as *bhakti-yoga,* always acting for Kṛṣṇa." For Śrīla Prabhupāda, this means varieties of activities. He created the ISKCON temples and the movement. He wanted us busy serving and spreading Kṛṣṇa consciousness. By that method of *sādhu-saṅga,* we can retire from material activities and transfer to spiritual ones. Make a radical break from newspapers, television—anything that is not *kṛṣṇa-kīrtana.*

❦

I am getting more self-conscious about this writing, adding cleverness to it so folks will like it. Decorating the Christmas tree with tinsel and balls.

❦

I have a picture of Rādhā-Dāmodara on my desk. It is up to Him whether I can do anything at all, whether I can even blink or breathe, whether I can think. Sometimes I imagine, "If I can write things down now, then later when my brain fails, this will remain." But things may not turn out as I expect. And what is it that remains? Who will judge it? What good will it do me when my body is burned and my soul has gone on? Prabhupāda often pointed out the absurdity of people honoring or mourning a great man after the soul had entered a dog's body.

Be a writer, but better to be in full submission to my guru's order and take a better next life. Neither can that goal be pursued with the mood of selfish salvation. Kṛṣṇa knows what is real devotion and what is counterfeit. No one can cheat Him. No one can impress Him with their razzle-dazzle. He sifts through and sees what they actually give, what they withhold, what their essential nature is made of. And although He kindly sees the good, He is always working for our rectification.

❦

When the leper Vāsudeva was cured by Lord Caitanya, he feared he would become proud and again be attracted by the material world. Lord Caitanya said, "O *brāhmaṇa,* never again will you forget the Lord, and never again will your heart become involved in the external things of this world. Why should you be anxious?" *(Caitanya-candrodayā,* Act 7, Verse 44).

With a blessing like that, one could be satisfied even if he had to take birth again in the material world.

All devotees are trying to pull free of material life. Our various tactics and plans, our temples and book distribution, are for teaching us devotion and renunciation from the world. Vāsudeva was already extremely tolerant and humble and renounced, and he constantly thought of the Supreme Lord. Still, he never claimed to be an advanced devotee, and Lord Caitanya embraced him.

❦

Kṛṣṇa Kṛṣṇa Kṛṣṇa.

Everything that comes out here is good for me. You don't have to disbelieve it. Sometimes you feel unworthy, sometimes proud, sometimes healthy, sometimes sick. Observe these changes and the mind's demands, and just tolerate them. You are not these ups and downs.

❦

I am grateful. Don't be afraid to repeat yourself before Kṛṣṇa. Don't think "I have praised Him enough." You have to sincerely feel it now. Meet this new moment with fresh contrition and thankfulness, thinking of Prabhupāda's kindness upon you.

11:00 A.M.

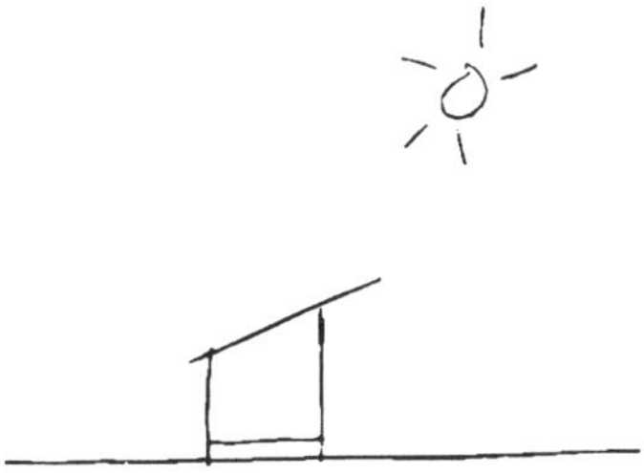

We discussed more on the wives of the yajñic *brāhmaṇas*. Fortunately, I have overcome my sleepiness, and Ananta was glad to be back after spending all day with the tow-away police in New York City.

Sometimes we are pulled away from regular hearing of Kṛṣṇa's pastimes. But we should not come to think that hearing *kṛṣṇa-līlā* is a kind of indulgence, as if the real world is calling us now. *Kṛṣṇa* book *is* the real world. Realness has nothing to do with the external world.

❦

When will we be able to go back to Godhead? If it is not at the end of this life, that is not cause for despair. When Kṛṣṇa tells a devotee he will return to the spiritual world "very soon," that could mean several lifetimes. Our prayer is *not to forget Kṛṣṇa wherever we have to go.* And never think Kṛṣṇa is being unfair.

❦

To hell with our pride in *varṇāśrama* status, to hell with our superior position over the *karmīs,* to hell with our record of austerities and obedience to the rules and regulations—"For we have not developed transcendental loving service to the Supreme Personality of Godhead who is beyond the speculation of the mind, body and senses . . . "

Here is a comment on women as a class: They are not so fortunate in many ways, not best suited for the life of renunciation and cultivation of knowledge, "but how wonderful it is that they have developed transcendental love for Kṛṣṇa, the Lord of all mystic *yogīs.*" Śrīla Prabhupāda writes, "Women in general, being very simple in heart, can very easily take to Kṛṣṇa consciousness, and when they develop love of Kṛṣṇa, they can easily get liberation from the clutches of *māyā,* which is very difficult for even so-called intelligent and learned men to surpass."

❦

I know a devotee who keeps a diary of his *japa.* His handwriting is tight and small, and he writes things like how attentive he was today, whether he was sleepy, how long each round took. I hesitate to write such a diary. I have tried it before. That kind of writing is not meant for readers other than oneself, but sometimes people read private diaries and criticize, "This person seems to be nagging himself, and he's not getting anywhere." Who can judge besides the diarist as to whether his entries are helpful?

This is an evasive introduction to the topic of my own *japa.* I feel a resistance to put it down here because it is too personal. And maybe my readers don't want to hear of my struggles in *japa.* But the real point is, I don't have good news. I would like to associate with someone like Madhu, for whom *japa*—prayer—is central to spiritual life.

Madhu says he has a terrible time controlling his mind while chanting—but maybe his sorrow over this is what pleases Kṛṣṇa. If at the end of life one sincerely laments, "I couldn't chant Hare Kṛṣṇa, although I tried. I couldn't control the mind," that will please Kṛṣṇa.

We *can* make progress, and I felt it recently. I gave a few classes on the practical aspects of *japa* at Gītā-nāgarī. I insisted that we cannot indulge in deliberate mind-wandering. I made the point enough times that I convinced myself. It stayed with me until I came here.

Sometimes I say that this writing is *kīrtana.* Maybe I have neglected the importance of *japa* while putting attention into my writing. I didn't want to broach this subject, but now I am glad I brought it out in the open. I know devotees sacrifice attention on *japa* for other duties in the *saṅkīrtana* movement. We justify it by saying, "This is an emergency time. It is not an age for *bābājīs*. Work now, and later we can chant." This attitude can easily get out of hand.

Let's look at the "worst scenario": I say I am beating a drum, the *bṛhat-mṛdaṅga*. Śrīla Prabhupāda told us that writing is that big drum. But *japa* is my spiritual heartbeat. If I develop palpitations of the heart or heart failure, I am finished. Do I want to come back next life as a materialistic talented writer who has to go through hell until he is forty years old and then join the Hare Kṛṣṇa movement?

Then again, do I really have to choose between the pen and my *japa-mālā?* The great *ācāryas* like Rūpa Gosvāmī, Sanātana Gosvāmī, Jīva Gosvāmī, and Śrīla Prabhupāda used both. I just have to keep everything balanced and do both in the mood of a servant. And I have to give prime mind-time to the holy name.

It is time to go back into the house and I'm glad for that. I'm glad I can go bathe, then eat and rest. These are the activities of a conditioned soul, the maintenance of "Brother Donkey," the body. Brother Donkey is a humble friend. He is helping me to write this book, and he is an old soldier for Śrīla Prabhupāda (although not the bravest). I know he is just a dead carcass, but as long as the soul is within, he is God's wondrous arrangement.

Let's go in. Water on my skin, ease my head, apply nice Vaiṣṇava *tilaka,* restrain my tongue while praying. Then eat, sending it to the eager belly. Rest awhile. Brother Donkey and I have got more writing to do today and I am depending on him to work.

All glories to Śrī Kṛṣṇa who told the wives of the *brāhmaṇas* to return home and think of Him always. All glories to those wives who at first made emotional arguments (based on scripture) to Śrī Kṛṣṇa, but when they saw He was serious, they obeyed His will wholeheartedly. All glories to Śukadeva Gosvāmī and Śrīla Prabhupāda for teaching us the art of surrender and hinting to each of us how we may do it in our own situations.

All glories to *Kṛṣṇa* book. Dear Lord, thank You for this little life of devotion. Prabhupāda is guru to this Hare Kṛṣṇa band. Please make us strong and loving.

All glories to the loving service You allow us to perform. All glories to Prabhupāda wherever he is now. I know he is with me.

3:30 P.M.

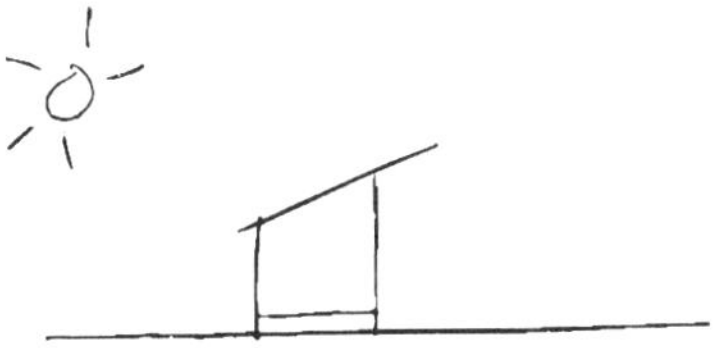

There is sometimes only a thin line between these notes and a diary, but these notes also have their purpose. I am trying to keep them up. I want to avoid manufacturing events to write about, but I suppose I should mention what Murray Mednick said about my writing.

He made his remark over a year ago, but I was remembering it today because a book by Beckett arrived in the mail. As I glanced over the book, I quickly saw that I didn't want to delve into the book, but somehow it reminded me of what Murray said to me about my poetry. After twenty years of no contact, last year Murray and I exchanged two letters. Then I sent him a book of my poems. He made a few favorable comments about lines he liked here and there, and then he made a constructive comment about the poems: "Sometimes you finish too soon. Keep going. You write about something and then quickly wrap it up in the canon." He meant that I write about experience, including dilemmas, but then I appear to introduce Kṛṣṇa consciousness (the canon, the dogma) abruptly as the solution. I took it as a valuable criticism, but it is not advice I can follow in an ultimate sense. Murray also recommended I read the Sufi poet Rumi, who he described as "classical" and "fearless." I have read some Rumi, and to me his "fearlessness" is that he is an impersonalist who thinks the ultimate is unknowable and unnameable.

Murray would prefer I drop the canon entirely. The atheists and agnostics rely on sense perception for knowledge. They claim one cannot talk of death or a next life because no one alive has "first hand information." To them, scriptures are human inventions. They assert that they know nothing, and therefore, everyone else knows nothing. Everything is futile, and nothing matters. Beckett even said his own dramas were "blathering about nothing in particular."

So Murray was hinting I should at least hang in there longer with my direct perception before turning to the solace and shelter of God and the Vedic way. I say this is valuable because I should not merely quote the scripture in an experiential poem. It shouldn't be obvious to a reader that I just tacked the scripture on at the end. A Kṛṣṇa conscious poem should *be* an experience. Rūpa Gosvāmī's prayers, pleading with Śrīmatī Rādhārāṇī and Śrī Kṛṣṇa to please accept him in Their service, are actual experience. Prabhupāda's prayer to Kṛṣṇa, written on the Boston pier in 1965, is not the tacking on of scripture to a thought in order to create a sermon. Prabhupāda was speaking intensely to Kṛṣṇa with his whole self: "Why did You send me to this land of demons so far away from Vṛndāvana? You must have some purpose. Then make me dance! Make me dance!"

Since my own direct experience of Kṛṣṇa is so tied up with my struggle to serve my spiritual master, it is fair to honestly say what it is like to struggle. Don't state prematurely, "Anyway, as Lord Kṛṣṇa says in *Bhagavad-gītā,* 'My devotee comes to Me.'" But tell what that coming to Kṛṣṇa is like, tell of your agonies, your doubts, of the actual nature of your turning to guru, of finding strength in his order. Tell us why you continue to chant even though you are not tasting the full nectar. Give us your doubts so we can be more convinced of your hope. Give us your actual experience so we can feel your conviction and be open ourselves to the universal values you find in Vaiṣṇava teachings.

I live by inviolable codes and *śāstra.* I am not a "fearless" voidist who makes atheistic jokes with apparently "no cost." I am one who lives by Vedic canon, and I am one who has been trying to be more honest about when and how the Vaiṣṇava way actually enters my consciousness—how its absolute answers provide solutions to my personal dilemmas. And I am struggling to live those solutions in my day-to-day life.

❦

I trust that I am neither intentionally nor unintentionally "blathering about nothing in particular." Vaiṣṇavas believe in the validity and the holiness of words. Words used in the service of the Supreme, even when imperfectly uttered, are appreciated by "those who are thoroughly honest." On the other hand, expertly constructed words that are filled with metaphor and universal symbolism (and earthy jokes and cosmic jests)—but which are devoid of appreciation for the Supreme Personality of Godhead—are garbage fit for crows. Beckett speaks of the "issueless predicament of existence," and he says of literature, "you would do better, at least no worse, to obliterate texts . . . to blacken margins, to fill in the holes of words till all looks like what it is—senseless, speechless, issueless misery." But he speaks only for himself and those like him; he speaks of his literature and the literature of all crow-like persons. He does not speak for my experience in Kṛṣṇa consciousness, or the experience of sages in Vaiṣṇava *paramparā.*

❦

Bhagavān: What should be glorified in song?
Rāmānanda: Kṛṣṇa's pastimes in Vraja.
Bhagavān: What is the best thing in the world?
Rāmānanda: The association of saintly devotees.
Bhagavān: What should be remembered?
Rāmānanda: Kṛṣṇa's name.
Bhagavān: On what should one meditate?
Rāmānanda: Kṛṣṇa's feet.
Bhagavān: What should make the ear happy?
Rāmānanda: Only Kṛṣṇa's pastimes in Vṛndāvana.
(Caitanya-candrodayā, Act 7, 62-73).

6:15 P.M. 

We started to read the Govardhana-*līlā,* just the beginning. We know it well, so we are trying to be as receptive as possible and to hear it as fresh. We visualized the opening scene as we have seen it in the paintings. Kṛṣṇa is smaller, more innocent and childlike than the big men. He is inquiring of His father, "What is the meaning of this sacrifice?" Nanda Mahārāja never became annoyed or acted indifferently toward his son, yet he was a little reticent at first to explain all the intricacies of the *yajña* to such a young child.

"If it is a secret," Kṛṣṇa encouraged, "still you could tell Me. We are confidential family members."

Then Nanda Mahārāja took the time to explain it to His beloved son. Nanda was in the superior instructing position at first, and they stood on Govardhana Hill and discussed it.

Not every reading is so intensely participatory. We mostly listen quietly as the pastime is read. *Kṛṣṇa* book is sufficient to pull us into the real world.

❦

Holes in the leaves now, where the caterpillars have eaten through.

❦

In our Kṛṣṇa conscious readings, we talk things out and often conclude, "The path of devotional service is like the razor's edge." It is easy to make mistakes. But if you do, Kṛṣṇa forgives you and you don't receive a reaction. (I heard Śrīla Prabhupāda being emphatic on this point in a lecture: Don't make mistakes if possible, but if you do, don't worry; there is no reaction for a devotee in His service.)

❦ ❦ ❦

July 17, 1:30 A.M. ◐

My Dear Lord Kṛṣṇa, please have mercy on this sinner.

❦

I often seem to express doubt in the process of working at writing. This is because part of me is not a good devotee and therefore, I am embarrassed to go through all *that* in writing. I also know my devotee readers need good, Kṛṣṇa conscious fare to nourish them.

Is writing absolutely good in itself? No, writing is a tool that must be wielded by someone who either directly glorifies the Supreme and the process of *bhakti,* or who instructs us in *bhakti.* And if it is used sincerely by a soul trying to find his own way to *bhakti,* then it is also valid.

Shack Notes is an experiment to prove to myself that I am motivated to work for my own improvement, and that I have worthwhile work to do on the page. *Shack Notes* is for self-help.

I have written quite a few books, and each of them has its own purpose. In *Lessons From the Road,* the writing evaluates experience, and it records travels and preaching: "How is ISKCON doing?" I ask myself. "How can I serve ISKCON?" Other books, such as *Obstacles on the Path of Devotional Service,* provide practical guidance to the reader and proclaim Kṛṣṇa consciousness as the supreme spiritual path. The purpose of books like the *Prabhupāda Meditations* series is clear, and even a book like *Journal & Poems* is an obvious sharing of my Kṛṣṇa conscious coping methods in my daily life.

But *Shack Notes* is special. To write *Shack Notes,* I have deliberately slowed down my outer experiences in order to think out Kṛṣṇa consciousness on the page. It is an attempt to explore the writing as Kṛṣṇa conscious experience itself, pushing it to the limits in hopes that writing will bring me deeper into my Kṛṣṇa consciousness.

And *Shack Notes* is an inside look at a writer's thinking.

❦

At least I have discovered that the mind's function is to make me miserable.

❦

As we grow older in Kṛṣṇa consciousness and see that we have to sustain our spiritual lives for an entire lifetime, it becomes more important to be satisfied. When we were younger, we thought satisfaction was sense gratification, something to be renounced. Of course, the scriptures tell us that spiritual satisfaction is the only true satisfaction. It comes from satisfying the Supreme Self, Lord Hari, Kṛṣṇa. But as neophytes, we think we are not qualified to experience that bliss, and, therefore, we renounce it. We perform our services for our spiritual master, and we are satisfied if he is pleased with us. But our guru wants us to be *personally* satisfied also. He knows we cannot work nicely unless we are.

There *is* a strong aspect of renunciation within spiritual satisfaction. Śrīla Prabhupāda said that one should accept whatever comes without much striving, and be satisfied with it. As soon as you want more materially, then you become dissatisfied. The quest for attaining devotional service should also generate a kind of dissatisfaction. We become painfully aware of our *anarthas,* our lack of love, our apparent lack of progress. That can be healthy. But this dissatisfaction does not counteract the need we have for personal satisfaction. We have to feel satisfied in our ordinary routines, our devotional observances, our chanting, serving, preaching, worshiping the Deity, our living with devotees. If we are not satisfied with our lives in devotional service, how can we go on? We are pleasure-seeking beings *(ananda-māyā)* by nature. If we don't find pleasure *now* in our spiritual routines, we will eventually reach out and seek pleasure in the material world.

Back from a Walk

My poor spirit is no concern of yours
and it's not even poor. No use complaining.
I do my little bit, exercising outdoors.
Maybe these days aren't meant for poetry.
Can I coax you out, Muse?

Give me the pen
and let me write in the shack—
My Lord, You are the center.
And this may be my worst mistake—
not to find You more important than I.

As we read in the story of
    the *brāhmaṇas'* wives,
they brought Kṛṣṇa into their hearts
through the eyes,
and embraced Him therein.
Prabhupāda says they
are like mystic *yogīs* in a union of One,
but both lover and Beloved continue to exist.
We can read it.

Walk looking up at the thrush
who every early morning
sits on a branch in the same tree
and sings an hour as the sun rises.
The tractors sit on the home sites,
and at this time of day I have nothing to say
but Hare Kṛṣṇa, Hare Kṛṣṇa, Kṛṣṇa Kṛṣṇa,
    Hare Hare—
and I ease up on my envy as I think
    of each person.

Walk quickly back,
stopping to pick a weed with big white
    flower atop—
it carries a yellow spider whom I flick away.
Now the flowers are in brass vases,
stooping over the picture of Rādhā-Dāmodara,
It's time to get out there and write,
stay awake!

6:30 A.M.

We have what no one else has. We look around for help from others, and we want to be understood. (By "we," I mean the community of Kṛṣṇa conscious devotees.) We are seen as intensely insular and sectarian, although some know us better as ordinary people with links to the world like everybody else. But the special thing we have is access to Kṛṣṇa, especially Kṛṣṇa in His name and in His Vṛndāvana feature. That is what we have and it should make us humble and eager to share Him with whomever we can find who wants to receive Him.

I am in one small corner of the Kṛṣṇa consciousness movement.

The spiritual journey is marked by questions. What are some of mine right now? "What can I write?" "When will I die?" I do not dare ask, "What will happen then?" That question is too big, and it is not meant for *now.* Now I should ask the one question Śrīla Prabhupāda asked his spiritual master, "How can I serve you?" Death will come in its own time, and I will go where the higher authorities decide.

Other questions devotees ask: Why am I not utterly submissive and obedient? But obedient to who? To Kṛṣṇa and guru? To their representatives? Which ones? The GBC? Which members of the GBC?

Who makes up the questions in your life? How do you know when you have actually *received* an answer? How do you know when to follow?

We need to ask ourselves these questions and understand that it will take time to get the answers. Even if Śrīla Prabhupāda answered you immediately, it would take time for his answer to sift down from your mind to your heart.

Another question: "What do I want?" That seems to be a realistic question. And another: "Do I even know yet how to ask a question?"

At least I know how to answer questions: I turn to the instructions of my spiritual master. "What do I want?" I have already assimilated his teachings enough to be able to answer that one: I want to be happy and strong, humble and renounced. I want to attain the twenty-six qualities of a devotee. I also want time to read and write. I want to behave properly as a *sannyāsī*. I want so many things, and each day I have to rethink this question. Answers are easy to come by, but they change with the passing of time. Getting to the unchanging essence is the difficult part.

❦

Kṛṣṇa, You know everything, and that certainly includes me and my rainbow soap bubbles and my fear and selfishness. I know You are guiding me. I hope it won't be *too* long before I follow You all the way and give up everything else. Please help me to like following You and to help others follow You also.

Please cancel out every nonsense desire I have and ignore my contrary foolishness. Find some good in me, and save me from this wandering birth after birth.

11:30 A.M.

We sat in the shack and read and discussed Govardhana-*līlā*. I tried to imagine the scene—impossible to do. We soon began talking about the observance of Govardhana-*pūjā* in ISKCON temples, especially in Vṛndāvana, India. I am a little talked-out from that right now and cannot summon it up in writing. It seems true when they say that if you intend to write something, don't talk it out first. Talking disrupts the creative tension and expends the impetus.

Still, a mellow remains. I sit alone and look up at the trees and at the space of sky between the treetops. Govardhana, Govardhana, Giri-Govardhana. What is it like to be a resident of Vṛndāvana? We strained our thinking and feeling as we heard the *līlā*—as they sometimes worshiped Kṛṣṇa as the Supreme Protector or played with Him as a friend, a son, a lover. They switched from one attitude to another, but they always loved Him as the all-in-all.

In this chapter, Kṛṣṇa is first treated as a younger family member. Nanda Mahārāja hesitates to speak to Him, afraid his child may not be able to grasp the import of the religious *yajña* they were about to perform. But soon Kṛṣṇa is treated differently, as His father accepts Kṛṣṇa's instruction to stop the Indra-*yajña* and instead hold a festival for Govardhana. They happily complied, and to us, it seems amazing and inconceivable.

Now Sarvesh is running the power lawn mower, and the kids next door are shouting. The mellow is fading. We will hear more tonight . . .

I look forward to my journey to Vṛndāvana, India, but I now know that the spiritual world is accessible to those who hear and participate in *Kṛṣṇa* book among the devotees.

❦

Kṛṣṇa. Flow-writing means to look at an object and go. Why am I offering resistance? Don't I have faith that deeper life is waiting below the surface? Trees . . . the yellow growth on the tree trunk, a putty-like mushroom . . . remember Śaraṇāgati? The black bear striding near where I wrote. I will never forget him, I think. What wildness!

So tiny I am, like an insect under a rock, looking out with furrowed brow at the big world. Time has slipped by.

"But the bears," I say, "the bears." Can they lead me to spiritual perception? Bears are excitement, fear, courage. They make me chant Hare Kṛṣṇa when I see them. Anything can lead to Kṛṣṇa, even if the connection is awkward. Someone's black hair can remind me of Kṛṣṇa's black hair. Simply seeing a bee can remind me of the *gopīs'* comparison of the bee to Kṛṣṇa. And a little pain in my heart can remind me that my end is coming. It can remind me to call on Him for all I am worth. How can I *not* think of Kṛṣṇa?

Here is a connection: "Ecology" note pad—it makes me think of something preachy. "Real ecology is to use everything for Kṛṣṇa in the *īśavasya* concept. Man should not exploit the resources of nature because they are supplied by God."

A tape recorder reminds me of Kṛṣṇa conscious work ahead. The Pilot pen reminds me of editing, of making rough versions that will become polished and tight.

Funny how things pop up. As I write I see the smiling face of Gaurahari dāsa. He was always a comedian in the community, and now that community is gone, replaced by a new one. Faces of friends . . .

❦

All glories to the Supreme Lord who accepts our words in His service. We praise Prabhupāda and bow at his feet. We join his servants and prosecute the *saṅkīrtana* movement. We pray that he clear our vision so we can serve him better. Prabhupāda, despite our faults, keep us in your service. Let us serve your own men and women. There is no other worthy purpose to life. Please keep us. We have no right to demand *bhāva.* We throw water on the fire of our progress. We are sputtering. But you don't stop teaching us, "Do like this, do like this. When will I make a man of you?"

All glories to Prabhupāda.

❦

Surrender

In material life, surrender conjures up the meeting of Lee and Grant at Appomatox Court House, or the Japanese, while thousands of U.S. sailors watched, sitting on the guns of the U.S.S. Missouri, while the ministers signed papers of unconditional surrender. The war was over.

But spiritual surrender is different. It means working for Kṛṣṇa. Book distribution is a hard test for a surrendered soul. I did some (but not much). It's so hard. It means finding a service and surrendering to it. Accepting the process and practicing it. Surrendering to the process means accepting its rules, putting aside reluctance.

In writing, I have to surrender to the traditional forms of "left brain"—essay-writing and rewriting. But I can also surrender to the discipline of free-writing practice.

Surrender—*śaraṇāgati*—is taught by Lord Caitanya. Śrīla Prabhupāda kindly gave us many different ways in which to practice surrender. Please teach us the ways of surrender.

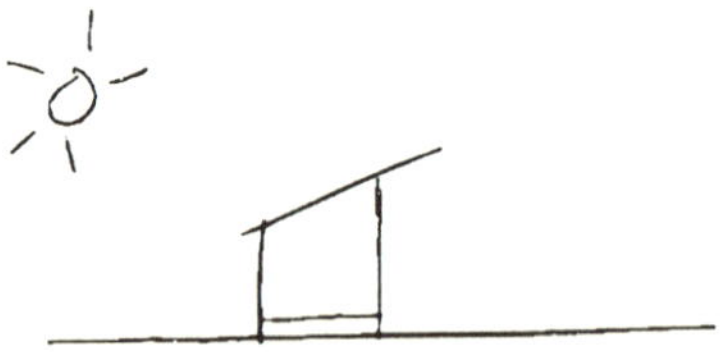

4:00 P.M.

Prabhupāda stated that the purpose of writing is purification. Purification occurs when we glorify Kṛṣṇa in *kīrtana.* Kṛṣṇa purifies us from within as we chant His holy name, as we glorify Him, as we serve. Our mind becomes cleansed by *kīrtana*—any *kīrtana*—including poem-*kīrtana*. Including *kīrtana* of doubt-airing, self-preaching, prayer-making.

When Professor Stahl wrote to Prabhupāda that constant *kīrtana* was not recommended in the Vedic *śāstra*, Śrīla Prabhupāda replied with passages describing the *kīrtana* of Śukadeva Gosvāmī to Mahārāja Parīkṣit. *Kīrtana* can be song, a discourse, or written down. Expressing doubts does not make it less of a *kīrtana*, as long as the *siddhānta* is served. When Baladeva Vidyābhūṣaṇa or Jīva Gosvāmī encountered the doubts of Māyāvādīs, they gave us the victorious conclusions of personalism. That *kīrtana* is as valuable as the *kīrtana* that does not deal in polemics.

I am not so learned that I can take on the world's big agnostics, but I can take on my own personal troubles, doubts, and deviations—my tendencies for karma and *jñana*—and when I come through with servicable Kṛṣṇa conscious replies, that is *kīrtana*. Purification in writing means to cope and struggle and serve.

❦

There is value in working things out for ourselves. We have to learn how to avoid constant bouncing off other people's points of view about us. We have to learn how to be alone *with* Prabhupāda and Kṛṣṇa and to hear their guidance. If I allow myself to be a soft lump of clay, and I invite anyone, "Please shape me," I will never be able to serve in my own way. I will never get down to the bones of offering my self.

A strong person is, among other things, not easily swayed. A grave or fixed person—how did they become that way? Did they find out by their own long processes what they wanted to do for guru and Kṛṣṇa, and now they are doing it? At the same time, they are not unresponsive to others' suggestions. They are careful not to be kicked around by over-eager advisors—those many advisors who differ so much in their analyses of other's situations that following them becomes bewildering. Both strong and weak people are in search of the one who will finally save them, but strong people don't look too far outside themselves for the answer.

Find out, make mistakes, be willing to change. Sincerely ask Kṛṣṇa every day for direction. Let *Him* kick us if He wishes. Let Him save us. I suffer from lack of confidence and an undeveloped will power. We may not have the exact same needs, but both of us can hear Lord Kṛṣṇa's instruction: "Whatever you do, do it for Me." All He wants of us is our *bhakti,* our *loving* service. Therefore, we should ask ourselves repeatedly and humbly, "What do I want to do for Kṛṣṇa? What service really interests me most?" This thinking leads to energetic acts of service. Those who are sensitive to our needs and who wish us well in Kṛṣṇa consciousness will help us work toward that self-determination. They may point out our naiveté or the obstacles that lie on our paths, but they will help us come to our own decisions about what we can actually offer to Kṛṣṇa. Ultimately, we are left alone again, just as I am alone in this shack.

❦

Please bring me closer to the meaning of Govardhana.

6:00 P.M.

Rāma-rāya is so faithfully absorbed in *kṛṣṇa-līlā*. Sometimes I have doubts though. Sometimes I think Kṛṣṇa's pastimes sound like imaginary stories. But Kṛṣṇa tells us through Arjuna: "The doubts which have arisen in your heart because of ignorance should be slashed with the weapon of knowledge." I try to slash my doubts by referring to statements Śrīla Prabhupāda made to confront doubts. That usually helps me.

Tonight I wasn't able to visualize—or imagine myself—in the scene. I was stuck with my doubts. But just by hearing, I was healing. I was able to be submissive and peaceful despite the doubts. Rāma-rāya finished reading the chapter and paused, waiting for me to speak as usual. But instead, I invited Rāma-rāya to speak his own realizations. Then I said, "Let's read the next chapter."

The next chapter is called "Wonderful Kṛṣṇa." The cowherd men expressed their doubts. How could Kṛṣṇa be the lifter of Govardhana Hill and yet appear also like a young boy in our village, a boy who likes us to coddle Him and appears sorry if we don't give Him attention? Nanda Mahārāja pacified their doubts by speaking of the predictions of Gargamuni that Śrī Kṛṣṇa was as good as Lord Viṣṇu.

By now, I was feeling more like talking. My strength was coming from hearing. "Read the next chapter," I asked, and Rāma-rāya read Indra's prayers to Kṛṣṇa. Indra was sorry he had been so puffed-up as to minimize Kṛṣṇa. My doubts seemed to be addressed on all sides by the powerful presentation of *Kṛṣṇa* book.

I remember a devotee once wrote to Śrīla Prabhupāda saying she was having trouble believing in the Kṛṣṇa stories. Śrīla Prabhupāda recommended more hearing of *Kṛṣṇa* book. We may advise newcomers not to read *Kṛṣṇa* book but to stick to *Bhagavad-gītā* if they have a problem with the "far-out" stories, but for initiated devotees, "descriptions of the Lord are the right medicine for the conditioned souls undergoing repeated birth and death. Therefore, who will cease hearing such glorification of the Lord except a butcher or one who is killing his own self?" (*Bhāg.* 10.1.4). When we are doubtful we can pray for faith, "Kṛṣṇa, please give me the knowledge to understand." Armed with yoga, stand and fight.

❦

A spiritual journal not only records your journey, but makes it. When one begins such a journey, superficial agitations ripple the mind's surface, as it strives to silence itself for concentrated prayer. These agitations are superficial garbage at worst, and intellectual symbols at best, and they can be moved out of the way by writing them down. It is important to understand, however, that they are not the Silence or the Godhead we seek in contemplation. There may be benefit in airing thoughts, becoming aware of them in order to lay them aside, but there is also danger. One must beware of becoming entranced by those thoughts, of mistaking them for spiritual musings, and thus identifying them with the soul instead of the mind. They should not be regarded as valuable records or as meditations in themselves.

On the other hand, experience can give voice to realization. Words are our only means of expressing our experiences. With words, we can record spiritual life. One may begin the record at the beginning, but by staying true to the act of recording, deeper levels can be uncovered. And it is possible that Kṛṣṇa could speak through a devotee in writing.

This has been my aspiration in writing *Shack Notes,* that I can honestly translate physical and mental experience into Kṛṣṇa conscious action, and that I can delve into my own inner meanings. I can only pray to Kṛṣṇa to help me, and pray also that the experience of writing *Shack Notes* will become a meaningful spiritual journey.

❦ ❦ ❦

July 18, 1:30 A.M.

Wake up. My eyes are covered with sticky sleep. I have been dreaming for over an hour and a half that I was back in the Navy.

Lately, I have been discussing with devotee friends the likelihood of a practicing devotee having to take more births in the material world. When a devotee of Lord Caitanya heard that he could not return to the Lord's direct association for many births, he danced in ecstasy. He was happy to hear that at least it was guaranteed that he would return. And in the story of Nārada Muni meeting the cobbler and the *brāhmaṇa,* the *brāhmaṇa* was angry and insulting toward Nārada when he heard that he would not be liberated for many births. The Vaiṣṇava prays, for my sinful activities let me be born in any species, but I beg that I may always remain in the association of devotees who are chanting and hearing the glories of the Lord.

I should prepare myself in this brief lifespan to imprint Śrī Kṛṣṇa in my mind. Pray to Kṛṣṇa for protection and the benediction that I may always remember Him.

❦

Now is the time to write. I search my motivation and honesty and I am certain to find imperfection there. But don't bother about it. I should use my pen to praise Śrī Kṛṣṇa. If some of His pastimes are not accessible to me, praise what little I can understand. Don't expect to know everything about the Unlimited, who is beyond the range of the mind and senses. Don't be surprised that He who is known only to those whose lives are free of sin is not attainable by me.

Even if I think I was a better devotee years ago, or that my practice of *sādhana* is *still* lacking, be patient, be grateful that I am still practicing at all. Keep moving in the right direction; keep trying to improve. Don't give up the constant attempt to engage in the transcendental loving service of Kṛṣṇa. Śrīla Prabhupāda writes:

> So, by the slow process of devotional service, under the guidance of the bona fide spiritual master, one can attain the highest stage, being freed from all material attachment, from the fearfulness of one's individual spiritual personality, and from the frustrations that result in void philosophy. Then one can ultimately attain to the abode of the Supreme Lord.
>
> —*Bg.* 4.10, purport

❦

Trucks rumble and rattle all night and all day along highways everywhere. Commerce paves the way. The American flag flies proudly across America. Business could be better, but at least we have the Mideast oil fields secured. We support our troops. It is a long summer, although we don't get much time off from work to enjoy it. What the hell, that's life. At least we were not born in some impoverished country. We have plenty to eat and freedom (of a sort). The planes and alert systems are protecting us while we sleep. We can read all about it in the newspapers and see it on T.V. That's life, and it ain't no other way.

❦

Supreme Lord, Regulator of all, I am sorry You are not the Lord of my dreams. How can I more deeply absorb myself in my working hours so that I can see happy, Kṛṣṇa conscious visions in that one-third part of my life spent in sleep?

I have gained trust that I can dive in anywhere and come up Kṛṣṇa conscious. But why dive in at a filthy place? Why not live in a holy land and swim in a holy river? But when that is not possible for us, then we may practice the method of turning to Kṛṣṇa anywhere and everywhere. As Śrīla Prabhupāda writes, "If he doesn't practice remembering Kṛṣṇa while he is struggling for existence, then it will not be possible for him to remember Kṛṣṇa at the time of death."

When we forget, at least let us remember. "Oh, I was doing something else. Now let me chant Hare Kṛṣṇa."

What is on our minds? Mostly nonsense. It is not all our fault. We came to this material world where it is impossible to be peaceful. The trucks and cars are always going. We are always going too. What is a truck anyway? Twenty wheels, tons of steel, and the truck driver is always harassed. People don't understand him. They treat him like a gypsy. When the police drag him in to pay fines, thieves strip the truck he parked outside the police station. A truck driver is driven on by economic survival. One truck driver says (speaking for truck drivers in general) that if he inherited a million dollars, he would use it to buy a new Peterbilt tractor-trailer. Then he would spend the rest of his life driving to make the payments. That is how they are, just like the man towing a barge who said if his greatest wish could be fulfilled, he would hope for cushions along the shore, so he wouldn't cut his feet as he pulled the barge. No one knows that it is possible to escape from these harassed conditions of life. No one knows how to break the chains. And when some of us follow the bona fide guru and break our chains, they accuse us, "Fools! Duped! Weirdos!"

A paper clip sits twisted on the desk. It is a bit cooler now. There is no end to the rolling and rumbling of the tires. America is always awake somewhere—drinking coffee, getting whores, working the graveyard shift, burning matches . . .

Let the devotees be awake and chanting. Let them teach the world what being awake is for, what it really means. Maybe a few new people will inquire into it. A few people always do. They spin off the wheel. Just as when we were standing on Second Avenue talking among ourselves, a man came up to us: "What's Hare Kṛṣṇa?" He was chewing a sandwich and balancing a cup in his other hand. He looked wild, like he was running loose in Manhattan.

(Is this the kind of person who asks about Kṛṣṇa? Is he mocking us? Just crazy? Just looking for a little human contact wherever he can find it in the huge, impersonal city? Does he see the devotees as crazy like himself?) He begged for a book, although he looked illiterate. He butt in to our conversation and we gave him mercy. He is an example of someone who has spun off the wheel.

I also spun off that wheel. I was spinning wildly until I bumped into Prabhupāda.

❦

Govinda, Govinda, Govinda Hari. Jaya Jagadīśa Hare.

❦

Back From the Walk

Nothing much happens on my walk,
I think of millions
of ideas within a few minutes
while chanting.
I can't remember any of it,
Walter Mitty "B" movies . . .
It's darker earlier now.
I do 20 push-ups, bend-overs,
the same highway nearby, bulldozers
parked.
Walk down the hill chanting and talking.
Pick a few milkweeds . . .

I don't care much for the past.
Today I kept looking around
at sounds in the woods.
The sun every day is a little different,
today orangish, and a strange car parked in
the driveway.
So many things to figure out in Vaiṣṇava
sampradāya.
I want to enter the mystery of it.
I thought on the walk of a letter to
Bhūrijana, I had said, "I will talk about
people's skepticism toward *kṛṣṇa-līlā.*"

Now I've overcome that. I could
write him a letter but by the time
he gets it things may have changed again.
Be happy-go-lucky 4 more days
in the shack.
Hope to learn to
continue always this writing practice.

6:30 A.M.

Imagine being the kind of preacher who can cut down all nonsense, as Prabhupāda did, without imitating him.

One of the devotees is chanting his *japa* too loudly—I can hear it way out here. Should I run in and tell him? Go ahead, and while you are at it, tell the trucks, "Please keep it to a low roar." Does the robin disturb you? Give him a warning.

❦

Baladeva back from another truck run. My mail in a pouch in the hallway.

❦

You have to go on your own in this life. That's all there is to it. One letter said, "The well wishes of devotees are of utmost importance to me," and I agree. Still, you have to go alone. For example, when you walk into a temple, maybe an ancient shrine while on pilgrimage, even if you are with a group of devotees, you enter alone. Something has to touch *you;* you are not a group, you are a person. When you bow down and make your prayer, your chest and legs and head touch the stone floor. You have to face your own attitudes toward the Deity, toward the monkeys and rats, not someone else's.

Face your aloneness, and then if you can, find and develop friendship with a devotee who can accept you with your little idiosyncrasies, someone you can also accept despite their quirks. Have mutual respect for each other. If you can pray together, then you have a good friend. (I know there is more to it than that.)

❦

The American eagle promises to deliver your mail overnight if you pay the price. In India, they make no such promise. In the spiritual world, they don't even worry about it.

❦

The mail is an excuse not to write. I can't think of anything to say.

Wait. Calm down.

These are just pen scratchings.

❦

News Report

At the end of the 20th Century the world is in turmoil. Kṛṣṇa consciousness is needed more than ever. The degradation is increasing year after year. A thoughtful person may wonder where it will all lead? Indeed, people are afraid to conceive children. Who wants their children to grow up in a polluted world, rife with corruption and the threat of nuclear holocaust?

These problems have no patchwork solutions. You cannot save the world while ignoring its spiritual needs. The world is dying of spiritual hunger, of ignorance of the self. We do not know how to shape the world's destiny around the self so we can experience real happiness.

We have to learn how to assess our situation seriously based on a higher, infallible knowledge. Who has faith that such knowledge exists?

But it does.

11.15 A.M.

We just finished reading the pastime of Varuṇa arresting Nanda Mahārāja. After going to the palace of Varuṇa to find His father, Kṛṣṇa showed the residents of Vṛndāvana their spiritual destinations by reflecting the spiritual world in the smooth surface of the water.

We too want to know our destinations. Rāmarāya keeps repeating how we have to earn that knowledge by service. *Yogamāyā* manifests only to those devotees who please the Lord and the spiritual master. If one insists on knowing the spiritual world without proper qualifications, one will only see a *mahāmāyā* version of Kṛṣṇa's pastimes.

It seems almost urgent that we tell people about the highest manifestation of God. Sometimes one meets people who perform real austerity in their attempts to understand God, but they do not know the topmost form of the Lord, the Divine Lover. They do not know the extent of His activities, and they do not know how they can personally participate in them. Prabhupāda calls this, "The nectar for which we are always anxious"—union with God.

I once read a recollection of someone's childhood. He said he was busily drawing a picture on the floor and was very absorbed in it. It was the usual abstract child's drawing. His parent happened to look and asked, "What are you doing?"

"This is a picture of God."

"Oh dear, no one has ever seen God."

The child replied, "Well, they will know what He looks like after I finish this picture."

The parent tried to instruct the child that it is not possible for anyone to know what God looks like, but it is natural that everyone wants to know. God's appearance is a great open secret, but as Kṛṣṇa says, "I am the silence of secret things."

This secret has to be introduced into world ecumenical exchange very carefully. First, the world has to accept personalism. If they continue to say, "I think God is beyond personal and impersonal," then it becomes hard to go further and describe Kṛṣṇa's personal features. It has to done from the beginning.

Kṛṣṇa! I want to break the silence, stop chewing my fingertips while looking into space.

As soon as I begin to write, the resistance begins. It is like a fault in the engine, grinding parts, conflicting selves—editor and writer.

If I can just keep going! The machine needs to rev up a little bit, get the oil flowing to all the moving parts—and then lift off.

What do we see as we rise? Vyāsadeva saw the Lord, the material energy, the suffering *jīvas*—and he saw the remedial measure, *bhakti-yoga.*

But what do I see? I see a city like St. Louis or New York from the air, the plotted streets and houses, tiny cars on the highway . . . and I feel the sense of mission. I see the books next to me in the cockpit—*Bhagavad-gītā, Kṛṣṇa* book, a new journal to write in. I want to read receptively above the fray—above the distractions of stale air, others' voices, the stewardess' requests . . .

I frown, then sigh. Get it out: "Kṛṣṇa I am trying by my own endeavor to improve, to read with real concentration, to write. But it is not the way. We do have to work, but we *need* You to please hear our call."

This forest gets thicker with summer. Now the locusts are buzzing constantly. Windows in the houses are left open all the way at night. The night itself is open. I love to rise in the middle of the night and pray in the freshness of open air. Whatever I may scratch here in pen is only one level. The other level is my intention. Please Lord, rescue my intention.

I cannot see much from here. I don't deserve to dip into the water of the Vṛndāvana lake, escorted personally by Kṛṣṇa, to be shown Goloka and my place there. But I hear of it and I relish it. And I pray to understand the deep exchange of love.

Bhaktivinoda Ṭhākura comments on the *anartha* represented by the pastime of Varuṇa arresting Nanda. He says, "By this pastime, Kṛṣṇa rectifies the misconception that the bliss of Bhagavān is increased by drinking wine or indulging in other kinds of intoxicants." Beware. You cannot see Kṛṣṇa by artificial stimulations. Keep a patient and lowly position, and Kṛṣṇa will reveal things as He likes.

❦

Dear Lord, I want to write and serve You. This *vrata* is nearing its completion. I want to go out strong. What is the meaning of it?

Bhaktivinoda Ṭhākura says that devotional service means to admit defeat before the Lord. Ideally, it is expressed with tears: "I cannot attain You by my own endeavors. All my endeavors end in failure. Please accept me." One stays at the lotus feet of Kṛṣṇa begging to be picked up.

How can I act out this mentality? By persisting in service—in plain, unsophisticated, loving service. And by crying: "Kṛṣṇa I could not attain You; I could not attain Mathurā."

❦

Flowing like an old leaf. Our bodies will soon be compost. One lady wrote me, "I am 35. I may be more than half way through my life . . . " Head in hand, he writes what he can.

All glories to the Lord who has pastimes in Goloka and who is also in the heart of every living entity. I crawl along the ground and beg Your mercy.

I am frying in the noon heat. Let me go inside and admit defeat. Take the Lord's holy names, and admit defeat. I cannot do it, I cannot do it, I cannot do it. O Holy Name, still You allow me to say the words, and I am grateful for that. I am too foolish and proud and dull to know that my interest lies in saying Your name with love. But You have not torn the beads from my hands, not yet. Let me at least touch them, even if my mind does not worship. At least my fingers will touch the *mālā* while my tongue speaks Your names over and over. If anything good comes of it, it is only by Your mercy.

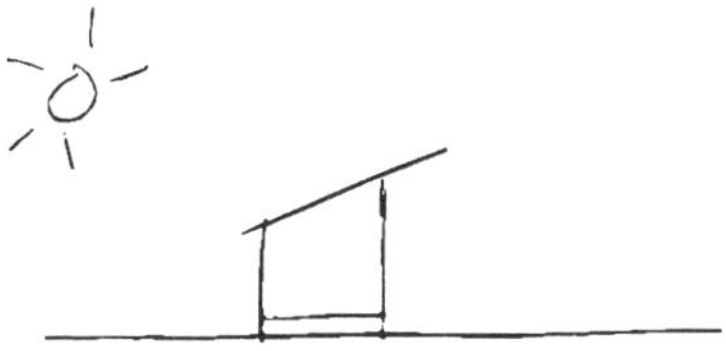

4:00 P.M.

Where's news—Sarvesh put an electric
fan in the shack, orange extension wire
across the forest floor.
Baladeva says, "The next challenge is
to write 24 hours a day.
Why not if that's your service?
At least say what you do all day.
Why do you brush your remaining teeth
if they are falling out?"

There are things I could say,
but I am too eager to wrap it up in the canon.
(This typewriter is also a Canon.)
Far away from Jayādvaita Swami's red pen,
I write amid pines.

Kṛṣṇa is becoming our friend,
as we keep on reading,
this is the *yajña*—
now in *Rāsa* Dance
with warning and no cynicism,
"Just see what the world religions are missing."

The leaves are rustling
my *dhotī's* too tight so I undo the knot.
I trust in thee, language, to carry me,
and I wrap it up in the canon:
man—(and woman)—and God are one in *bhakti*
without losing their identities;
and death shall have no dominion.

Writing

It's my promise that I write for the Master.
He didn't ask me to do it—
He says, Whatever you do, do it with love.
God doesn't need our food,
but if He asks us to give up
stolen goods,
that's good for us.
We develop free love.

My spiritual master says, Preach and

serve Kṛṣṇa.
Have faith he says,
you already have faith
that the airplane won't crash,
so why not faith in sages?

This form of writing I chose,
and thought it could be my offering.
I didn't ask them to build a shack,
"I didn't ask to be born,"
but here I am. A product of my times,
formed by my guru and by America.
Let me take the blame for my own false ego—
and I hope this offering is acceptable.
Place it in pages on the altar
beside a 20 pound bag of rice,
and a few dollars in the donation box.
The poems,
it's the devotion that counts.

Keep off the bodily platform. We are not anti-physical, we don't love flesh and bone, but the spirit of life. Enlightened masters wake us to the fact that we never knew our brother; we mistook him for his body. The person is the spark of life, and while residing in this body, we may learn to love Kṛṣṇa, the Supreme Person.

Dear Lord, this is the preliminary conclusion, and we have to learn it from a spiritual master. We cannot approach this conclusion only by reading books, but we must serve Your devotees and be blessed by them. The devotees have to recognize us, give us service. Your devotees guide us in our offering of food and direct us to proper conclusions. This is the test of Your devotees, our gurus: They give everything to You and then tell us how.

I hear Śrīla Prabhupāda lecturing about Bali Mahārāja. Without even flinching, he states, "Bali was the emperor of all the planets." Bali was a devotee, yet he was creating a disturbance with his attitude of false proprietorship. Therefore Lord Vamana (the dwarf) came to beg from him.

Bali said, "Yes, I am a *kṣatriya.* I will give You whatever You want." But Bali's so-called guru said, "This boy is actually Viṣṇu. If you give, He will take everything."

"He is God?" asked Bali, "Then I must give."

"No," said his so-called guru, "I forbid you."

"Then I reject you," said Bali. "I don't want such a spiritual master who refuses to give to God."

Winter morning '66, hearing from the Swami, this and more. Laughing with him, coughing, going out into the cold.

❦

This is my offering to God. Last November, Turīya dāsa went up the hill and collected dead creepers. He turned them into Christmas wreaths, sold them, and then used the money to fix his shack. The man he sold them to said, "It's a typical Turīya wreath. You either love it or hate it. They were too bulky, and I couldn't sell many of them, but I bought all he had." These are my wreaths.

❦ ❦ ❦

6:30 P.M. 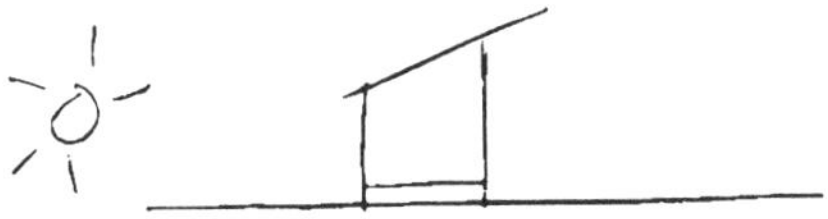

Prabhupāda says "Lust means sense gratification, and love also means sense gratification—but for Kṛṣṇa."

❦

We read the rest of the chapter, "The Rāsa Dance: Introduction." Prabhupāda describes the *parakīya-rasa* as the topmost *rasa.* When it is perverted by the material world, it becomes abominable, but in the spiritual world, it is the highest form of love. I spoke a little about how anyone who is promiscuous in youth, but who later becomes chaste, always regrets those misspent times. We know that any sin committed can easily be forgiven by Kṛṣṇa. But hearing Prabhupāda explain that the *parakīya-rasa* is the topmost spiritual relationship—and in that *rasa,* Kṛṣṇa relates to the *gopīs* as paramours—has given me a realization. We have really polluted our minds, consciousness, and bodies by our promiscuity. Not only do we now have to struggle to forget the impressions of illicit sex-life, but we are contaminated in our attempts to understand this very fine, subtle *rasa.* Little did we know how serious a reaction we were forming. Little did we know how difficult savoring this *rasa* would become. If we could have only understood how contaminated our material heroes were—the ones in books, in movies, in our material friendships—where the man tries to play the role of Kṛṣṇa with his many female companions. It is *so* regretful that we indulged our minds and bodies in irreligious sex-life, and it is so difficult now to crawl out of the material conception into the understanding of spiritual *rasa.*

❦

> The appearance of the moon increased Kṛṣṇa's desire to dance with the *gopīs.* The forests were filled with fragrant flowers. The atmosphere was cooling and festive. When Lord Kṛṣṇa began to blow His flute, the *gopīs* all over Vṛndāvana became enchanted. Their attraction to the vibration of the flute increased a thousand times due to the rising full moon, the red horizon, the calm and cool atmosphere, and the blossoming flowers. All these *gopīs* were by nature very much attracted to Kṛṣṇa's beauty, and when they heard the vibration of His flute, they became apparently lustful to satisfy the senses of Kṛṣṇa.
>
> Immediately upon hearing the vibration of the flute, they all left their respective engagements and proceeded to the spot where Kṛṣṇa was standing. While they ran very swiftly, all their earrings swung back and forth. They all rushed toward the place known as Vaṁśīvaṭa. Some of them were engaged in milking cows, but they left their milking business half-finished and immediately went to Kṛṣṇa. One of them had just collected milk and put it in a milk pan on the oven to boil, but she did not care whether the milk overboiled and spilled—she immediately left to go see Kṛṣṇa. Some of them were breastfeeding their small babies, and some were engaged in distributing food to the members of their families, but they left all such engagements and immediately rushed towards the spot where Kṛṣṇa was playing His flute.
>
> —*Kṛṣṇa,* Vol. 1, p. 191

This is one of the main scenes to meditate on without transgressing the etiquette—how the *gopīs* were all in different places in their homes and were running to Kṛṣṇa, drawn by the sound of the flute. We can visualize them passing through the dangerous forest with its hanging snakes and thorns and wild animals. And we can hear this theme stated at least briefly in many of Śrīla Prabhupāda's lectures, telling the audience how the *gopīs* loved Kṛṣṇa so much that they ran to join Him on the full moon night in the autumn season. He would just give a little description of the *gopīs* rushing to be with Kṛṣṇa, and his speaking about it was always very enchanting.

Spirit souls going to God. Even the beginner in Kṛṣṇa consciousness can relate to this pastime—the fearless giving up of all other things in search of the Beloved. The *gopīs* are not running through the forest with the idea of finding some personal sense gratification. They are going to give Him enjoyment, to serve Him in a way that He wishes to be served. Therefore, the *gopīs* are the most highly qualified devotees of all—*vraja-vadhu*. Lord Caitanya praises their worship as the best of all.

❦

The Stroudsburg neighbors are having an outdoor party. "I don't believe it! Get the hell out of here!" That high-pitched hilarity from adults drinking liquor reminds me of my childhood when I would listen to it from another room. I could sense my parents and their guests getting out of control, and I never liked it.

The blue wooden duck oversees the party. His wings move in the evening breeze. This noise reached us while we were reading *Kṛṣṇa* book, but we managed to hold it off. Now the reading is over, and the party rolls on. I prefer to hear only the rustle of leaves in the wind and to think of Kṛṣṇa. Kṛṣṇa-thought requires a sanctified mind.

Words all culminate in the Hare Kṛṣṇa mantra, when your own words rest and you call out to Kṛṣṇa with pure intention to serve Him in words: Hare Kṛṣṇa, Hare Kṛṣṇa, Kṛṣṇa Kṛṣṇa, Hare Hare/ Hare Rāma, Hare Rāma, Rāma Rāma, Hare Hare.

❦ ❦ ❦

July 19, 1:30 A.M. ◐

Move on this morning while you can.

❦

When anyone does something for purifying the self and for purifying the world with Kṛṣṇa consciousness, it is what Śrīla Prabhupāda called "a hammer blow against *māyā*." He saw preaching as war. Whenever our movement met with resistance, he said this was a sign of our effectiveness. What a fighter he was. Yet he was peaceful. He spoke of "innocent devotees" who were persecuted by the world. Jesus Christ in the West, Prahlāda Mahārāja from the *Bhāgavatam*. Becoming Kṛṣṇa conscious is risky, but Prabhupāda assures us, "Don't be afraid, Kṛṣṇa will protect you."

Prabhupāda is with us. We have departed radically from our societies, but Prabhupāda is on our side. We turn to him sometimes with doubtful looks. "Go on," he assures us. "You are doing the right thing. Kṛṣṇa is God. Do not doubt it."

❦

The Supreme Lord is inconceivable, and when we try to make Him fit into our limited conceptions, He appears contradictory. Queen Kuntī says, "Of course, it is bewildering, O soul of the universe, that You work though You are inactive, and that You take birth although You are the vital force and the Unborn. You Yourself descend among the animals, men, sages, and aquatics. Verily, this is bewildering" (*Bhāg.* 1.8.30).

I cannot directly reach out to Kṛṣṇa in my life. I mean, it is almost like there are two different Kṛṣṇas. There seems to be the Kṛṣṇa who resides in the spiritual world, and then there appears to be one who lives here in the material world. I know and accept the philosophy that Kṛṣṇa is one and that He expands Himself into many energies and presences, but sometimes I sense duality. And I sometimes feel left out of the association of either Kṛṣṇa.

I try to be patient about my distance, and I reconcile myself to this feeling of duality because there doesn't seem to be any way to immediately change it. We come to the world of *māyā* and give ourselves over to the vast, all-powerful, controlling energy. By the grace of Kṛṣṇa and guru, we know we don't belong. They have enrolled us in Kṛṣṇa consciousness to teach us that. But neither have we claimed our eternal position within the internal energy, dancing with Kṛṣṇa, eating lunch with Him, swooning as we chant His name. That is what I mean by the duality.

Here is another example: My chanting doesn't bring me the nectar for which I am always anxious, yet I will never give up chanting. I feel as if I belong in the material world, and yet I am certain that I definitely *don't* belong. There is nothing unusual about my situation—all I am saying is that I don't fully realize Kṛṣṇa consciousness even though I practice it. I see Kṛṣṇa as far away, both in this world and in His pastimes in the spiritual world; yet even that distant or faint contact is enough to set me apart from the Queen of Illusion and all her disciples.

❦

Chanting Hare Kṛṣṇa comes straight from Kṛṣṇaloka, but my chanting doesn't seem to make the connection. Day and night, I am burning in this dark world without even seeking to make that connection.

You know what I mean, you support me. Then *you* talk. You say how *you* feel about Kṛṣṇa consciousness, the material world, and your relationship with Kṛṣṇa. It is a different feeling than what I said, but the same in some ways. It is another random shot. Neither of us can say the whole thing for all of us. I think I understand what you mean. I support you. We speed through the end of night. Chanting Hare Kṛṣṇa is the best way to solve this incoherency. We share it. We are traveling together to help spread it on the order of Śrīla Prabhupāda. Keep the faith, brother.

4:30 A.M.

Part of the shack experiment has been to relax and see how Kṛṣṇa conscious I am in a natural way. A preacher has to constantly speak perfect truth in lectures, often twice a day, and in letters and private meetings. He represents the Absolute Truth at all times. If one isn't really *there,* he may sometimes feel out of touch with himself. He may even feel a strain, "Am I being honest? Do I believe this, or do I just say it as policy?" In discussions with Lord Caitanya, the *tattvavādīs,* and also the followers of Prakaśānanda Sarasvatī, admitted that they spoke according to the "policy" of Mādhva or Śaṇkara, but their hearts were not satisfied.

Audiences also detect when a preacher is speaking policy, exalted ideals, and theology, but when he is not quite in synch with it. So if I didn't "have to" preach the glories of Kṛṣṇa, would I want to do it anyway? If I didn't have to speak against the folly and misery of material life, would I gravitate toward sense gratification, or would I be convinced of what I repeat from *Śrīmad-Bhāgavatam?*

The experiment in being freer to express myself has proven to me that although I don't take naturally to long speeches on the perfect philosophy, I am convinced of it. I talk more of the little things in life that surround us—but I still go instinctively to "the canon" to give the purport. I find myself preaching vigorously to myself. And what inner debates!

I think I have gained a greater ease in my presentation of the philosophy and the freedom to speak as a "real person."

Other gains—honesty, aversion to clichés.

❦

Coming Back From a Walk

Since yesterday, the smaller bulldozer has
evened out
the piles of granite chips into a road.
The other tractors looked like
they didn't move all day.
Now this is not good enough—
You have to start talking
something Kṛṣṇa conscious,
or what's the difference between you
and an ordinary person?

That's a good question.
The difference is I don't eat meat or smoke,
am celibate, do 3 hours daily chanting,
walk around in saffron "robes."
These, you could say, are external
differences.
I chant and someone else doesn't, so what?
The difference is Kṛṣṇa accepts my offering.
Besides that there is no difference—
the wise person sees all alike as spirit soul.
All are one in Kṛṣṇa.
I'm trying to follow.

How different I am from somebody
ordinary—
that's not so important.
A better question is "Who am I,
and how can I improve?"
I would like to improve. Wouldn't you?

That will come with time, let's go
write in the shack, Kṛṣṇa consciousness
as it comes to mind
from Śrīla Vyāsadeva and Śrīla Prabhupāda.

6:30 A.M.

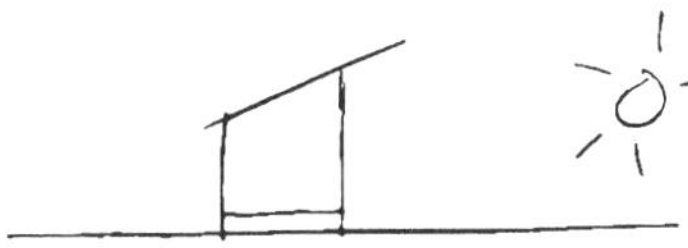

A young kid asks himself, "What do I want to do, who do I want to be?" I figured that out twenty-five years ago, (Or the Swami figured it out for me, and gave it to me). Before I met Prabhupāda, I thought my vocation was to be a marijuana smoker. It was an identity. "Heads" (as we called ourselves) were different from everyone else. We saw through the world. We lived in the special dimension of "high." I saw myself as a writer, but only within the context of being a head.

That is one thing I left behind. Good riddance. I am no longer a kid trying to figure out what to do. I have no parents to contend with, no more formal schooling, and I am too old for military service. I am an established mendicant. I don't need to look for a job. My goal is clear and specific as the eternal servant of God. I follow the teachings of Lord Caitanya as enunciated in the books of His Divine Grace A.C. Bhaktivedanta Swami Prabhupāda. I can live in any number of places in order to carry out my activities, in ISKCON centers throughout the world.

Sounds like I have it made. And I do.

The only thing is that I have to surrender. Surrender is the only way to attain the spiritual kingdom. If I don't go back to Godhead, then all my activities are exposed as failures. The life of *sannyāsa,* of proclaiming myself a follower of Lord Caitanya, is meant to result in joining Kṛṣṇa's eternal entourage. And that is attained in this lifetime when one is fully absorbed in worshiping and serving Lord Caitanya in His *saṅkīrtana* movement.

Externally, I am doing that, but internally, I am lacking. I am also lacking in ways obvious to others. Therefore, I may say the same thing as a young kid, "Who am I and what am I going to do?" In my case, I am not asking, "Should I become a doctor? Should I get married?" But I am asking—"What kind of a so-called Vaiṣṇava am I? Why am I afraid of surrender? How is Kṛṣṇa going to deal with me?" Are some big changes already arranged by Providence?

Or is my surrender to accept—*this is it, you are who you are?* Without becoming a spiritual hero, prosecute humble duties unto death and be steadfast in a little way.

At least I know that I haven't got everything figured out. Whatever comes, I have to remain in Kṛṣṇa conscious practice.

❦

One thrush sings and another replies. They stay a considerable distance from each other and trill, twerp, and bubble their songs. This begins in the morning and continues all the way up until evening. This morning I saw a bat fluttering overhead.

Stick to Kṛṣṇa at the end of a thought or line . . . Write to help yourself.

Two years ago I discovered "*Japa* With Pen." It was in a book by a Hindu lady named Vandana. I tried it and started writing the Hare Kṛṣṇa *mantra* over and over in a notebook. I promised myself to do at least a full page daily and two pages if possible. When Pragoṣa dāsa in Ireland saw it he said, "This reminds me of being in school when the teacher made you write a sentence over and over as punishment. It is amazing that you can do this. I could never do it."

Was it like a punishment to write the Hare Kṛṣṇa mantra a hundred times? No, it was an attempt to use writing to chant. But after awhile it became too mechanical, like everything else.

❦

I am writing little segmented thoughts and not tying them together. Tying them together can make this *too* neat, like a sentimental movie or a propaganda piece. Thoughts come and go. In Kṛṣṇa consciousness they are tied together by your attempt to keep yourself on the path of best behavior. You veer off a little, then bring yourself back. You push ahead, then have to slow down. It is like a mosaic—your total life in Kṛṣṇa consciousness. You put together all the little pieces of colored stones, and you end up with a picture of Kṛṣṇa with His devotees. You are in the picture too. Whenever you have time, you add some pieces to the mosaic. There's room for anything you want to add, provided there is sincerity in it. And there is always room for more. The picture will never be finished. It is done as an offering to Kṛṣṇa.

❦

Caitanya-candrodayā relates the same incidents that are contained in *Caitanya-caritāmṛta,* but with some interesting new touches. In Act 9, a *kinnara* explains to his wife how Lord Caitanya appears in different ways: in His personal presence, within empowered devotees, and "by appearing in His devotees' thoughts."

I was reading the story of Nṛsiṁhānanda meditating on Lord Caitanya, and how this "brought Him" from a distant place to come and take the *prasādam* cooked by His devotee. Śivānanda heard this and he began to doubt: "Is this appearance of Lord Caitanya simply a story made up by Nṛsiṁhānanda, or is it the truth?" A year later, Lord Caitanya confirmed in the presence of many devotees (including Śivānanda and Nṛsiṁhānanda) that He had indeed gone to take *prasādam* at Nṛsiṁhānanda's house, and that He had enjoyed it very much.

Can the Lord appear in the writing of a devotee? And even if He does not appear, may we write *to* Him and *for* Him? May we beseech Him and pray to Him in written words?

My dear Lord, if You do not appear in my words, at least a little bit, then I may go on writing, but it is a vacant cry. Please give me Your mercy so that when I write, at least I feel separation from You and the expectancy of Your presence. This is the goal of writing practice.

(Murray Mednick was right when he said I shouldn't "wrap it up in the canon" too soon. I cannot prematurely claim, "There, I have given the instruction of Kṛṣṇa, I have quoted scripture. This means Kṛṣṇa is present in my heart and words." The reader *knows* it isn't true. I have to keep going, keep writing, keep praying for the Lord to use me as His instrument through the medium of the written word. My duty is not to write only *after* the Lord appears in what I write. My duty and my love is to write to Him, and for Him, and to praise Him—whether He "handles me roughly in His embrace or leaves me broken-hearted by not being present before me." He is always the object of my writing and I may always write, if He allows.)

❦ ❦ ❦

11:15 A.M.

*L*ast night's *Kṛṣṇa* book reading was about the pastime of Kṛṣṇa calling the *gopīs* to the forest with His flute. While listening to Rāma-rāya read this pastime, I was struck by the difference in the *gopīs'* mood in approaching Kṛṣṇa, and in His own dealings with the *gopīs.* Often we read of Kṛṣṇa being aggressive or demanding the *gopīs'* attention. He blocks their path or breaks their milk pots or tricks them in some way, and the *gopīs* often respond by joking with Him or speaking angry or insulting words, even mocking Him. But here, the mood is different; here the mood is one of intense conjugal love.

The *gopīs* pray to Kṛṣṇa, "Please accept me, I am unworthy." All devotees can identify with this prayer and this desire to surrender wholeheartedly to Kṛṣṇa, but the *gopīs* are offering this prayer in the pure conjugal mood. They make long, eloquent speeches—romantic music in answer to Kṛṣṇa's flute call—expressing their yearning, and presenting the pain of their love. There is no break in the mood, no joking, no playfulness. Their song gets stronger and stronger, and Kṛṣṇa is moved to reciprocate.

> Dear Kṛṣṇa, as women, we are certainly satisfied when our hearts are engaged in the activities of family affairs, but our hearts have already been

> stolen by You. We can no longer engage them in family affairs. Besides that, You are asking us repeatedly to return home, and that is a very appropriate instruction, but unfortunately we have been stunned here. Our legs have no power to move a step from Your lotus feet. Therefore, if even at Your request we return home, what shall we do there? We have lost all our capacity to act without You.
>
> —*Kṛṣṇa,* Vol. 1, p. 200

Who but the *gopīs* could make such a presentation before the Lord?

❦

Thinking of India. I imagined I was in Māyāpura and someone asked me "What do you do?" I answered, "I'm just coming now from East Europe. And sometimes I go to America. I travel wherever my disciples are." That's the ten second version of what I am doing. If they want to hear more, I add, "I take some time to write also." That is about all I will ever say, and then I usually inquire about them. Are you *hurt* that people don't deeply understand or appreciate you? Do *you* care for others for more than ten seconds?

No, I am not hurt. I am a bit amused at devotee interaction, especially in our large family:

"Are you still working out of Bombay?"

"No, I haven't been there in ten years."

❦

I just got a letter from a *bhakta*. He said he has been traveling and distributing books and has heard inspiring lectures by leaders of book distribution.

One lecture was titled, "Think Big." He said this seemed different than a lecture I gave about "The Little Way." I replied that leaders have different points of view, and that that doesn't mean they are conflicting. But he has to make a choice about what guru he wants to follow, what mood he can relate to. "I have to re-evaluate," he said. Big or little?

What's my version of "Think Big"? That ISKCON devotees may become pure and potent and loving? Why not? It could happen. There is no limit to the spiritual potency.

I cannot claim to be so modest that I don't harbor big aspirations. But I tend to aspire in the closet. I tend to work at the immediate, to get through the day with no headaches, to get my mail answered, to go where I am supposed to go, preach what I am supposed to preach. And I do have a strong tendency to think small—I mean to achieve something like humility. How can I dare claim, "I will go to Goloka in this lifetime"? I can only try to go to Goloka, but the rest is up to Kṛṣṇa. (My hand trembles as I write this. Do I *dare* to think big?)

Prabhupāda had a bold vision of ISKCON growing like Varāha. He appeared from Brahmā's nostril, but expanded to half the size of the universe. Armies on the march, millions of books distributed, thousands of people joining ISKCON, skyscraper temples growing, government power to the Vaiṣṇavas, *bhāgavata-dharma* taught in all schools, high court judge with *tilaka* . . . That was Śrīla Prabhupāda's version of "Think big."

I want to be one of Prabhupāda's many successes. That is thinking big. I want to do what seems impossible—to chant and read and hear *kṛṣṇa-kathā,* until one day I feel actual love. One day I *will* chant with attention, I *will* spontaneously talk *kṛṣṇa-kathā*, I *will* be humble and unafraid of others' opinions . . .

11:30 A.M.

Surrender to these last writing sessions. Be attentive, deep, easy. Relax and say what you want to say.

❦

I would like to remember the lessons of last night's *Kṛṣṇa* book reading. After reading "The Rāsa Dance: Introduction," we went on to read "Kṛṣṇa's Hiding From the Gopīs." In this chapter, the *gopīs* search the forest for Kṛṣṇa after having been left by Him. They ask the plants and trees if they have seen Kṛṣṇa, and when they get no response, their feelings of separation increase unlimitedly. Finally, they find Rādhārāṇī alone, lamenting that She has been left by Kṛṣṇa. They then attempt to alleviate their feelings of separation by imitating Kṛṣṇa's childhood pastimes.

Śrīla Prabhupāda gives us a glimpse of his own realization here as he ends the chapter with the Hare Kṛṣṇa mantra:

> When they saw that it was getting gradually darker, they stopped. Their mind and intelligence became absorbed in the thoughts of Kṛṣṇa; they all imitated the activities of Kṛṣṇa and His speeches. Due to their heart and soul being completely given to Kṛṣṇa, they

began to chant His glories, completely forgetting their family interests. In this way, all the *gopīs* assembled together on the bank of the Yamunā, and expecting that Kṛṣṇa must return to them, they simply engaged in the chanting of the glories of Śrī Kṛṣṇa—Hare Kṛṣṇa, Hare Kṛṣṇa, Kṛṣṇa Kṛṣṇa, Hare Hare/ Hare Rāma, Hare Rāma, Rāma Rāma, Hare Hare.

—*Kṛṣṇa*, Vol. 1, p. 207

The *mahā-mantra* is not just a temporary mantra to be chanted in this world; it is the way to call to Kṛṣṇa. We can learn from the *gopīs* that Kṛṣṇa is present in His holy names, and that we can associate with Him by chanting. Our own feelings of separation are dull and unawakened. Our love is frozen compared to the burning love of the *gopīs*. The *gopīs* are calling to Kṛṣṇa out of their deep love for Him; we are chanting to awaken that deep love within ourselves.

❦

To be a devotee, I must be prepared to experience whatever is necessary for me to attain devotional service. I cannot be timid, and neither can I conform to social pressure so much that I miss the real point of service. Neither can I be whimsical or ease-loving, doing only those things that please me in a way that misses surrender.

❦

Kṛṣṇa kṛṣṇa kṛṣṇa kṛṣṇa
kṛṣṇa kṛṣṇa kṛṣṇa *he!*

❦

I would like to introduce some simple techniques for preparing to hear receptively and with concentration. I have been practicing these techniques myself for over two years, and I have introduced them to our little group of three or four who read *Kṛṣṇa* book with me. These techniques help me to better hear the scripture, and to speak on it with more clarity.

The first is relaxation of the body. I began this about five years ago in the attempt to reduce headache pain. Although bodily relaxation cannot actually subdue a headache once it starts, it does help to prevent them. Aside from that, relaxation before study or prayer is now something I do automatically. I immediately notice the difference in my own mental state if I neglect this step—my attention is much less focused.

Bodily relaxation can take as much as five minutes or as little as five seconds. First, relax the tensions in your body, one part at a time. After relaxation, or as a continuation of it, take a few deep breaths. I do not practice full-fledged yoga *prāṇāyāma,* but that is where this practice originates. Fill the lungs. Slowly and gently inhale, then exhale. Hold the breath in between. Deep breathing can change your mental state immediately from preoccupation with surface agitations to a deeper sense of the "other world." *Śāstra* is another world, so ease into it.

I like to accompany my deep breathing and relaxation with vocalized expressions: "I am going to quiet down now, and by quieting the body, the mind will be quieted. We are going to hear *kṛṣṇa-kathā* from Śukadeva Gosvāmī. Prabhupāda wanted us to do this, and he will be pleased."

These two—relaxation of the body part by part, followed by deep breathing—are sufficient. But I like to go two steps further. One is a method I learned when practicing to remember for *Prabhupāda Meditations*. You notice the sounds, then touch sensations, then sight sensations. Right now I hear the leaves rustling and the distant highway. I say aloud, "I hear the leaves rustling and the highway." Then I notice what my body feels, "It is warm in the shack. I feel the weight of my backside as I sit in the chair." And sight: "My eyes are closed. I see a darkness with yellow speckles." Or, "I see a young fir tree just outside the shack. It has horizontal lines on its bark and some stubs of broken branches." Doing this produces a kind of "tunnel vision" that helps me to concentrate on *śravaṇam*.

As a final act to induce favorable aural reception, I count down from ten to zero. I have been doing it with my friends lately, and saying, "I am going down the stone steps of a *ghat* near a holy river. As I go down, I have to give up my bodily designations and prepare to hear about Kṛṣṇa. 10 . . . 9 . . . relax . . . 8 . . . Prabhupāda wants me to hear about Kṛṣṇa . . . 7 . . . he is inviting us . . . "

All these methods take me no more than five minutes, but it produces a gentle, altered state of consciousness and improves my hearing noticeably.

4:00 P.M. 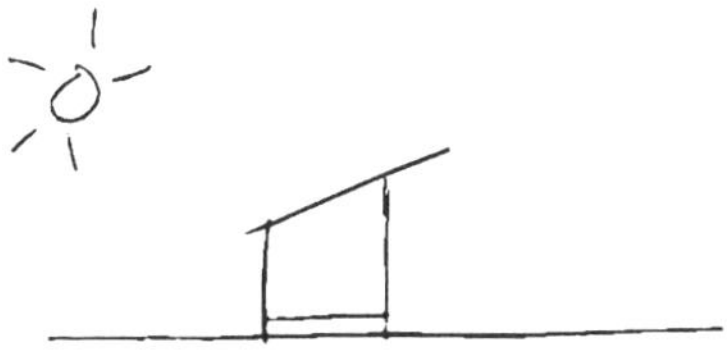

Ishta Devata

Rāma-rāya was writing something, &
looked up as I passed through the room.
Expressing his thoughts maybe—how best
to deal with an attraction to serving
Rādhā-Kṛṣṇa and serving by book distribution,
which earns him the right.

What is my right to come here and
  make a poem?
A desire to express, beginning in 1966,
little free verse poems
"On chanting," I showed to Swamijī
who smiled approvingly.
That's the basis of it.

Turn to
praises unto your *Ishta-devata* (favorite
  Kṛṣṇa Deity).
But I never get to see Him much,
I keep His picture, think of Him when
  I am away,
even in Jagannātha Purī—
the homing instinct,
"Let's go back and live in a room,
walk to see Dāmodara,
Rādhārāṇī and the *gopīs.*"
Wrap it up in the canon—
poor heart at His lotus feet—
or what good is living?

The second poem is harder,
when the neighbor shouts.
Dried up leaves, I suddenly see you.
Peck away here imagining I could be
a Vaiṣṇava *kavi* whose thoughts dwell in
Goloka Vṛndāvana.
I am carrying Rūpa Gosvāmī's *Stavamālā.*
6 volumes with a rubber band around them,
repeatedly reading the benedictions—
"Whoever reads with attention these 8
    excellent verses
to Rādhā-Kṛṣṇa,
shall soon gain loving service at Their
    lotus feet—"
I like his cries as a fallen person
asking for Their mercy.
I cannot write like that but I study
the spiritual mentor for all of us
    in ISKCON.

Maybe I can put together some lines
in Vṛndāvana. Put the Deity in your poem,
and no fuss about your mind and body . . .
As for right now,
I pray in the morning,
bathe and worship with incense the pictures
of Kṛṣṇa and Rādhārāṇī,
completing a 21 day vow of writing
which attempts to love the Lord
from a Pennsylvania shack.

I have half an hour. It is clouding over but it is still warm. We live on this planet and talk about the weather. Śrīla Prabhupāda tells us, "You say, 'Good morning,' but what use is the good morning unless you do something with it?"

❦

Two days left in this writing *vrata*. We all cheerfully joke about time running out. In that sense, everyone is brave about impending death. I measure up my accomplishments: "That's another thing I did before death."

We tend to count based on the average life expectancy of seventy years. We imagine what it is like when all the days have run down, when there are no days left. Fifty still feels young to me. Baladeva told me that I had maybe ten or fifteen years left. I was shocked he thought I had so little.

People are smiling and making money. Young people are trying to look good. Older people are trying to preserve themselves—"Oh, another summer, and after that . . . "

❦

Hare Kṛṣṇa, Hare Kṛṣṇa, Kṛṣṇa Kṛṣṇa, Hare Hare/Hare Rāma, Hare Rāma, Rāma Rāma, Hare Hare . . .

❦

When someone would sigh in our house, my mother used to say, "Are you sighing for Killarney?" Her mother used to say that to her. Irish immigrant in New York. Well, Mom, I'm not sighing for Killarney. I am sighing with hopes for Kṛṣṇa consciousness.

Love between Kṛṣṇa and the *gopīs* is beyond any psychological analysis. Although some scholars describe a man's love as equal to a woman's love in the conjugal relationship, they do not understand the love between Kṛṣṇa and the *gopīs.* Kṛṣṇa says the love of the *gopīs* is so much greater than His own love that He can never repay them. And Rādhārāṇī's love for Kṛṣṇa is the highest manifestation of love possible. The word "love," as we understand it, cannot capture either the essence or the intensity of Rādhārāṇī's love. Therefore, we should not glibly say, "I know what *kṛṣṇa-premā* means, it means love of God." Only the lover of Kṛṣṇa really knows what it means to experience *prema* for Kṛṣṇa.

Even in the beginning stage, though, love for Kṛṣṇa acts on us in the same way it acted on the *gopīs:* It nullifies our attachment to family and friends, to 20th Century sense gratification, and to mundane thought processes. Kṛṣṇa sometimes appeared before the *gopīs* and accepted their service, and sometimes He disappeared in order to allow them the bittersweet taste of separation. Separation increases love. Kṛṣṇa gives us that taste too. Sometimes we think that Kṛṣṇa does not reveal Himself more to us because we are so unqualified. If we think only of our unworthiness, we may become hopeless and defeated. Kṛṣṇa deals with us lovingly; He works for our rectification and tries to stir our love for Him. He may do that by *not* appearing before us, just as He disappeared from the vision of the young Nārada Muni.

To appreciate this, we have to follow Lord Caitanya's instruction: *tṛṇād api sunīcena . . .* we have to have a humble state of mind. And we have to chant the holy name constantly. We cannot imitate the *gopīs;* neither should we imagine ourselves in their places. We have to start by honestly assessing our position and then practice our *sādhana* under the direction of our guru in disciplic succession. Prabhupāda writes that in the beginning, one is attached to service. By laboring in devotional service, we begin to taste the love of doing that service for Kṛṣṇa. From that, love of God develops.

7:00 P.M.

Busy clerk filing papers and books for travel. In this way I avoid writing. Now I come back to the shack, with the the aura of reading about the *rāsa* dance still washing over me. Rāma-rāya stunned me with his statement that unless I go out and preach, I will have a mundane conception of the *rāsa* dance. He is right. Can I surrender without surrendering by writing *Shack Notes?* My critic-self is waiting in the wings with even tougher questions than these, but I am reluctant to fight with him.

I am trying to capture moments in two more days, surrender to a process, dive in and come up Kṛṣṇa conscious.

The first heavy drops of rain, now in full rhythmic pattern—an early evening shower. This rain is welcome.

I like to think of rain in terms of my own needs for the rain of *bhakti.*

Śamīka Ṛṣi's little children are squealing with delight, excited by the earthy fragrance of the rain drifting through the screen of their porch. The wind moves the tree tops, which are at the peak of summer lushness. A wet bunch of leaves breaks off and floats down.

Maybe I have not done anything at all. As Prabhupāda once asked me with a penetrating look, "What *are* you doing?" At that time, in his presence, I felt I was doing nothing at all, just driving around making a show of *sannyāsa.*

Pour down rain and tell me the truth. Have I opted for a soft life? The rain eases off; the heavy shower was brief. A refreshing bath. What about my exposure to truth? Can I only take a little at a time? Was the criticism true, or was it just self-immolation, the enemy mind taking on a deceptive appearance? Whatever it was, I still have to live with myself.

❦ ❦ ❦

July 20, 1:30 A.M.

About a week ago, I drew a cartoon depicting Baladeva holding off the world (an on-rushing truck) while I sat writing in the shack. Last night Baladeva said that the cartoon should be changed. It should show him no longer able to stop the oncoming world. I added, "It should also show me about to leave the shack before the world crashes in on me."

We both have to go. No more endless mornings hearing the crickets. We are both Kṛṣṇa conscious travelers, committed to devotional service. We know we cannot stay here. Crickets in Pennsylvania, crickets everywhere we go. Kṛṣṇa provides for us wherever we go.

❦

There is always a new life. It makes us dizzy to comprehend it. Nothing is old and worn out in the spiritual sense. Spiritual vision always sees Kṛṣṇa's energy as ever-changing. For a devotee, that means there is always an opportunity to praise Kṛṣṇa and render Him service. In a small way, we can infuse the day and the people around us with Kṛṣṇa conscious vision.

❦

Prabhupāda began his letters to his disciples, "Please accept my blessings." Vaiṣṇava authorities also traditionally begin books and end poems offering benedictions. "May that Gopīnātha, the Master of the *gopīs*, Kṛṣṇa, bless you. . . . As He attracted the *gopīs* by the sound of His flute, so the author desires that He may also attract your mind by that transcendental vibration" *(Teachings of Lord Caitanya).*

We can bless others by wishing them well in Kṛṣṇa consciousness, or simply by saying, "Hare Kṛṣṇa." And if the idea of giving blessings embarrasses us, then let us simply have faith that we are rendering devotional service by constantly praising Kṛṣṇa. "Always engaged in chanting My glories . . . the great souls perpetually worship Me." If our praises seem more like crazy dances of false ego or wranglings with the mind, then we can only hope to improve by repeated practice. "And so by the slow process of devotional service . . . "

Devotional writing is a process. We are safe in the process of *bhakti;* writing is within that process. By any one process of devotional service, we can go all the way back to Godhead.

I am starting to sound my farewell. There is not much difference between hello and goodbye for one who is here so briefly.

Look around. Fill paper. Admit poverty and greed. Pick up the clanky *karatālas* (the only pair I have) and sing in the only voice I have with whoever happens to be with me: Hare Kṛṣṇa, Hare

Kṛṣṇa, Kṛṣṇa Kṛṣṇa, Hare Hare/Hare Rāma, Hare Rāma, Rāma Rāma, Hare Hare. Bless the page with *mahā-mantra.* Bless the reader with Hare Kṛṣṇa. You can't go wrong. Find truth in every line, every moment.

All glories to Śrī Kṛṣṇa. Let us praise Him directly. Out of a false modesty we think we cannot say His name and state His glories. We may fear an unsympathetic audience or think ourselves unworthy. It is at these times that the critics jump in and work against our natural spontaneity. All glories to Śrī Kṛṣṇa. All glories to His enchanting flute-playing on the night of the *śarat* season. All glories to the *gopīs,* the greatest authorities on Kṛṣṇa consciousness. All glories to the learned *ācāryas* of *bhakti,* who protect the Vedic knowledge from the Māyāvādī attacks. All glories to our spiritual master, who gathered together the valuable conclusions of millions of years of Vedic science and presented them strongly and simply in our present day.

He gave us courage to face our body's decay. He ordered us to go into the world and spread Kṛṣṇa consciousness. He ordered us not to be "sleeping members," not simply to ring a bell for the Deity in the morning and then sleep the rest of the day. He ordered us to always be active, to be alive, and to try for something wonderful.

Our spiritual master keeps us awake and honest. We cannot go to him with pretention or dirty hearts. Chant Hare Kṛṣṇa and be cleansed. According to our capacity, we must preach. Thank you, Śrīla Prabhupāda.

On Saying Goodbye

We are always saying goodbye in little ways, and we are usually afraid of too much sentiment or of being so truthful that we invoke tears. We usually try to make it as cheerful as possible.

Where are we always going that we keep saying farewell? The Vaiṣṇava is going off to preach, the father to work. They will be back, we think, but one of these goodbyes will be final. We prefer to take them in many small doses while we wait for the one crashing goodbye at the end.

Lord Caitanya appeared cruel when He finally left His friends at Jagannātha Purī. They had delayed Him for a year in His desires to go to Vṛndāvana, but finally they released Him. He walked away and didn't look back to see Sarvabhauma Bhaṭṭācārya fainting. Lord Caitanya wasn't really cruel; His devotees just loved Him "too much."

When Kṛṣṇa went from one place to another, His "goodbye" also threw His devotees into grief. They thought Kṛṣṇa was cruel, although He was going away to give mercy to people in another place.

Kṛṣṇa's coming and going is like the sun, but what about ours? Where are we going? Is our farewell just a forced croak, a death cry? The servants of the Vaiṣṇava should do better than squawk like a parrot at the time of death. They are going home.

Return from a Sunrise Walk

I see rabbits on Brislin Road;
someone left a light on all night;
and the construction site is muddy from
  the rain.
But I want to know
how is the stuff we see in the street
and woods, like the thrush's breast,
and an open rural mailbox—how is it
directly Kṛṣṇa consciousness? If you say
this is not Kṛṣṇa, He is only
in His internal pastimes and Holy name,
then what do we do with this stuff
that greets our senses?
If it is *māyā*, why is there so much of it—
trillions of leaves and skillions of insects,
and some of them land on my neck and bite?
Why is there anything?
Apart from the philosphical answer,
what I want to know is
how to greet the morning?
Am I in *māyā* if I say hello?
Should I see the earth as vacant?
I do chant the holy names as I walk
and this helps. But I would like to know more.
I think it is all a miracle
how the brain works, and the planets spin,
God is in control.
It's easy to enjoy all this in summer,
but I aspire to something more than
what I knew as a boy.

6:30 A.M. 

No stopping in this dripping forest.

On long overnight flights to India, they offer you breakfast, sometimes twice. It comes on a plastic dish with compartments, and with the customary orange juice. "No thanks." The stewardess doesn't care if you don't take it, but she has to ask, "Nothing at all?" You look out the window at clouds, and then below to see the snaking Ganges on the plain.

Breakfast here consists of fruit and yogurt. What a topic of interest—breakfast! Do I love fruit more than I love Kṛṣṇa? Which is best, offering the fruit to Prabhupāda, or gobbling up blueberries like a bear? Offer and eat, a one-two punch.

12:00 Noon 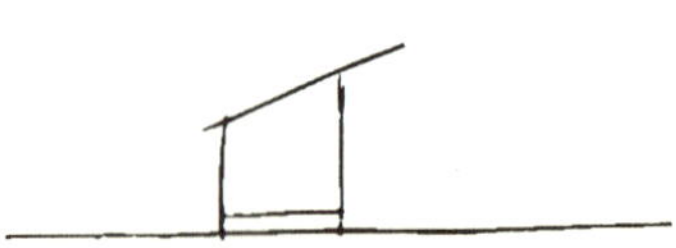

Dear Rādhā-Dāmodara,

Please accept my humble obeisances at Your lotus feet. All glories to Śrīla Prabhupāda.

Someone wrote me a letter recently in appreciation of my little free verse poems to my *"Iśta-devatā* (favorite Deity), Rādhā-Dāmodara." This made me think, "Are Your Lordships my favorite?" I think You are. But I am serving Prabhupāda as a *sannyāsī,* and I cannot stay much at Gītā-nāgarī. I have to think of Your Lordships wherever I go, and I keep Your picture with me to receive Your *darśana.*

I have been reading of Kṛṣṇa's Vṛndāvana pastimes, and today we heard of the *rāsa* dance. Then I brought up the topic of a favorite temple Deity. Rāma-rāya and I agreed that if the *paramparā* orders us to change our *prabhu-datta-deśa,* we may have to change worshipable Deities of Rādhā-Kṛṣṇa. Or, we might have to take with us the mental image or picture of our favorite Deity wherever we go. In that way, we can consider ourselves sent out in the service of our worshipable Deity.

I realize that this may be sentimental talk. It is shameful in a way, how my devotion is nearly nonexistent, and yet I dare to talk of myself as a Rādhā-Dāmodara-lover. Maybe just by repeating the names of "Rādhā-Dāmodara," something favorable will happen. I write this as I am about to travel even further away from Gītā-nāgarī. Let me serve You everywhere, Goddess of Kārttika, and Lord who was tied by ropes of love in His childhood.

❦

Hot and humid. Even the page feels damp.

❦

Someone wrote something about my book-writing that hit the nail right on the head. She said, "You are trying to combine your knowledge of devotees' struggles in Kṛṣṇa consciousness with your personal realization of Prabhupāda's teachings . . . for devotees who need extra help in applying Śrīla Prabhupāda's teachings to our lives."

Let me help. I know what it is like to have problems. And I know what Śrīla Prabhupāda teaches. So let me preach on how to solve problems. It is a big field, categorically called "preaching to the devotees."

❦

Be perfect—at least in following the four rules and chanting sixteen rounds (even if they are of poor quality). And regardless of whatever imperfections we have now, we should preach and help the other devotees.

One time, I was rolling white flour *purīs* in Śrīla Prabhupāda's room. He came in, picked up one of my rolled *purīs* and said, "This is not standard."

"Should I throw it out?" I asked.

"No, it will have to do," he said.

We must try to learn how to do *everything* better. Have we learned *anything* over the years? Never boast that we are teaching based on our own success or our so-called long years of experience. We can help only because Prabhupāda has blessed us and requested us to, and because of others' willingness to hear.

Our worst faults can be consumed by the service of advising others. We are forced to practice Kṛṣṇa consciousness if we are going to propagate it to others with any sincerity or effectiveness. And we are forced to participate in our own purification, forced to become "standard," not allowed to throw ourselves out. Prabhupāda has blessed us with the association of other struggling devotees, and he has blessed us with knowledge of the standard of perfection. We have to become perfect.

❦

What is the connecting thread to all this? I am out here, writing. That is my perfectly unified theme.

The forest is still, muggy, settled into summer. Locusts buzz, humidity hangs heavy in the air, the sun hides itself in a haze of unclear air. Maybe there will be rain today.

Look around your shack room at the notes taped to the beams: "Give me the moment," "If this were my last piece," "A Kṛṣṇa conscious reflection is always worthwhile, and I always have one," "The skeptical nondevotee says, 'I know better,'" "The whoozies are not going to get me (I am going to write on with confidence in this project.)"

Kṛṣṇa. Kṛṣṇa. Kṛṣṇa. You are the Supreme Person, let all persons worship You. Let all literate persons read Prabhupāda's books and be pleased and enlightened with sublime, thorough God consciousness. Let scholars and theists and sincere seekers—everybody—somebody—read and be awakened and desire to become a follower of Kṛṣṇa. That is what I say. That is why I have come to the shack—to say that.

❦

My dear Lord Kṛṣṇa, thank You for bodily health. Please let me use it in Your service. Let me advise others to do the same. Health is fleeting. Even the healthiest become decrepit in a relatively few years. Up until the end, let us serve You with our bodies.

And thank You, Lord, for the ability to communicate. Let us learn to always communicate Your glories. Let us fashion our words into plain, clear, *paramparā* utterances. We can only do this by Your mercy, but You also want to see our efforts. The pewee birds peep, the crows caw harshly, a dump truck crashes its load of rocks to the ground—and we humans can make a thoughtful speech for sanity and peace and Kṛṣṇa consciousness. Please help us to use speech until it is time to stop. No Māyāvādī silence. No speculation. No hurting others.

And thank You for allowing us to think of You. The mind is meant for that. We have so misused this faculty that it is now quite out of control. We please beg for special mercy. It is nearly impossible, Lord, to control the raging mind. Please create a miracle—enable us to control our minds. The pure mind of a pure devotee is like a clear pool after the rains. May we worship the mental control of the pure devotees and learn how they do it bit by bit. Body, mind and words in Your service, that is our desire.

❦ ❦ ❦

3:30 P.M. 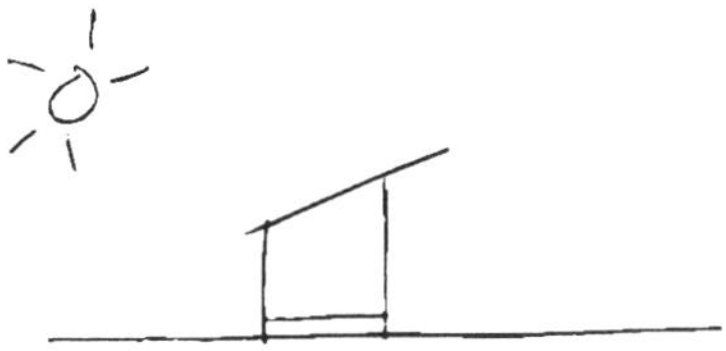

Manuscripts and people are arriving here today. It is humid, and I have the first stage of a headache. We will probably have to cancel our *Kṛṣṇa* book reading this afternoon. And this may not be a full-fledged writing session because of all this.

Just try to have the presence of mind to appreciate and savor what you have been trying to do here.

The breeze moving through the leaves makes a deep sound. When I would hear that sound at Gītā-nāgarī, it used to remind me of an approaching train. Gītā-nāgarī is deep in the forest, and by comparison this is only a backyard patch, but it is sufficient. Even at Gītā-nāgarī, I don't think I let go to writing as much as I was able to do here.

There is definitely a knocking on the door.

It's Just a Scene

It's just a scene and I am leaving.
There is nothing to say,
and there is everything to say.
All I can do it seems to me,
is thrust aside the world,
and chant Hare Kṛṣṇa.
Push aside my life and repeat what I
    have heard.
The nondevotee would prefer his own
truth, no matter how grimy.
But I say his is illusion.
It is good to push aside or cut through
the illusory world and repeat what
    you've heard
from your spiritual master.
Eventually, it becomes your own life.
T-shirt and sitting drinking beer
is not the only truth. There is
the life of the spirit which drives
    your heartbeat.
This world is the garbage heap of dead bodies.
Living bodies are driven by eternal spirit,
but eternal spirit wants to get out of here—
wants to breathe and live in spiritual form.
So let us hear and repeat the codes
    passed down,
and not be intimidated
by a humid July 20, 1991.
If I can subdue this pressure in the head,
I will enter Kṛṣṇa's pastimes
by hearing them at 5 P.M.

❦

It is harder to write freely in these last days. You want to show people, "I ended triumphantly." You want to prove the process works. And to do that, you think an eloquent finish will be needed. But process means there is no final product as distinct from process itself. As Śrīla Prabhupāda said, "Chanting produces chanting." The beginning stage of *bhakti* is a mango (unripe), and the later stage is a ripe mango.

❦

Round and round she goes, and where she stops . . . my Seiko watch is always running. I look at my watch more times than the face or lotus feet of any Deity. Even during the night. I never get enough of it! It is endlessly fascinating and always pertinent. It has a black background and fluorescent hands that I can read in the dark. No one knows the intimate relationship I have with my watch. Even travel over borders cannot disrupt that relationship; it is so easily adjusted.

My watch runs fast. Every day it is three or four minutes ahead of the world. It is better than being slow, but I don't know how much longer we will last together.

Can meditation on my friend Seiko lead to Kṛṣṇa? I am confident that it can. Seiko is the constant companion of a *sādhaka's* day. I feel happy when I sit down to write and it says 1:30. It is as if I have been granted life. If I wake late, at 2:00, I am very upset. Seiko's pronouncements are heavy. Sometimes I am able to circumvent those heavy pronouncements, "Oh well, it is only relative time."

Seiko marks the lines of devotional service: When to pray, when to wake the Deities, when to begin *japa,* when to stop *japa* and ring my intercom, when to go on the walk, when to return—every minute, every hour . . . Yes, Seiko, you are very much part of my Kṛṣṇa consciousness. You are just a mechanical aid, but for the stage I am in, I need you very much.

Seiko warns me that *bhāva* (steady ecstasy) consists in not wasting a minute of devotional service.

Now that I have been glancing at my watch for the purpose of writing this portrait, I have forgotten to notice the time. It says 4:45. Time to go up together and hear of Kṛṣṇa in the *rāsa* dance. But only for an hour. In the midst of *śravaṇaṁ-kīrtanam,* I will glance down confidentially to Seiko and get its signal, "The hour is up." Time to move on.

❦

Reading "Description of the Rāsa Dance." Such a shower of metaphors! In the *Caitanya-caritāmṛta,* Rāmānanda Rāya says, "Unless one can speak with metaphor, he cannot understand the pastimes of Rādhā-Kṛṣṇa." A devotee is poetic, and the real perfection of poetry is to describe the pastimes of Kṛṣṇa and the *gopīs.*

Prabhupāda tells us that the *ācāryas had* to use metaphors because they were trying to describe things that were inconceivable in this world. It is impossible to appreciate spiritual beauty with mundane eyes, but the *ācāryas* tried to give us the eyes to see spirit by the use of metaphor.

It appeared that Kṛṣṇa was a greenish sapphire locket in the midst of a golden necklace decorated with valuable stones. While Kṛṣṇa and the *gopīs* danced they displayed extraordinary bodily features. The movements of their legs, their placing their hands on one another, the movements of their eyebrows, their smiling, the movements of the breasts of the *gopīs* and their clothes, their earrings, their cheeks, their hair with flowers—as they sang and danced these combined together to appear like clouds, thunder, snow and lightning. Kṛṣṇa's bodily features appeared just like a group of clouds, their songs were like thunder, the beauty of the *gopīs* appeared to be just like lightning in the sky, and the drops of perspiration visible on their faces appeared like falling snow. In this way, both the *gopīs* and Kṛṣṇa fully engaged in dancing.

—*Kṛṣṇa,* Vol. 1, pp. 214–15

6:30 P.M. 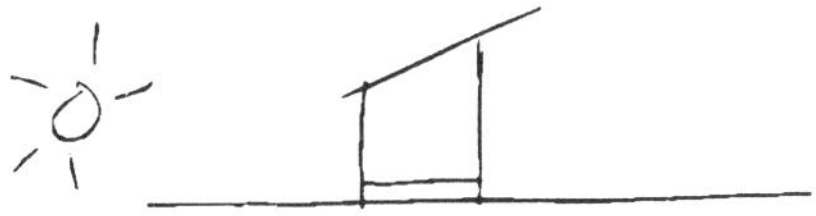

I am game for a full final day tomorrow, but it may not be possible. People are arriving. We go to Europe in four days, so various matters have to be settled. I am trying to write for one more day in the shack as if it were not like this. But, "Why not tell what's happening?"

❦

Kṛṣṇa, this day is ending and I am facing the window and the backyard forest. The writing retreat is coming to an end. How tiny I am! It is silly in the face of my tininess to say, "*the* writing retreat." Śrīla Prabhupāda said that the universe we live in is a small one among universes, and all the universes rest on Lord Ananta's head with so little significance that He barely notices them. Beyond these material universes is the spiritual sky. So within this insignificant universe, the earth is a tiny planet, and on the earth I am most unnoticeable, like a grain of sand on the beach. Yet I say, "The writing retreat is ending," as if it is a cause for general melancholy. What fools these mortals be.

But more amazing than my foolishness is Your compassion. You expand to be with each of us. Therefore, we are not insignificant. Śrīla Prabhupāda says You are clapping Your hands and the *gopīs* are dancing to Your rhythm. In the same way, each of us is meant to dance to Your tune, Your clapping. In the words of my spiritual master, "Please make me dance."

❦ ❦ ❦

July 21, 1:30 A.M. ◐

Today I may keep a regular diary at any hour I get the chance. It is the last day to "sell" my product. As you sometimes see a sign in a store window: "End of lease sale! All items must be sold today! Prices slashed!"—So I must release my devotional sentiments in any form I find, in any spare moment.

It won't be the usual day and I have already accepted that fact. We will not have time for the *Kṛṣṇa* book readings. I am supposed to proofread a manuscript, and I have to meet with Madhu. I will get *some* time in the shack, but it will be at budget prices.

❦

Last night I woke at 10:00 P.M. and then couldn't get back to sleep. A headache and noises in the house.

❦

I am grateful for the gift of reading *Kṛṣṇa* book with visualization and participation. This came during these twenty-one days, and I hope I will be able to continue it.

❦

If I remember anything for ongoing writing practice from these twenty-one days, it should be the willingness and confidence to do flow-writing in Kṛṣṇa consciousness. If I lose that touch . . .

When I have less time to write—when I open the diary for only five minutes just to say "hello" and "no time to write today," "We just missed our plane," then the inner censors have a firm grip on the writer. They say, "There is no way you can say anything worthy off the top of your head. Besides, time is precious. Just write down 'had lunch' and close the writing book. Get back to serious duties." This is how it is with most non-writers, but writers have to be willing to play a little and give themselves more time.

"Another Bright Idea . . . " Śamīka Ṛṣi's note pads stare me in the face. "Another Bright Idea"—it becomes a sarcastic, cynical remark, a meaningless bit of print.

The *gopīs* talked to all creatures in Vṛndāvana, speaking out of their pain of separation from Kṛṣṇa. O does, you must have seen Kṛṣṇa, did He pass by here? Banyan trees, did He touch you as He passed? You all seem ecstatic and cheerful, tell us, where did He go? The *gopīs* saw the world as alive with Kṛṣṇa consciousness, and even if the surroundings didn't respond, the *gopīs* were overflowing.

We want to speak our own little monologues of devotion to the Lord. We always *think,* and our thoughts always go to Kṛṣṇa consciousness, even if only to say, "I did not remember the Lord again, could not keep Him constantly in my thoughts." This is still worthwhile.

Writing helps us focus our attention on Kṛṣṇa consciousness, and saves us from the mind's tendency to sprawl in inner space. And writing allows us always to speak intimately regardless of our situation. The journal accepts our thoughts and invites more, as long as there is paper and pen and a hand that can move. I am grateful to have discovered that writing is my *bhajana.*

Devotion for Its Own Sake

The *gopīs* discovered the greatest reward for devotional service: To be satisfied with their own acts of loving service to Kṛṣṇa. Anything else Kṛṣṇa could give them would be less valuable than this reward. This open secret is known only to the *gopīs* and their followers, and Kṛṣṇa suggests we follow their path.

I can consider this point in my writing practice. Śrīla Prabhupāda told us we write for our own purification. Get permission to write, and then don't be anxious to see it published. All your desires will be fulfilled by writing sincerely in devotional service.

I intend to keep coming back here throughout the day. I don't need an actual shack. The theme is already given by Śrīla Prabhupāda, "Never mind two lines, three lines, but write." Write your realization (not listening to the inner critic who sneers, "Realizations! You have none!"). The essence of this book: Writing in Kṛṣṇa consciousness always can be—and should be—done by me.

Madhu is back. I took him with me on my walk and introduced him to the wood thrushes singing to each other.

"They are in the same place every day."

M: "They probably say the same things to each other every day like humans do."

And so we talked. He told me news of the devotees in Europe where we will be going. It sounds as if people welcome me, although I know I cannot make a big contribution. Mostly we talked of arrangements for travel and mutual friends. Now I am back here, and these lines don't seem like they are coming out with any depth.

❦

Soon I will be lecturing in Belgium, Germany, Czechoslovakia, and Poland.

❦

My dear Lord Kṛṣṇa, when I address You in writing, I realize it is presumptuous. Diary-writing specialists advise the writing of "unsent letters," but I send my letters to You, and I know they are heard by You. It is not presumptuous to communicate with You . . . but I don't do it deeply. I should write to You more from the heart. I am scattered on the surface, stuck in thoughts about travel arrangements, and so on. Please let me render service to You even in these affairs, as a member of the Kṛṣṇa consciousness movement.

❦ ❦ ❦

6:30 A.M.

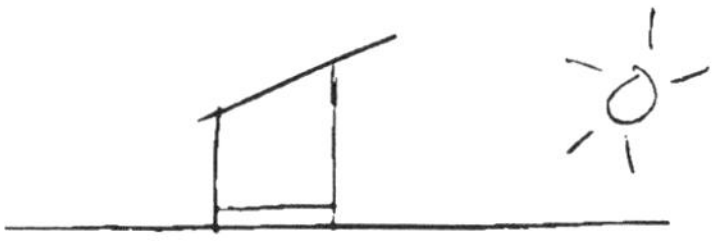

I already sense that I will be unable to write in a driving way while I travel. It will become a "had lunch" daily diary. It will say, "Dear Diary, I am anxious, as we are about to catch a plane over the Atlantic. I am in New York and have two meetings scheduled today. Duty calls. My diary in the shack seems long ago. There's no time for such writing now."

But it doesn't have to be like that.

How can I write things as they are or love things that way? This place and this situation is *māyā.*

My hand writes, and I watch it move like a machine.

Kṛṣṇa consciousness—there are people waiting in the house to talk with me.

11:00 A.M. 

A pain is beginning behind my right eye. It will be difficult to go out to the shack and write. I hear it is a hundred degrees in New York. There is something special in the shack, but once I go out there, I will probably start "melting down" fast.

I am proofreading my story, *Śrī Caitanya-dayā: The Diaries of Harideva and Chāyadevī.* I noticed that my Harideva story has similar themes to *Shack Notes*—a devotee who is preoccupied with his own struggle, but who occasionally praises Lord Caitanya. They say no matter what you write, you tell your own story. So I might as well tell it directly, and also live a better life so that my story will improve. It is not to be done entirely by the weight of the pen cutting through the underbrush of *anarthas.* Do good things, and write humbly. Now I sound *exactly* like my character Harideva.

❦ ❦ ❦

11:30 A.M.

Eye pain. Can't write so much on this last day. Go lie down. You have done enough.

At least I ain't lookin' askance at you. I am waiting for more nectar as soon as you are able. Please think of Kṛṣṇa, take in His mercy, see Him everywhere—and tell us more. It is as easy as falling off a log.

❦

A chipmunk has come close to the shack. He is lovable, but wild. You would like to hold his warm little body, but you don't dare. He would probably bite. Besides, you could never catch him as he scurries over the leaves. Big fanning trees . . . soon I will be leaving this place. It's hard to enjoy my last day.

❦

May Lord Kṛṣṇa bless the readers of *Shack Notes*. May Lord Kṛṣṇa, who is beautiful and kind, and who forever enjoys His pastimes in Goloka, bless all devotees of Prabhupāda and all living entities so that they may progress beyond the fruitless cycle of *saṁsāra*. May He especially guide the followers of Prabhupāda. If they become pure and sincere, then others will be attracted to the service of the Kṛṣṇa consciousness movement, because without devotional service to Kṛṣṇa, the world has no purpose.

Acknowledgements

I would like to thank the following disciples and friends who helped produce and print this book: Baladeva Vidyabhūṣaṇa dāsa, Mādhava dāsa, Kaiśorī-devī dāsī, Caitanya-rūpa-devī dāsī, Kṛṣṇa Kumarī-devī dāsī, Lalitāmṛta-devī dāsī, Keśīhanta dāsa, Vegavati devī dāsī, and Charlie Sullivan.

Special Thanks to Vincent and Vivian Lim, and Kailash Mahajan and family for their kind donation to print this book.